Urbanization and Religious Tolerance

Urbanization and Religious Tolerance

Study of Hindu-Muslim Interactions in Varanasi

Anupama Pandey

RAWAT PUBLICATIONS
Jaipur • New Delhi • Bangalore • Hyderabad • Guwahati • Kolkata

ISBN 978-81-316-0664-3

The publication of this book was financially supported by the ICSSR. The responsibility for the facts stated, opinions expressed, or conclusions reached, is entirely that of the author and that the ICSSR accepts no responsibility for them.

ICSSR Consultant: Professor Anand Kumar, Centre for the Study of Social Systems, Jawaharlal Nehru University, New Delhi.

Published by
Prem Rawat for **Rawat Publications**
Satyam Apartments, Sector 3, Jawahar Nagar, Jaipur 302 004 (India)
Phone: 0141 265 1748/7006; Fax: 0141 265 1748
E-mail: info@rawatbooks.com
Website: www.rawatbooks.com

New Delhi Office
4858/24, Ansari Road, Daryaganj, New Delhi 110 002
Phone: 011 2326 3290

Also at *Bangalore, Hyderabad, Guwahati* and *Kolkata*

Typeset by
Mukesh Technologies Pvt. Ltd. Puducherry

Printed at Nice Printing Press, New Delhi

Dedicated to

Mahamana Pandit Madan Mohan Malviya

a visionary, patriot and crusader of intellectual revolution.

Contents

Acknowledgements

I acknowledge the immense intellectual, emotional and financial efforts from diverse sources that have made the completion of this volume possible. I thank Prof. M.K. Chaturvedi, Prof. J.K. Tiwary, Prof. A.K. Joshi, Prof. S.R. Yadav, Prof. A.K. Kaul, Prof. J.N. Singh and Dr D.K. Singh of the department of Sociology, BHU, for their kind cooperation and affectionate encouragement and for providing me necessary facilities for completing the work. I thank all the faculty members from my own department as well as from other departments and faculties for their continuous support and affection during the preparation of the manuscript.

I owe gratitude to Prof. A.K. Srivastava (former Dean of Students, Banaras Hindu University) who always encouraged me and provided a lot of support. I thank Prof. S.M. Dubey (former Vice-Chancellor, Dibrugarh University) for his suggestions in improving my work, and I convey my regards to Prof. I.S. Chauhan (former Vice-Chancellor and High Commissioner, Fiji) for his academic suggestions.

I thank my husband Sri Manish Shukla and his elder brother Sri Rajanish Shukla who despite their busy schedule helped and encouraged me to complete this assignment. I express the profound sense of gratitude to my grandfather-in-law Pt Bhaum Dutt Shukla, my father-in-law Sri R.P. Shukla, retired Chief Engineer K.D.A. (Kanpur), my mother-in-law Mrs Sunila Shukla for their moral support and encouragement.

Mr Mukesh Srivastava needs special mention here as he has shared every moment related to this work. His valuable suggestions and timely interventions at the time of need helped me enormously.

I am extremely lucky to have a wonderful family that has been always with me throughout. I cannot express the sense of gratitude I feel for them in words. My parents Prof. P.N. Pandey, Professor of Sociology and former Dean, Faculty of Social Sciences, Banaras Hindu University and Dr (Mrs) Indra K. Pandey, Medical Officer and former Joint Director, Health and Medical Services, UP Government, have been the driving force behind me all throughout my life. Their love and affection keep me motivated to face different crises and challenges in life. I shall remain extremely grateful to them. I have all the reasons to thank my brothers Prashant Pandey and Santosh Pandey and my 'Bhabhi' Mrs Purbi Pandey and younger sister Meenakshi for always managing to bring the best out of me and for being a source of constant encouragement at all times.

I thank the staff of the Central Library, BHU, Faculty Library, Social Sciences, BHU, and the staff members of the libraries of Delhi University and JNU for their kind cooperation.

I thank ICSSR for providing grant-in-aid for the publication and also to BHU administration for providing academic facilities.

I also express my gratitude to all the office bearers in my department for their support and cooperation.

Finally, I must add my responsibility for any limitations or errors of judgement in this work.

Anupama Pandey

CHAPTER 1

Prologue

The present study is concerned with the examination of the nature and magnitude of social reciprocity and religious tolerance in an urban setting. The problems of social reciprocity and religious tolerance have been selected for the study because these two hold the key to an understanding of the nature of urban social structure in modern societies. Urbanism as a way of life can be measured and analysed effectively through the interactional pattern of the residents of a city. Urban social structure is used for a specific community that is full of heterogeneity, anonymity, superficiality, impersonation, associative individualism and dominance of secondary relations rather than primary and high degree of dependence upon others. This social structure indicates the environment that is created by man himself for his own well-being. On the other hand, urbanism has been defined differently by various social scientists, demographers and statisticians who conceived it as a specific mode of life. Anderson (1959) observed that urbanism as a way of life is not confined to cities and towns only, although it enlarges from the great metropolitan centres. It is a way of behaving, and this means one can be very urban in his or her thinking and conduct although he or she may live in a village. On the other hand, a very non-urbanized person may live in a most urbanized section of a city, whereas urbanization is the concentration of humanity into cities. Urbanization redistributes population within a society and transforms many patterns of social life.

Urban society is a representation of modern society. Hatt and Reiss (1963) observed urban society in such a way that the enormous significance of the city in determining pattern of life throughout modern society is obvious. The very term 'modern society' connotes a way of life characterized by a rationalized industrial structure, complex markets, rapid transportation and efficient communication. More than this, modern society connotes a way of life so related to the environment of the city that it is almost the equivalent of urban society. Keeping this view in mind, it becomes a necessity to explain the underlying processes of an urban social structure in the light of the factors of modernization. Various sociologists and social scientists have studied the process of urbanization. Ferdinand Tonnies (1963 [1887]) studied how life in the new industrial metropolis differed from life in rural villages. Durkheim (1965) agreed with much of Tonnies' thinking about cities. But, Durkheim countered, urbanites do not lack social bonds; they simply organize social life differently than rural people. For Durkheim, urban society offered more individual choice, more tolerance and personal privacy than people found in rural villages. George Simmel (1971 [1903]) offered a microanalysis of cities, studying how urban life shapes individual experience and mentioned that individuals perceive the city as a crush of people, objects and events. To prevent being overwhelmed by all this stimulation, urbanites develop a 'blasé attitude', turning out much of what goes on around them. According to Simmel (1978 [1907]), modernity concentrates in city, and money economy and modern society exhibit a clear-cut distinction between the objective culture and subjective culture and lead to atrophy of individual culture and hypertrophy of objective culture.

Robert Park et al. (1925) found the city to be an organic mosaic of distinctive ethnic communities, commercial centres and industrial districts. The urban society is full of heterogeneity of population in terms of age, occupation, education, caste, language, religion and so on. The cities have attracted people from every nook and corner from all regions to come over here and stay either temporarily or permanently. The study is focused on social reciprocity and religious tolerance in an urban centre. This social reciprocity can be understood better in terms of informal and formal reciprocation. Informal reciprocity refers to the relationship with the members of friendship circles, neighbourhood, kinsmen and other informal interest groups. The formal reciprocity includes many aspects, each of which is important to community structure and change. The urban society is the structure that is directly affected by the changes brought about by modernization, industrialization and globalization. For some, it is very difficult to distinguish the borders of rural and urban societies. For MacIver and Page (2000 [1950]), there is no sharp demarcation to tell where city ends and country begins. Rural and urban societies depict modes of community life, not simply geographical location. The urban social structure is composed of the various communities. These communities are meant to live their lives by their own way. The urban social structure has the occupational specialization and the emphasis on competitions. The social structure of an urban set-up is necessarily as complex as its culture, presenting a variety of extremes and modulations. The urban society has the prestige of power, wealth and specialized knowledge. It holds the key of finance. It is the market for all.

In this study, reciprocity and religious tolerance have been treated as the basic indicators to explain the nature of urban social structure at a particular place and over a particular time period. Social reciprocity may be perceived in various social situations such as family, kinship group, friendship circles, neighbours and caste members, at work and recreation and in formal and informal associations. Most of the societies in the world, either developed or developing, have felt a universal need for cooperation and equality. The dimensions of interpersonal relations among different religions are changing in contemporary society due to this demand. The causal factor behind these changes can be termed as techno-economic development. This *techno-economic development* is the outcome of modernization. Modernization is a way of thinking in which rationality is dominant in ideas, thinking, habits and behaviour patterns (Jan dt, 2006; Sarvacs, 2008).

Modernization is a process of social change that consists of new values, ideas, thinking processes and different forms of technology by which traditional and semi-traditional societies are transforming themselves into a definite and required social structure. These social structures, by the process of modernization, are accommodated with new technologies, value orientations, motivations and ideals. Thus, modernization is a process of transformation and change by which new values, ideas, norms, technology and socio-economic relations are transforming the pre-existing social system. This transformation can be observed as modernizing the social system. This very process of modernization has occurred during the seventeenth century in Western European and North-American social, political and economic systems, and it later on appeared in South America, Asia and Africa during the nineteenth and twentieth centuries. Eisenstadt (1969) presented the explanation of modernization in the same manner.

Different models to explain the process of modernization have been perceived in Western countries. For example, Western Europe, North America and Russia have different models of modernization, whereas Japan in the East has different model of modernization. The nature of modernization in Indian society is different from that of Western models of modernization. The major causes of the differences are modern values, ideas, and continuity and synthesis of tradition and modernity. Modernity indicates the behavioural patterns, that are historically found in contemporary urbo-industrial and technological society. The social systems of Europe, America and Russia are the best examples in this regard.

The development of science and technology has placed the social life on such a place where humanity is trying to dive in future and is changing the pole of its national and international character. The social, cultural, economic and religious changes and tendencies of social, cultural, economic and religious perspectives during the twentieth century were unique that could not be seen for the past 5,000 years (Jan dt, 2006).

The emergence of intellectual society is trying to develop a new system in society, which is based on equal rights of human beings besides class, caste, community, colour or religion. The modern idea of socialism is the product of the twentieth century although it was found in ancient Indian epics and culture such as Rig Veda and Buddhist philosophy.

Socialism in India, as a philosophy of economic and social construction, is developed and became popular due to Western influences. Development of modernization in India was an outcome of the communicative devices and availability of better transportation and communication. The printing work in India was started by Portuguese during the early sixteenth century, and the first printing press was established in Mumbai due to the motivation of the British. Although the written newspapers were started during Mughal dynasty, the credit for printed newspapers goes to the Britishers. In modern societies and industrial settings, the means of transportation and communication are commodities such as railways, roadways, airways and waterways, vehicles, press, radio and television, mobile, computer, postal services and Internet banking. Various activities in human life in contemporary social structure are being completed by machine and other scientific tools. The control of human beings on nature is gradually increasing. This state of affairs in society is termed civilization. Civilization can be defined as the whole system and organization that is formed by human beings to control the conditions of their life. The civilization includes the infrastructure and social techniques. The major goal of infrastructure techniques is to enhance the control of human beings on natural phenomenon. Social techniques that involve economic organizations, institutions and law are basically related to the regulation of human behaviour. Despite various disparities, disputes, discriminations and disappointments, the world is stepping towards a unified structure. Art and culture are being common assets. The boundaries have been broken. Today, the sky is limited in the sense that the distance from one place to another place can be covered within few minutes. The farther states have become neighbours, and the formation of an international society is a possibility. The society is moving towards new cyber systems and informatics putting the global network into the choice category of human interactions.

Religion is closely related to culture and civilization. At the primary level, religion is an integral part of culture. Modernity has added sophistications to religious practices and usages. It is no more a Pandora's Box of superstitions. Rationality has added new attitude and perception towards religion. Thus, it can be concluded sociologically that religion has been bifurcated from culture and civilization. Culture is a human-made part of society and as such refers to the totality of all human creations, and civilization is the utility of the cultural contents. In primary societies, religion was a concern of belief; whereas in modern societies, it is a utility. Thus, religion has covered the distance from culture to civilization.

The contemporary society is lying at the gate of burning and excited period of history. The modern science and technology is full of beliefs of the modern age. Science has presented such tools and techniques that can manage material prosperity for all. The new sources of power are being used to change the system of transportation and agricultural work. The communicative devices have opened the new possibilities of interactions and inter-relations of human beings, their attitudes, ideas, beliefs and rational sentiments. Modern scientific developments in society are actively engaged in bringing up the nature of humanity at a global level. The religious explanations have been differentiated by interpretations, traditional superstitious beliefs due to scientific developments and innovations. As a result, the religions are now accompanied with rational outlook. This rationality is creating such a mindset in individuals that they perceive themselves free from religious boundaries, narrowness and differentiation and far from emotional attitude regarding life. As a result, all the communities are behaviourally adopting the reciprocal relations and developing tolerant behaviour. Religion is closely associated with culture. At the primary level, religion itself was an integral part of culture but in modernized societies, religion is accompanied by civilization.

In other words, the religious beliefs and values have been changed due to the development of science and technology and have adopted the novel values in terms of utilitarian and consumption values. It can be concluded that religion has also led towards civilization from culture. Culture is a creation of human being and civilization is the utility of that creation. In primitive societies, religion was a creation and in this modernized world, religion is a utility. In traditional societies, religion played a central part in social life. Religious symbols and rituals are often integrated with the material and artistic culture of the society music, painting or caring, dance, story telling and literature.

Tradition and modernity exhibit specific patterns of time, place and activity in a particular period. Religion is universally found in all societies as either traditional or modern. Religion has had a strong hold over the lives of human beings for thousands of years. The study of religion is a challenging task which places quite special demands on the sociological imagination. Sociologists define religion as a cultural system of commonly shared beliefs and rituals that provide a sense of ultimate meaning and purpose by creating an idea of reality that is sacred all-encompassing and supernatural (Durkheim, 1965; Berger, 1967; Wuthnow, 1988). In many cases, religion is being considered as a major source of social solidarity. Religious beliefs, rituals and bonds help to create a moral community in which all members know how to behave towards one another. Sociologists tend to explain the appeal of religion in terms of social forces rather than in terms of purely personal, spiritual or psychological factors. For many people, religious beliefs are a deeply personal experience, involving a strong sense of connection with forces that transcend everyday reality. Some sociologists argue that people often 'get religion' when their fundamental sense of a social order is threatened by economic hardship, loneliness, rise of grief, physical suffering or poor health (Berger, 1967; Schwartz, 1970; Glock and Bellah, 1976; Stark and Baindbridge, 1980). Sociological approaches to religion are strongly influenced by the ideas of the three classical sociological theorists: Marx, Durkheim and Weber. Being a non-religious person, Marx contributed much to the explanation of religion.

Durkheim (1965) defines religion in terms of a distinction between the sacred and the profane and labelled religion as the sacred. He considered religion as a social fact. The differentiation between the sacred and the profane and the elevation of some aspects of social life to the sacred level are necessary but not sufficient conditions as needed. (1) There must be the development of a set of religious beliefs; (2) a set of religious rites; and (3) a religion requires a single overarching rural community (Ritzer, 1996).

Becker and Boskoff (1957) divided social facts into sacred secular typology and considered religious beliefs and mysticism in the category of sacred. Weber (1921) considered that religion and social change are interconnected and perceived that religion is not necessarily a conservative force.

Religion is a continuous process of interaction, and in a particular group or community, the quantum and affectivity of modernity may differ, but there cannot be complete vacuum of religion. The bases of the differences are based on rational calculations.

Religion and morality are also interrelated. Morality is a set of directives that emerges from religion. According to Durkheim (1965), it is a social sanction, which is the outcome of religion. No matter whether the society is traditional or modern; both continue in some measures. There is no scope for complete vacuum; when such condition appears, it is termed as anomie in Durkheimian sense, and is a syndrome of sick society. As a matter of fact, no society in the wave of modernization is ready to accept the moral vacuum.

It appears that religion is a perennial system of beliefs. It is an ongoing process and superimposed on social continuity; and as such, religion is a superimposed and socially accepted social reality. Religion is a reality in the context of modernization. Malinowski (1954) observes religion as a mode of beliefs and practices—a personal experience as well as a sociological phenomenon.

The origins of Islam, today the second largest religion in the world, overlap with those of Christianity. Islam derives from the teachings of the prophet Muhammad in the seventh century CE. The sole God of Islam, Allah, is believed to hold sway over all human and natural life. On the other hand, Hinduism is the oldest of all great religions still prominent in the world today. Hinduism is a polytheistic religion. It is being considered as a cluster of religions rather than a single religious orientation.

Islam supports the view that excessive growth of materialism leads to decay of great nations. Some historians illustrated the fact that the loss of Greek and Iranian cultures was caused by atheistic materialism. The disputes on religion created a rift in the Christian world as a result of which the very concept of social justice and philanthropic concerns were disregarded. The Prophet Muhammad himself heralded the slogan that 'almighty is one and all human beings belong to one fraternity'. The Muslim realized that this humanity is immortal and its destiny is not sure. The only immortality is the Almighty himself. In the latter courses of history, the Maulvis and the interpreters of Quran created a rift between the Almighty and human beings. The very Quran, the Hindu treatises such as the Vedas and the Epics such as the Bhagavad Gita believe that the Almighty is omnipresent, omnipotent, free from odour, colour and form. He is endless, kind, unbecoming and present everywhere (Aktar, 1992; Williams, 2007).

All other communities and sects, such as Buddhism, Christianity, Jainism, Confucianism and Judaism, differentiate between idolatry and non-idolatry forms of God; even then under specific sanctions, all such sects substantially emphasize on the self-entrant of human mind, self-enlightenment and a realization of the combination of nature and dynamic force, which moves the nature. Buddhism believes that human beings can escape the reincarnation cycle by the renunciation of desire. The path of salvation lies in a life self-disciplined and meditation, separated from the tasks of the mundane world. The overall objectives of Buddhism are the attainment of 'Nirvana': complete spiritual fulfilment. Confucianism was the basis of the culture of the ruling groups in traditional China. It seeks to adjust human life to the inner harmony of nature, emphasizing the veneration of ancestors. Various structural changes in society have led to a massacre in the religious lives of people. The differences in life style concerning religious values, fanaticism, superstitious beliefs, fundamentalist and extremist outlook and irrational demands for religion have created a rift between individual and society, especially in terms of religious values and ideology. Sociologically, the communal beliefs wrapped in the clothes of superstitious beliefs and irrational values cannot be termed 'religion' because religion has the ability of adaptability.

Sankhya Darshan denotes that religion is that which leads to overall upliftment and well-being. Thus, this definition of religion, based on Sankhya and Gyan Mimansa, is the soul of all communities. It means that all religions such as Hinduism, Christianity, Buddhism and Jainism have defined their religious glossary and language according to the above-mentioned descriptions.

The social reform movements launched during the fourteenth century under the Bhakti movement, and the nineteenth-century Renaissance were excellent examples of social reforms movements. A religious movement is an association of people who join together to spread a new religion or to promote a new interpretation of an existing religion (Giddens, 2007). Religious movements tend to pass through certain definite phases of development. The movement usually derives in life and cohesion from a powerful leader. Max Weber (1921) has classified such leaders as charismatic. The examples include Arya Samaj of Dayanand Saraswati in North India, Brahmo Samaj of Raja Ram Mohan Roy in Bengal and Prarthna Samaj of Keshab Chandra Sen in Mumbai. These are the outcomes of nation-wide awareness and the expansion of liberal ideology of the West.

The nature and the needs of society during British India were different from those of ancient society. The people who have been educated in Western culture have identified their necessities and started reform movements and tried to bring the changes in social institutions, religious approaches and traditional moral ideas. They believe that the political, cultural and economic developments of new societies are possible only by individual freedom, social equality and liberalism. That is, the emergence of an egalitarian society. The nineteenth century was the period of transition in the socio-cultural history of India, and modern India is the outcome of this transitional period. The contacts of Indian and European continent can be divided into two parts: (1) before 1948 and (2) after 1948.

Historical sources justify the contacts between India and Europe before the first century BC. The different forms of relationship are being observed between India and Europe. The first is in the form of trade relations that can be explained with the help of roman coins found in the excavation of 'Aadit Nalur' situated in the Western Ghats.

The second stage of relationships is being started after the attack of Alexander. The invasion of Alexander on India was very important in the sense that after this invasion a mutual sharing in the field of art, music, literature and science and technology were initiated between Indians and Greeks. It is believed that this intruder created the first cultural reformation in Indian society. The invasion of Alexander had left an important influence on Indian society, and the process of this mutual sharing was continuing till the spread of Islam and the emergence of political dominance of Mongols. Due to the collision of European civilization, Indian society has realized the changes that are referred to as renaissance by the historians of India and they prefer to call renascent India due to the nationalist and reformist cultural changes, upliftment and development in India from the emergence of Brahmo Samaj (AD 1828) to Sarvodaya (AD 1949).

In European history, the period between thirteenth and seventeenth centuries is defined as renaissance by the historians of nineteenth century considering that period as a specific cultural age. Modern historians consider the renaissance as the transition period of medieval Europe of twelfth and thirteenth centuries and modern Europe. The contemporary social order and system is predominated by the forces of modernization. One important question for the sociological and psychological perspectives can be pointed here that, in what sense do religious superstitions and dogmas present hindrance for the society and man in the modern world?

The novel scientific developments in contemporary societies have established a uniform religious structure. The communal differences between Hindus and Muslims are still alive but in the midst of some, certain boundaries, and it must be accepted that the approaches of modernization and the current explanations of modern lifestyle, especially in urban communities, will indispensably lead to religious reciprocity. Industrialization, urbanization, science, technology, communicative devices, easy availability of life amenities and spread of education have broken the traditional beliefs, superstitious customs and narrowness in developing societies such as India and have given birth to new values, ideas, thinking and behavioural patterns that are being considered as helpful in the modification of existing ideas with regard to religion. The process of modernization has converted the religion into an indispensable means rather than the end in itself that was found in ancient Indian society.

MODERNIZATION AND INDIAN SOCIAL STRUCTURE

Historically speaking, modernization is a process of change in system during the seventeenth century in Western Europe and North America, which later on appeared in other European countries and, especially, in South America, Asia and Africa during the nineteenth and twentieth centuries. Thus, the contemporary societies have evolved from the confluence of traditional and pre-industrial societies. In Western Europe, these changes are found in the form of feudalistic to utilitarian states and in the form of larger urban centres. In Eastern Europe, these changes are borne out from the totalitarian states and small urban societies; on the other hand, in different countries the birth of modernization passed by colonialism, imperialism, migration, religious movements and religious faith (Singh, 1999 [1977]; Bryant and Peck, 2008).

The process of modernization in India has also covered its journey from feudalism, imperialism to colonialism under the Western influences. Thus, modernization is a process of change in some certain kind of technology, values, orientations, motivations and ideals of social structure found in traditional or semi-traditional social structure. The interpersonal relations, adoptability of others' values and religious dogmas and traditional character of society have been changed due to modernization, industrial development and Western cultural contacts. The process of modernization has brought new values, ideas and beliefs in the social set-up and as such is also predominant in the Indian society. Thus, a novel culture and religion have replaced the older cultural and religious beliefs. Indian society is a confluence of tradition and modernity; the traditional features of Indian society have not been abolished in the wave of modernization but have got a new shape and mode of presentation. In such a state of affairs, both tradition and modernity are running for the better accommodation. The modern forces in society such as science, technology, industrial and urban development have developed better facilities for life and novel occupations in the social system. In this set-up, unique business elites with urban values have been borne out who are beyond the communal conflicts and communalism. This class of business elites has developed a new way of life full of religious reciprocity, tolerance and social participation. It can be said that the outcomes of modernization are the emergence of multi-cultural system, multi-religions, multi-languages and multi-communal interactions. These processes can be easily found at global level, and in the Indian context, it is observed in urban and industrial societies. The observation of Varanasi city reflects that besides an oldest orthogenetic city, only Hindus are not in dominant position ; rather it is developing as a confluence of different religions. It can be mentioned that all the major religious prophets and founders had frequently visited Varanasi; for example, the prophets, the saints, preachers and ideologists of Hinduism, Islam, Buddhism, Christianity and Jainism were concorded with the city.

Besides different variations in life and traditional differences, both the communities are closely linked to each other, and a new pattern of social reciprocity, tolerance and accommodation has been observed. This unique configuration of Hindu–Muslim relationships in Varanasi can be credited to the social structure of the city. There are various examples that can better explain the forbearance character and reciprocal relations. After the bomb blast in Varanasi (2006), the people from both the communities have presented one of the best examples of religious reciprocity and tolerance. Both the communities come to the rescue of the victims by sharing together. Again on 7 August 2006, both the communities prayed for the welfare of all societies. Both the communities sang communal harmony songs. The theme behind this auspicious prayer in Varanasi was to take oath to stop terrorism and to stop corruption. They prayed for the country's progress and prosperity (*The Times of India*, 8 August 2006).

STATEMENT OF THE PROBLEM

Modernization has worked as a facilitator for behaviour-friendly religion rather than stereotypic, superstitious and traditional values of the society. The observations in the field of social sciences have accepted that the appearance of modern life style and modernization have narrowed the religious orthodoxy. The modern man has also found himself biocide with the religious faiths and beliefs. Here, the assumptions and observation of Prof. Yogendra Singh (1999 [1977]) are suited well that the Indian traditions are going to be modernized. The studies of Milton Singer (1964), McKim Marriott (1955) and M.N. Srinivas (1952) are also the testimony of reciprocal relations.

The study attempts to analyse the nature and form of social reciprocity, religious tolerance and mutual relationships between the two communities: Hindus and Muslims. It has been attempted to explain the extent and the quantum to which Hindus have adopted the beliefs and traditions of Muslims, and Muslim communities have adopted from the religious traditions, rituals and beliefs of Hindus in their social and occupational life in the wave of modernization. Modernization has been adopted as a key factor to analyse this mutuality because urban structure is much affected by this process.

The empirical study was conducted in Varanasi. In this study, attempts were made to trace out the nature and quantum of mutual interactions and reciprocity in the course of social and economic life of the city. The specific context of modernization was adopted because the modernizing forces have enabled both the communities to be intermingled to exchange the ideas, sharing of occupations and participation in religious activity and rituals. It can be observed in the society that during Hindu religious festivals, Muslims participate and during the Muslim ceremonies, Hindu communities participate actively. It has been tried to find out the trends of inter-religious and social interactions. It has also been tried to locate the emerging trends of participation of the two religious communities in festivals, commensalities, social occasions and cultural as well as festive celebrations. Not only this, there is a very positive interpretation of both the communities in running the business, trade, commerce and occupational enterprises. This reciprocity seems to be inevitable in the wave of techno-economic developments, although the historicity of the reciprocity of the two communities unlike other urbo-industrial centres is distinct and age old. The attempt in this empirical study is made to highlight the ever-accelerating social reciprocity and religious tolerance in the city of Varanasi, which is supposed to be the stronghold of traditional Hinduism. Such study by its very nature happens to be of sociological interest and arrests the attention of travellers, visitors, social scientists, economists and technologists to this peculiar dynamic blend of urban social texture. That is why this present study is conducted to unveil and highlight the social reality of religion and society in an orthogenetic city and to trace out the changing scenario of communitarian relations in the light of modernization.

MODERNIZATION AND INDIAN TRADITIONS

The structure of rural society has been changed due to the impact of British rule in India. The traditional socio-economic institutional bases of society have been changed. Sociologists have explained this situation as the confrontation of tradition and modernity. In other words, it is a war between Indian and Western philosophy. The social structure and culture of Indian society are changing rapidly due to the impact of the Western culture. The Western cultural contacts basically attracted the process of modernization and different traditional institutions have also been influenced by this process. The cultural reformation of Indian society started after the British regime.

The British rule in India led to the emergence of bureaucracy, law and order, army, postal services, railways, new elite class and risk-bearing people. The process of modernization has led to the development of social, economic, cultural, educational, religious and developmental aspects of structure. The ideas of Gandhiji, Vivekananda, Aurobindo, Gokhale and Tagore created a mark on the brain of the people of India. The Western influences on Indian society have brought about some radical changes. Besides these radical changes, Indian society has retained its tradition. Thus, a confluence of tradition and modernity is being perceived in Indian society. On the one hand, positivism, science, technology and excess dependency on material resources have developed; and on the other hand, ritualism, monotheism, reverence, spiritualism and traditional beliefs have been strongly communicated. This aspect has been expressed as continuity in indigenous traditions (Singh, 1999 [1977]).

The subject of social change in modern India is vast and complex, and an adequate understanding of it is necessary for better explanation. A number of scholars from various fields as Economics, Social and Cultural History, Law, Politics, Education, Religion, Demography, Psychology and Sociology have tried to explain the changes in Indian social structure. To explain some features of religious, cultural and social changes in India, Srinivas (1962) used the concept of *Sanskritization* and *Westernization*. Sanskritization seems to have occurred throughout Indian history and still continues to occur and was used to describe the process of cultural mobility in traditional social structure of India. In his study of the Coorg in Mysore, he found that lower castes, in order to raise their position in the caste hierarchy, adopted some customs of the Brahmins and gave up some of their own, considered to be impure by the higher castes. Westernization is a simpler concept and refers to changes introduced into Indian society during British rule and which continue, in some cases with added momentum, is not confined to any particular section of the Indian population and its importance, both in number of people it affects and ways in which it affects them, is steadily increasing. It can be said that Sanskritization is the process by which a 'low' Hindu caste or tribal or other group changes its customs, rituals, ideology and way of life in the direction of a high, and frequently 'twice-born', caste. On the other hand, Westernization refers to radical and lasting changes in Indian society and culture. Srinivas prefers the term 'Westernization' to modernization. He explains that modernization presupposes rationality of goals that in the ultimate analysis could not be taken for granted, since human ends are based on value preference and rationality could only be predicted of the means not of the ends of social action.

Westernization is an inclusive, complex and many-layered concept. It covers a wide range from Western technology, at one end, to the experimental method of modern science and modern historiography, at the other. Its incredible complexity is seen in the fact that different aspects of Westernization sometimes combine to strengthen a particular process, sometimes work at cross purposes and are occasionally mutually discrete.

On the other hand, various other social scientists such as Almond and Coleman (1960), D. Learner (1962), McClelland (1961), Ethiel Pool (1963), W.W. Rostow (1990 [1960]), Frisby (1992), Giddens (1991) and Young (2007) have pleaded the process of modernization. In the Indian context, S.C. Dube (1967), Y.B. Damle (1976), M.S.A. Rao (1970), A.R. Desai (1959) and Yogendra Singh (1999 [1977]) have advocated the concept of modernization to explain contemporary changes in Indian society rather than Westernization. There are various differences between both the processes with regard to conceptual and theoretical explanation.

INDICATORS OF MODERNIZATION

Various studies have been conducted from time to time to explain the process of modernization. In this respect, Learner (1962–1963), Almond and Coleman (1960), McClelland (1961) and Moore (1963) are notable theorists. Some basic indicators of modernization as described by these social scientists, theorists and philosophers can be summarized as follows:

(i) Empathy
(ii) Mobility

(iii) High participation—Learner (1962–1963)
(iv) Interest articulation
(v) Interest aggregation
(vi) Institutionalized political competition—Almond and Coleman (1960)
(vii) Achievement orientation—McClleland (1961)
(viii) Rational means-end calculation
(ix) New attitude to wealth, work, saving and risk taking
(x) Faith in the desirability and possibility of change
(xi) Social, economic and political discipline
(xii) Capacity to put-off immediate and short-term satisfactions for higher satisfactions in the longer run—Ethiel Pool (1963), Moore (1963), S.C. Dube (1965)

Inkeles and Smith (1974) presented a list of 24 indicators to explain the patterns of modernity. But for the present empirical study, some of them have been selected for the verification and analysis as follows:

(i) Active participation
(ii) Orientation towards change
(iii) Reality
(iv) Expression and orientation towards communication
(v) Planning and attitude regarding controlling the size of the family

Thus, various social scientists have adopted and analysed the views regarding modernization given by Learner, Almond and Coleman, Dube, Moore, McClelland, Ethiel Pool and Inkeles and Smith. Besides these, some indicators have also been selected in this empirical study of an urban social set-up. These are as follows:

(a) Associative individualism
(b) Intercultural tolerance
(c) Voluntary associations
(d) Occupational relations
(e) Techno-industrial organizations
(f) Materialistic attitude
(g) Demographic heterogeneity
(h) Social transactions

(i) Religio-cultural pluralism
(j) Changes in religious beliefs and standard of morality and
(k) Rational and humanist attitude.

The content of the empirical study is *psycho-sociological*. The study is aimed at highlighting the attitude of both the communities, Hindus and Muslims, regarding value orientation, aspiration, mentality and level of satisfaction in the mutual exchange with their counterparts in urban social set-up. These are the psychological aspects of the study. On the other hand, attitude regarding reciprocal behavioural and participatory behaviours, social exchange and transactions have been regarded as the sociological aspects of the study. Thus, the study is a joint venture of both the approaches. *In this empirical study, the responses of the respondents, mentality and level of activity have been explained in the light of the indicators of modernization*. In contemporary urban social set-up, two categories have been prepared to analyse these indicators and to provide objectivity to this study:

(a) Psychological Indicators

In this category, the indicators presented and discussed by earlier social scientists, and the indicators found in urban environment have been collected. There are as follows:

1. Empathy
2. Interest articulation
3. Interest aggregation
4. Achievement orientation
5. New attitude towards wealth, work saving and risk-taking
6. Faith in desirability and possibility of change
7. Capacity to put off immediate and short-term satisfaction for higher satisfactions in the longer run
8. Exposure to mass media
9. Associative individualism
10. Religious tolerance
11. Rational and humanist attitude
12. Materialist attitude
13. Change in religious superstitions and standards of morality

(b) *Sociological Indicators*

1. Mobility
2. High participation
3. Institute analysed political competition
4. Rational ends–means calculations
5. Social, economic and political discipline
6. Intercultural contacts
7. Voluntary associations
8. Occupational relations
9. Techno-industrial organizations
10. Demographic heterogeneity
11. Social transactions
12. Religio-cultural pluralism

Thus, in this study, the findings concerned with the above indicators have been verified and justified.

TRADITIONS AND ATTRIBUTES: A DEBATE ON MODERNIZATION

In contemporary society, where the forces of industrialization, globalization and modernization are predominant, religion is being observed in a rational and positivist approach leaving aside the iron cage of superstitions and narrow boundaries, and various communities and sects are observing the social relations in a new mood and order. The people of various religions and communities are engaged in urban structure by maintaining the continuity of their religious values. The modern man has developed the rational idea that the ultimate goal of all religions is one and universal. All religions are promoting the affectionate values; the tolerant nature; and the values of truth, non-violence and good moral conduct. This awareness in the urban social set-up has forced the people to form social reciprocal relations and participatory behaviour (Schramm, 1964).

Indian society is an embodiment of various religions. The followers of various religious groups are here, and they are practising their religious and ritual activities. In this empirical study, the Hindu and Muslim communities have been selected for the purpose. Both the communities have observed the impacts of modernization, urbanization, industrialization and Western cultural contacts. Modernization has facilitated the rationalist view of life in both the communities and has shattered the nerves of narrow religious beliefs. After all, the great traditions of both the communities are not disappearing but are being observed in the form of a social exchange. Besides various differences, both the communities participate in the religious activities and rituals of each other, and they all believe in the universal existence of God. Although the forces of modernization have elapsed some of the traditions, myths regarding religions and values, the continuity is still prevailing. People from both the communities have frequently visited the religious places for worship. For example, the Hindus visit the mosques, tomb or idgah for their well-being, and as such Muslims also visit the Hindu pilgrimages and saints. This behaviour is not only frequent at a national level but can, easily be observed at an international level. The observations of both the communities reveal that the accommodative social exchange is also predominant besides all the variations in sociocultural lifestyle, values, traditions and norms (Pandey, 1987). The elite classes from both the communities have expressed a serious concern regarding religious values and faith in religions despite the impacts of science, technology and modernizing factors. These people always have a positive attitude regarding the religions, faith, worship, prayers and consequences of planets on the life. The various Hindu pilgrim centres such as Badrinath, Kedarnath, Amarnath, Puri, Rameshwaram and Vaishno Devi have observed the frequent visit of the masses each and every year. These people may be common men or the modern men. The development at these pilgrim centres has attracted much more people from far and wide to come over here and to spend days or months for the religious and ritual activities. Not only have the people from India, but from various nations such as France, Britain, Italy, Germany and America, had also a serious concern about these pilgrim centres. This concern is not for the leisure or tourism, but this is mainly enchanted with the psychological perfectionism of the mindset regarding the fulfilment of the needs and desires (Parsons, 1951). In the same manner, a lot of people from different communities visit Muslim religious places such as Ajmer, Fatehpur Sikri, Agra and even Mecca. For the fulfilment of the needs of life and goals, the Hindus also frequently visit these places. In contemporary society, it can be observed that Muslims also celebrate the Hindu festivals such as Holi and Deepawali with their Hindu friends and Hindus also participate actively in the Muslim festivals and festivities. The mutual religious interactions and interdependence, as in the case of Varanasi, is much frequent. The famous festival of victory of evil forces or devil, known as Vijayadashami, is finished with the help of Muslims in the city. The dummy of devil emperor Ravan is made by Muslim families, and this is celebrated by Hindus. In a famous play, 'Ram Leela in Varanasi', the characters are Muslims who play the role of Ram and their family members (*The Times of India,* October 2007). The traditional Indian society is based on the principles of hierarchy, holism, continuity and transcendence (Singh, 1999 [1977]). These four value themes were deeply interlocked with other elements of Indian social structure. Hierarchy was engrained not only in the system of caste and subcaste stratification but also in the Hindu concepts of human nature, occupational life cycles (ashrama) and moral duties (dharma). Holism implied a relationship between individual and group in which the former was encompassed by the latter in respect of duties and rights; what had precedence here was community or Sangha and not that which persisted all along the line of traditional social structure, for example, family, village community, caste and political territory of nation. Communalism in traditional social system was reinforced through the value system of continuity, which in Hinduism was symbolized by principles of karma, transmigration of soul and a cyclical view of change. Historically, social structure and tradition in India remained impervious to major elements of modernity until the contact with the West began through colonization. The earlier encounters with Islam only reinforced the tradition since Islam despite being exogenous to the Hindu tradition was basically organized on value themes that were traditional; ideally, Islam had no place for hierarchical differentiation of individuals within its community of believers; its worldview was messianic-historical in contrast to the Hindu view of continuity; the principle of transcendence in Islam was strictly monotheistic, and here too it differed from Hinduism. The principle of holism, which no doubt, was present in both Islam and Hinduism also varied in sociological meaning in the two civilizations. In Hinduism, holism implied individual's social and moral subordination to the group without theocratic implications, hence basic in Islam. Despite these dissimilarities in ideal value, themes of the Hindu and Islamic traditions, there is a synthesis between these two, which reinforced the traditional character of Indian society without significant breakdown in its organization.

Modernization in India started mainly with the Western contact, especially through establishment of the British rule. These contacts had a special historicity that brought about many far-reaching changes in culture and social structure of the Indian society. Not all of them, however, could be called modernization; Srinivas (1966) prefers to call it Westernization. The basic direction of this contact was towards modernization; but in the process, a variety of traditional institutions also got reinforced.

The Islamic tradition in India came from a heterogenetic source; its establishment by conquest introduced a complex emotional variable right from the beginning, which has continued through time. Value themes of Islam were holistic, but the principle of hierarchy or caste was not accepted in theory; the idea of continuity was also less pronounced as Islam, like all religions of Semitic origin, was based on the conception of historical time; its value theme on transcendence too was rooted in the principle of absolute monotheism. These contrasts of history and value themes could not; however, render Islam as a systematic exogenous source for radical transformation in the Indian tradition. Despite the apparent dissimilarities, the contact between the great traditions of Hinduism and Islam was only a contact between two traditional systems. The national democratic awakening of Indian people found expression also in the religious sphere. The contradiction between the old religious outlook, practices and organizations, on the one hand, and the new social and economic reality, on the other hand, gave rise to various religious-reform movements in the country. These moments represented attempts to revive the old religion in the spirit of the new principles of nationalism and democracy that were the conditions for the development of the new society. Modern society, established in India by the British conquest, is a capitalist society resting on the principles of individual liberty, freedom of competition, contract and freedom of the individual to own and manipulate property at their own will. Individualism was its key note in contrast to the pre-capitalist society that was authoritarian in character, maintained social distinctions based on birth and sex, and subordinated the individual to caste and the joint family system. The new society demanded, as the very condition of its development, the abolition of privileges based on birth or sex. The early religious reformers strove to extend the principle of individual liberty to the sphere of religion. In fact, these religious reform movements, such as the Brahmo Samaj, the Prarthna Samaj, the Arya Samaj and others, were in different degrees endeavours to recast the old religion into a new form suited to meet the needs of the new society. The early religious reform movements in India were attempting to build a religious outlook that would build-up national unity of all communities, the Hindus, the Muslims and others, for solving such common national tasks as the economic development of India on modern lines, the removal of restrictions put on the people's free evaluation, the establishment of equality between man and woman, the abolition of caste, the abolition of the Brahmin as the monopolist of classical culture and sole intermediate between God and the individual. The Indian religious reformers were not rehabilitating any past period of society but only consolidating the rising new society. Another characteristic of the religious reform movements was that their programme was not restricted to the task of merely reforming religion but extended to that of the reconstruction of social institutions and social relations. This was due to the fact that in India religion and social structure were organically intercoined. Caste hierarchy, gender inequality, untouchability and social taboos flourished because of the sanction of religion. Social reform constituted a part of the platform of all religious-reform movements. Religion dominates and determines the life of the individual; his or her economic activity; his or her social life; and marriage, birth, and death and physical activity. It was dispensable for the religious reform movements to have an all-embracing programme for religious, social and even political reform.

In India, the religious reform movements launched a crusade against medieval religion, which sanctified such institutions as caste, which was a powerful obstacle to the national unity of the Indian people and to the development of the new economy in the country. Some major religious reform movements that have nation-wide popularity and prospects are as follows:

The *Brahmo Samaj*, established in 1828 by Raja Ram Mohan Roy (1772–1833), who can be correctly described as the father of Indian Nationalism, was the first religious reform movement in India.

Raja was essentially a democrat and a humanist. In his religio-philosophic and social outlook, he was deeply influenced by the monotheism and anti-ideology of Islam, deism of Sufism, the ethical teachings of Christianity and the liberal and rationalist doctrines of the West. He tried to assimilate and interpret into himself the highest elements of Islam, Christianity and modern rationalism or Humanism, and transformed them into a single creed that he found in the ancient Upanishadic philosophy of his own community (Buch, 1939). He attacked the polytheistic degeneration of ancient Hindu monotheism. He attacked the idol worship of the Hindus as degrading and expounded the concept of one God of all religions and humanity.

The Brahmo Samaj, under the leadership of Raja, launched an offensive against the caste system branding it as undemocratic, inhuman and anti-national. It crusaded against '*Suttee*' and child marriage. He stood for the freedom of the widows to re-marry and equal rights of man and woman.

Debendranath Tagore (1817–1905), who succeeded as the leader of the Brahmo Samaj, developed scepticism about the infallibility of the scriptures and finally repudiated scriptures.

Keshab Chandra Sen (1833–1884) was the next leader of the Brahmo Samaj. Under his leadership, the doctrine of the Brahmo Samaj was more and more adopted to the doctrine of pure Christianity. In later stages, he propounded the doctrine of 'Adesha' according to which God inspires knowledge in some individuals whose word must therefore be considered infallible and true. A section of Brahmos did not accept this doctrine. He then left the 'Samaj' and started the 'Sadharan Brahmo Samaj' (ordinary Brahmo Samaj).

The *Prarthana Samaj* was founded in 1867 in Bombay by M.G. Ranade and Keshab Chandra Sen. It had a programme of religious and social reforms on the same lines as those of the Brahmo Samaj. Its founder Ranade was one of the leaders of the Indian National Congress and the Indian Social Conference which held their first sessions in 1885 and 1888, respectively. The Arya Samaj was founded in 1875 by Dayanand Saraswati. It had more revivalist character. It declared the Vedas infallible; and further, an inexhaustible reservoir of all knowledge, past, present and future. Its slogan 'Back to Vedas' was inspired with the urge to bring about national unity and to kindle national pride and consciousness.

The *Arya Samaj* had a programme of social reform also. Although opposed to the literary caste system, it stood, however, for the four social categories, that is, the Varna system of society to be determined by merit and not by birth. The Arya Samaj stood for equal rights of man and woman in social and educational matters. This was a distinct democratic conception. It, however, opposed co-education since in the Vedic period co-education did not exist. The Arya Samaj organized a network of schools and colleges, in the country, both for boys and girls, where education was imparted in the mother tongue. The Dayanand Anglo-Vedic College was founded in 1886. The conservative section of the Arya Samaj thought the education imparted in this college to be not sufficiently Vedic in character. Its members led by Munshi Ram, therefore, started Gurukul at Haridwar, where the education, both in content and method, was given in the ancient Vedic manner.

In all its activities, the Arya Samaj was generally inspired with the spirit of nationalism and democracy. It attempted to integrate the Hindus by destroying the subcastes. It spread education among the people, proclaimed the principle of equality irrespective of the distinctions of caste, creed, community, race or sex. It has tried to destroy their inferiority complex, the inevitable product of their status as a subject nation.

The Arya Samaj represented a form of the national awakening of the Indian people. Restricted to a narrow Hindu basis and with a negative attitude to Islam, it, in course of time, led the Muslims to mobilize on a corresponding communal basis. It played a progressive role in the earlier stages when the national awakening was just sprouting.

The national awakening of the Indian people found expression in the movement inspired by Ramakrishna, a great Hindu saint, in direct line to such saints as Chandidas and Chaitanya. It is primarily based on the principle of Devotion or Bhakti. Its principal advocate was Swami Vivekananda, a disciple of Ramakrishna who established the mission on 1 May 1897 and an intellectual of a very high calibre who, after the death of the saint, founded the Ramakrishna Mission to propagate his teachings. The Ramakrishna Mission aimed at protecting India from 'the materialist' influences of Western civilization. It idealized Hinduism including its practice of idol worship and polytheism. It aimed at the spiritual conquest of the world for revived Hinduism.

Thus, the Bharat Dharma Mahamandal Society having for its programme the reforming of the Hindu religion and dissemination of religious and non-religious education among the Hindus was started in 1902. In 1890, Shri Narayan launched the movement of the Tiyas, a community that worshipped demons and formed one of the lowest castes of the Hindu society, with the programme of building of temples and establishing schools for the community.

Theosophy introduced in India by Madame Blavatsky and Henry Steel Olcott in 1879 and mainly popularized by Mrs Annie Besant was another religious reform movement started in India under the impact of the new Indian and international conditions. The uniqueness of this movement consisted in the fact that it was inaugurated by a non-Indian who was a great admirer of Hinduism. Theosophy subscribed to the spiritual philosophy of ancient Hinduism and recognized its doctrine of the transmigration of the soul. It preached universal brotherhood of men irrespective of distinctions of caste, creed, race or sex (theosophy – the connotation theo = truth and sophy = vision, that is, the vision of truth). It stood for the development of a national spirit, among the Indians. 'The needs of India', Mrs Besant wrote in 1905, 'are, among others, the development of a national spirit, an education founded on Indian ideals and enriched, not dominated, by the thought and culture of the West' (Desai, 1976). Theosophy stood for making a comparative study of all oriental religions. However, it considered ancient Hinduism as the most profoundly spiritual religion in the world.

In addition to these organized national religious reform and religious revivalist movements, individuals of outstanding capacity and political pre-eminence, such as Bepin Chandra Pal, Aurobind Ghose, Tilak and Gandhiji, without organizing any distinct movements, contributed to the work of religious reform.

Nationalism in Bengal was, though becoming increasingly secular, for some time religious in character. It was influenced by the Neo-Vedantic movement of Swami Vivekananda. Hence, the attempt on the part of the Bengalee Nationalists to base the movement for 'Swaraj' on the ancient Upanishadic ideal of the search for *The Metaphysical Absolute* in one's own innermost self. Hence, the worship of the Mother—the country symbolized as the Goddess 'Kali'.

Tilak reinterpreted the Gita and declared action to be its central teaching. The very kernel of the Gita's philosophy, he said, was missed by the Indian people who had, as a result, sunk into inertia and fatalistic moods. The Indian nation could be roused to dynamic effort only if they recognized this. Tilak tried to provide nationalism with a dynamic philosophy by drawing from the ancient Hindu religion.

Islam arose out of the democratic ferment of the common people of Arabia against the privileged strata of society. As such, it has a democratic ring. Islam preaches the principle of social equality. This makes the international socialism more successful among the Muslim.

Despite this relative inertia of the Muslims, from the point of view of their development on nationalist lines, there sprang up, in course of time, a number of religious revivalist and even religious reform movements among them. These movements were, however, not as powerful as their counterparts among the Hindus. Besides, most of them lacked the national note. There were four such main movements started by (1) Shah Abdul Aziz of Delhi, (2) Syed Ahmad of Bareilly, (3) Shaikh Karamat Ali of Jaunpur and (4) Jahi Shariat-ullah of Faridpur. These four movements were more of a revivalist character.

The *Ahmadiya Movements* founded by Mirza Ghulam Ahmad in 1889 was more or less based on liberal principles. It described itself as the standard bearer of Mahomedan Renaissance. It based itself, like the Brahmo Samaj, on the principles influenced by western liberalism, theosophy, the religious reform movements of the Hindus. The Ahmadiya Movement opposed Jehad or the sacred war against non-Muslims. It stood for fraternal relations among all people.

The movement spread Western liberal education among the Indian Muslims. It started a network of schools and colleges for that purpose and published periodicals and books, both in English and vernaculars.

Despite its liberalism, the Ahmadiya Movement, such as Bahaism that flourished in the West Asiatic countries, suffered from mysticism. It, however, represented an attempt on the part of Islam to assimilate the principles of Western liberalism.

The first national awakening among the Muslims found expression in a movement that aimed at making the Indian Muslims politically conscious and spreading modern education among them. Saiyad Ahmed Khan was the founder of this movement. He had such able collaborators as the poet Khwaja Altaf Hussain Hali, Maulvi Nazir Ahmad and Maulvi Shibli Numani.

The liberal social reform and cultural movement founded by Sir Saiyad Ahmed Khan is known as the Aligarh Movement because it was at Aligarh that the Mahomedan Anglo-Oriental College was established by it in 1875. This college developed into the Aligarh University in 1920.

The Aligarh Movement aimed at spreading Western education among the Muslims without weakening their allegiance to Islam. The religious education reinforced the secular education, which was imparted in the educational institutions. The second task it undertook was to introduce social reform in the Muslim society. The Aligarh Movement was based on a liberal interpretation of the Quran. It tried to harmonize Islam with the modern liberal culture.

Sir Muhammad Iqbal, poet of worldwide fame, played an important role in the history of the Indian Muslims. Although he supported the Liberal movement, he asked the Muslim Liberals to be on guard so that the broad human principle, which Islam stood for, was not thrown in the background by emphasis on the nation and the race. In the course of time, the movement for the emancipation of the Muslim women and for combating such institutions as *'purdah'* came into existence (Smith, 1976). Tyabji, an enlightened and progressive Muslim, was the founder of his movement in Bombay. Shaikh Abdul Halil Sharar (1860–1896), an outstanding author and journalist, organized a veritable crusade against *purdah* in the United Provinces. Individual Muslims and Muslim organizations established an increasing number of educational institutions for the Muslim women all over India and slowly education began to spread among the Muslim women.

Thus, the religious reform and social reform movements grew and gathered momentum among the Muslims also. The rise of Turkish and Arab nationalism and the establishment of a national secular state in Turkey had the effect of broadening the outlook of the Indian Muslims. Modern Turkey had the effect of modernizing the mind of an increasing number of the Indian Muslims. The rise and development of the Indian National Movement also increasingly brought the Muslims into the orbit of the Indian nationalism. The independent workers' and parents' movements developed rapidly in India later on and were mostly led by the communists, the socialists and the Left nationalists such as Jawaharlal Nehru and class-conscious activists.

THEORETICAL APPROACHES TO THE STUDY

Sociologically, social structures are the determinant of cultural activity and interactions. When one individual interacts with another, the reciprocal and social exchange is being perceived. These facts have been considered as the basis of the approaches in the theoretical interpretation of social exchange by Homans (1961,1974), Blau (1964) and Rose (1962). George Mead (1934) accepted the importance of social interactions in his role theory. *In this study, interactional exchange approach has been adopted to analyse the reciprocal relations and tolerant behaviour of both the communities.* The interactional approach is of much relevance due to its real presentation of the social exchange and interdependency. The social configuration of Indian society—with its structural components, such as caste with its over 3,600 units, the joint family, marriage, the village community consisting of the jajmani system and predominant agricultural economy, on the one hand, and the cultural components and inherent institutional attributes, such as varna, ashrama, purushartha, the doctrine of karma and dharma of Hindu population along with a number of other communal, sectarian groups, a jumble of languages, dialects, eco-cultural demarcations such as the tribal, the rural and the urban, on the other hand, present a peculiar and complex profile of the social system. It demands a highly rationalized body of conceptual schemes or approach to analyse and account for social and cultural changes occurring in the system. It was this institutionally organized framework fortified with institutional norms, values, beliefs, transcendental ideas, caste sanctions and taboos that protected itself from the damaging effects for thousands of years. The historical survey reveals the arrival and invasion of the Aryans, the Scythians, the Parthians, the Bactrians, the Turks, emerging changes with different dynasties such as Gori, Gazanavi, Khiljis, the Lodis, the Great Moghuls and then the Britishers right from 4000 BC to the sixteenth century AD. They conquered many estates, established their Sultanates and Empires, ruled over the country by inculcating their own religio-social and legal norms and beliefs. But despite all the thundering shocks of outward changes, as the historians, indologists and social scientists perceive, these shocks resulted only in positional, attitudinal and cultural changes, whereas the structural framework with minor modifications functioned as a shock absorber to the outwardly changes and perpetuated the continuity of orthogenetic attributes and traditions vis-à-vis Western urbo-industrial and modern forces of change (Koshambi, 1956; Majumdar, 1958; Nehru, 1960; Ghurye, 1961).

As far as the present situation is concerned, the modernizing forces arising out of modern education, Western technology, industrialization and urbanization and above all, the growth of materialism and rationalism, have sapped most of the potential traditional social sanctions concerning caste hierarchy, segmentation, the doctrine of Karma and the myth of purity and pollution (Dube, 1965). The sure and serious impact of all these have brought about many more changes in the structural as well as institutional or cultural aspects of society. This has resulted in socio-cultural and positional changes among the caste Hindus as well as among the backward classes, the Scheduled Castes and other sections. The urbo-industrial forces have paved the way for socio-occupational mobility, rural–urban migration and a shift from ascription to achievement, from particularism to universalism, from diffuseness to specificity, from quality to performance, from affectivity to affective neutrality and from private interest to common interest in terms of the Parsonian dilemma, or, in a word, from traditional to modern, or orthogenetic to heterogenetic transformation. The present critical analysis attempts to focus on the following objectives:

1. To re-examine the relevance and functional utility of the existing theories and approaches of social change in India;
2. To highlight and trace the cause, problems and conditions leading to irrelevance and inactivity of the existing approaches in the contemporary situation, if they have happened to be so;
3. To discover to establish the new and probable approach in the context of problems and causes making the pre-existing approaches dead and dormant so that it can enable us to furnish an objective explanation of the trends and patterns of changes occurring in the network of social plurality and peculiarity of Indian society.

In this context, the following theoretical formulations or approaches are prevalent in the sociological literature on Indian society:

1. Sanskritization and Westernization (Srinivas, 1952, 1962, 1966).
2. Little and Great Traditions focusing upon parochialization and universalization (Singer, 1964; Marriott, 1955, 1961; Redfield, 1955; Pocock, 1957).
3. The structural approach with functional and dialectical models (Mukherjee, 1942; Desai, 1959).
4. Historico-indological approach (Dumont, 1970).
5. The multiple traditions approach (Dube, 1965).
6. Integrated approach (Singh, 1999 [1977]).

As far as the approach of Sanskritization and Westernization is concerned, we find that the concept of Sanskritization is based on a single factor, that is, rituals. In contemporary situations where higher caste Hindus themselves have vacated their platforms and gone up to higher levels in the wave of modern techno-industrial development, they have consequently left their ritual and sacramental precincts far behind. Therefore, they do not appear as an attractive model or imitative reference group for the scheduled castes and scheduled tribes (Gould, 1963 [1961]). Besides, the approach of Sanskritization does not have the potential to explain cross-cultural mobility movements occurring outside India. The concept of Westernization, no doubt, is partially useful in exploring socio-cultural changes. But this too has failed measurably in pointing out the quality, the quantum and the rate of such changes as there is no definite model of Westernization or modernization. The United States, the USSR, France and the United Kingdom (in the occidental world) and Japan (in the oriental world) are the modernized societies. They have different models of modernization.

As regards the approach of the Little and Great Traditions, it focuses mainly on the indigenous changes and inhibits the direction of change. It also suffers from a culturological bias. Hence, it would not be wrong to say that this approach is sceptical, replete with social biases and prejudices and does not refer to structural changes.

The structural approach with functional and dialectical models applied by D.P. Mukherjee (1942) and A.R. Desai (1959, 1984), is a derivation of European, American and Marxist interpretations of economic history and does not systematically explain the indigenous changes. It is useful when applied to small sub-systems and sections of society. That is why this approach does not account for indigenous changes occurring in India.

When we look into the Indian context, we find that most of the studies of social change are based on the cultural approach. The studies of the structural approach to change are either very few, or they are based on historical analysis rather than the empirical and experimental base. Although some studies of structural changes have been made in regard to the village community, caste, class, jajmani system, family, kinship, urban structure, leadership, administrative structure and bureaucracy, the models of such structures are not properly specified. Some structural studies such as power structures, youth organizations, labour movements, change in leadership, and so on, are no doubt brilliant studies on structure but are not properly specified. Some structural studies on structural change are such that they lack consistency and uniformity from the methodological point of view. Whatever studies have been made of changes in social relations from the view point of the dialectical approach, they do not exhibit clearly the development of the tradition of thinking and research. D.P. Mukherjee has been one of the exponents of dialectical approach in regard to social change in India, and he focused mainly on the encounter of the Indian tradition with that of the West which, on the one hand, unleashed forces of cultural contraction and, on the other hand, led to the growth of a new middle class. The rise of these processes according to him generates the dialectical process of conflict and synthesis. In this way, the ideas of Mukherjee in the context of social change give accord to the dialectical approach that he observes as a process of synthesis emerging as a result of interaction and conflict between two paradoxical systems of value and class interest. The process of conflict and synthesis in social structure emerged as a result of the impact of Islam in India and henceforth, continued. According to Mukherjee, the establishment and expansion of British imperialism and colonialism after Moghul rule gave rise to a middle class whose roots are neither in Indian tradition nor in modernity.

A.R. Desai has followed the same dialectical model. He pleads that nationalism in India is the product of the conditions created by British colonialism, which were not in existence in pre-British India. How can this be accepted as a fact? The historical survey of Indian society reveals that the specific forms of nationalism and nationalistic movements were active even before British colonialism. It is true, however, that there was the lack of a powerful and conscious public force behind such movements. An important drawback of the dialectical approach is the lack of substantial empirical data in support of its major assertions that are generally historiographic and can be challenged. It reveals merely a historical description of the past.

The historical-indological approach of Dumont (1964, 1970) fails to account for cultural and heterogeneous change in India. Therefore, is the case with the multiple traditions approach of Dube (1965). It is a general classification but practically too confusing since it does not indicate a clear dividing line between classical tradition, national traditional, regional tradition, local tradition, Western tradition and subcultural traditions. It is also overlapping. The integrated approach of Yogendra Singh

(1999 [1977]) is comprehensive and useful but when applied on two different levels of micro and macro structures. It also appears to be a via-media type of assimilative approach and is not very satisfactory.

If we apply the adaptational theory of social exchange (Homans, 1961, 1964; Blumer, 1962; Rose, 1962; Blau, 1964) under emulative reference (Friedl, 1964), in the present techno-industrial and urban environment of society, it gives more sociological scope for systematic analysis of structural as well as cultural aspects of Indian society as a whole. The adaptational theory of exchange is based on action and interaction situations that frame up the social network with institutional and attributive aspects of a group, or any social aggregate, be it a caste, a family, a school and an industry, a workshop, a church or a religious centre. It enables with explanatory power the analysis of changes occurring in the caste structure and functions under the influence of modern urban industrial contacts and adjustments. It allows one to focus on an emerging picture of multidimensional changes and rise in caste hierarchy in the urban social network and the relationship through the adaptation process in the field of social living and occupational arrangements. It is an aspect of structural transition by social exchange. As far as cultural attributes and institutional changes are concerned, it is dependent on emulation and exchange. The process of exchange in cultural aspects has a long history in Indian society. It is perceived in the domain of customs, rituals, languages, deity worship and celebrations, style of life and living arrangements. Most of the customs, habits and norms have been exchanged and adopted by different caste groups and communities. Some of the Muslim cultural attributes have been imbibed by Hindus and vice versa. So also, some of the Western, European and American cultural norms and attributes are being absorbed by Hindus, Muslims and other groups and people of other sects and vice versa. Hence, the emulative process under adaptational exchange in theoretical formulation suits the analysis of time and situation best. In terms of eco-cultural transformation, a process of adaptation is seen, where tribal and rural adapt to urban and urban to urbo-industrial and urbo-industrial to super-industrialism.

Although super-industrialism has emerged more clearly in the Western world, its glimpses are seen in the developing societies as well.

The process of adaptation and exchange which found its place in the past quarter of this century in the works of Homans and Rose already has its roots in ancient Indian society. For example, the inclusion of the fifth order, that is, the Svapochas, 'Mritapas' and 'Chandals' into the Sudra Varna during Manu's time. The replacement of matriarchal families by patriarchal family formations among the Sudras and Untouchables is yet another instance of structural change through the adaptational process. The changes in the structural network and kinship organization among Muslims are other examples of a creative aspect of structural change through adaptation and exchange. For example, in a Muslim family, the structure of relations was such that a son and a daughter of two brothers within the family generally married each other. There is a taboo on marriage only if the son and daughter are born out of one mother. Even the son and daughter of the same father but born out of different mothers, married each other. This practice is being minimized with marriages being arranged between different families. It is an adaptation of the Hindu family structure. Hence, is the case in the cultural-institutional circle. For instance, the dower is being replaced by dowry. This, Sanskritization cannot explain. Muslim religious places are revered by Hindus (and Christians). For instance, every year thousands of Hindus (and Christians) go to pray in the tomb of Sheikh Salim Chisthi. Westernization has not done away with traditions and rituals. No doubt, some have vanished but at the same time we find that the continuity of orthogenetic attributes and rituals has accelerated vis-à-vis Western forces. The growth of railroads and other means of transportation have helped this process. When there was no means of transport, barely a thousand people visited Gaya, Vaishno Devi, Badrinath, Amarnath and other places. Now the district record of pilgrims of Gaya indicates that 3,500,000 Hindus visit Gaya to offer *Pindadan* and observe the rituals to their dead ancestors. More than a lakh people visit Badrinath, Kedarnath and Puri every year to observe rituals. Can Westernization offer an explanation for such orthogenetic continuities? Perhaps, but it has miserably failed.

M.N. Srinivas' approach of Sanskritization has a historical base. First, he applied and defined it as a tendency to move higher in the caste hierarchy in a generation or two with respect to his study of Coorg in Mysore. He termed it Brahaminization. Later, he redefined it as 'a process by which a low Hindu caste, or tribe or other group changes its customs, rituals, ideology and way of life in the direction of a high and frequently twice born caste.' Here, he termed it Sanskritization by having recognized the existence of Kshatriya and Vaisya models and again, later, even assuming the Untouchable as a model in terms of the dominant caste. He assumes that the term *Sanskritic* is inclusive of both the sacred and secular elements of culture. Although the scheduled castes have been able to imitate only the secular status symbols such as dress, ways of life and dietary patterns, they have not been able to imbibe the ritual and sacred elements.

A number of studies by Cohen (1955), Shah (1964), Singer (1964), Barber (1968), Damle (1968), Silverberg (1968), Lynch (1969), Rao (1970) and many others showed that the main causative factor in the social mobility of scheduled castes are modern education, democratic privileges, land reforms, industrialization, urbanization with subsequent growth of a number of occupations and economic choices. As far as Westernization is concerned as a tool of heterogenetic changes, Srinivas (1952, 1962, 1966) observed it as the change brought about in Indian society and culture as a result of over 150 years of British rule in India with the establishment of scientific, technological, educational and legal institutions, rise in nationalism, new political ideology, growth of means of transport, railroads, printing press and diffusion of knowledge through English medium. He further says that Westernization and Sanskritization go together and the former accelerates the latter. Thus, the two focus mainly on the 'culture change' not on the 'structure change'. He accepts the weakness, 'to describe social change occurring in modern India in terms of Sanskritization and Westernization is to describe it primarily in cultural terms not in structural terms.'

This is indicative of a simple minded approach and a flight from what is 'difficult'. Thus, we see that it is a dramatization of mere 'culture change' with some historical evidences and stories and not a focus on 'structure change'. The main focus of study for professional sociologists, however, is the analysis of structure first and of culture next.

The two processes are confusing and do not explain the quality, the quantity or the extent of orthogeneity and heterogeneity. With regard to social change and mobility among the scheduled castes in the contemporary situation, our assumption and perception is that a caste is an 'adaptive structure' and not only a cultural category (Pandey, 1987, 1988). The 'socio-political potentialities' enable the people of a caste to develop adaptability to go up in hierarchy and status. One of the comprehensive surveys made by the author indicates that there is an 'emulative tendency' or a process of 'lagging emulation' among scheduled castes to adopt the secular norms, habits and style of life of the elite sections and urbanities living under urban values rather than the rituals and traditions of Hindu systems. The higher caste Hindus themselves have a tendency of de-Sanskritization (Majumdar, 1958; Srivastava, 1959). They have left their places and gone up to higher levels of living in the wave of modernization. Thus, by adapting the habits, manners and customs of people of urban areas, the scheduled castes themselves achieve an elite status for emulation by the rest of the masses of their castes.

Our studies in this regard indicate that the growth of education and changing socio-economic status among the scheduled castes are closely related. Consequently, there is reluctance to accept the traditional socio-occupational structure. Since the modern socio-political environment is embedded with modern education, democratic secularism and provisions for 'protective discrimination', it has provided the most effective measures to introduce radical changes in their socio-economic and cultural status leading them to be status conscious with new aspirations, expectations and value orientations. Further, the new situations of interaction, adaptation and exchange, new economic and political opportunities and incentives motivate them to set their fingers on the pulse of changing socio-cultural situations and modify and transform their status in the direction of elite sections of people of any caste or creed, living under urban values as models for emulation and do not look at Sanskritization on the lines of traditional Hinduism, which once imposed on them numerous disabilities and was to them a veritable chamber of horrors. This has made them conscious of achievement and, therefore, the ascriptive structure of caste Hindus has no practical appeal and attraction for them. In this regard, we perceive the existence of two incompatible systems in India: (a) ascriptive systems of caste and (b) democratic secularism oriented towards achievement and equality of status. In such a situation, the traditional means, such as Sanskritization, has absolutely failed to work. Moreover, it is too deceptive, culture bound, mythical and heterogeneous, appearing as a bundle of concepts, lying dead and dormant and becoming a record or testament of history only. It involves numerous mythical and ideological considerations such as strong vegetarianism, teetotalism, donning the sacred thread, frequent baths and ritual observance, abstaining from eating meat and beef, all of which are not in keeping with the demands of modern techno-industrial situations. Hotels, restaurants, canteens, clubs, recreational centres, health and educational centres, are more modern and secular places and are being increasingly patronized by upper castes as well as low castes as a symbolic mode of life of modernity and modern taste. The socio-economic changes have brought about a similarity of status attributes (sophisticated and prosperous way of life), which has provided a basis for imitative reference group behaviour vis-à-vis upper castes and wealthier castes in the Mertonian sense (Merton, 1957). Economically and culturally, the relative deprivation of scheduled castes in the past enables us to marshal an argument that they are very reluctant to tread on the path of Sanskritization. The modern social climate provides them new avenues in terms of achievement. Hence, they are on the road to neither Sanskritization nor de-Sanskritization since both presuppose the existence of some Sanskritic values which were never found among scheduled castes. As a marginal and peripheral class of the Hindu social organization, they have always been subjected to cultural shocks and conversion to Christianity, Buddhism and Islam.

Democratic secularism and protective discrimination have provided the scheduled castes tremendous potentialities for their socio-cultural upliftment. In this regard, changes in the external relations of scheduled castes with other castes in terms of marriage, participation in common dining and ceremonies occur in such a way as to maximize for them their share of power, prestige, wealth, high status and so on, by which new social forms emerge out of old ones—new caste names and nomenclature, new identities and status links with upper castes. For example, the titles of 'Singh', 'Prasad', 'Gupta' and so on. There is a section that has adopted secular titles such as 'Shastri', 'Bhaskar' and 'Rashtrapal', which do not have any caste connotations. It is many steps beyond Sanskritization. We find that democratic secularism along with modern education itself works as a functional alternative to Sanskritization.

The magical and hypnotic effect of Sanskritization that prevailed over India for more than 30 years on the sociologists of young generation and fellow admirers of Srinivas is almost over. The adaptional theory of exchange is inclusive of the concept of lagging emulation and provides the basis for structural mobility (not only cultural and ritual mobility through Sanskritization). It provides the basis for cross-cultural comparisons of mobility movement studies in India and abroad.

ANALYTICAL CONCEPTS

The concepts and facts that have been used in this study need some explanation for better understanding.

Urban Area and Urbanity

An urban area is an area with an increased density of human-created structures in comparison to the areas surrounding it. Urban areas may be cities, towns or conurbations, but the term is not commonly extended to rural settlements such as villages and hamlets. Urban areas are created and further developed by the process of urbanization. Measuring the extent of an urbanized area helps in analysing population density and urban sprawl, and in determining urban and rural populations. Urbanity refers to the characteristics, personality traits and viewpoints associated with cities and urban areas. People who can be described as having urbanity are also referred to as citified.

Modernization

The idea of modenization comes from a view of societies as having a standard evolutionary pattern, as described in the social evolutionism theories. According to this, each society would evolve inexorably from barbarism to ever greater levels of development and civilization. The more modern states would be wealthier and more powerful, and their citizens freer and having a higher standard of living. This was the standard view in the social sciences for many decades with its foremost advocate being Talcott Parsons. This theory stressed the importance of societies being open to change and saw reactionary forces as restricting development. Maintaining tradition for tradition's sake was thought to be harmful to progress and development.

Hindu–Muslim Traditions

The social, cultural, religious beliefs, social sanctions, customs, accepted norms and regulators of behaviour are considered as the Hindu–Muslim traditions in this study.

Inter-Religious Tolerance

Religious tolerance can be better understood by the participation reciprocation and the process of exchange between the communities.

Social Reciprocity

In social psychology, reciprocity refers to responding to a positive action with another positive action, and responding to a negative action with another negative action. Positive reciprocal actions differ from altruistic actions as those only follow from other positive actions, and they differ from social gift giving in that those are not actions taken with the hope or expectation of future positive responses.

SUMMARY

The universal character of cooperation and homogeneity in all the societies of the world has been observed as a basic need. The process of transformation and change for the fulfilment of this universal requirement has been termed as modernization by the economists, psychologists, political scientists and sociologists. Basically, modernization is a process of change, by which new values, ideals, norms, behavioural and thought processes have been dissolved in the social structure and by which the traditional and semi-traditional societies are moving towards definite and required social milieu. This social structure is decorated with the novel technology, new value orientations, motivations and ideals.

In other words, modernization is a process of transformation and change, by which new values, ideas, technology and economic relations are formed and transform the social order. This transformation can be perceived as the modernized social system. The urban social structure by its very nature is a centre for the diffusion and dispersion of modernization. The mutual interrelations and interdependency among the communities have been affected by the process of modernization.

Historically, modernization was a process of change in system during the seventeenth century in Western Europe and North America, which later on spread to other European countries and, especially, in South America, Asia and Africa during the nineteenth and twentieth centuries. Thus, these modern societies have been developed from different traditional and pre-industrial societies. In Western Europe, these changes are found in the form of feudalistic to utilitarian states and in the form of larger urban centres. In Eastern Europe, these changes are borne out from the totalitarian states and small urban societies; on the other hand, in different countries the birth of modernization has passed by colonialism, imperialism, migration, religious motivations and religious faith. Various models have been observed with regard to modernization. The European countries have different models of modernization whereas Japan has its own model and the model of modernization, for Indian society is much different from any other model in the world. This is just because of the confluence of tradition and modernity along with synthesis of values, norms and ideals.

The process of modernization has been routed in Western countries and expanded to Indian subcontinent. The process of modernization in Indian society has created a network where specialization in socio-economic structure, division of labour, interdependency and cultural contacts has accelerated. In Indian society, the processes of structural change in the form of either Westernization or modernization have been perceived in a specific manner. Various sociologists have studied the process of modernization and presented certain indicators to explain this very process. The indicators carry on psychological and sociological characters. Apart from these, some indicators that are active in urban structure have also been selected.

In this study, attempts have been made to analyse the social reciprocity and religious tolerance between Hindu and Muslim communities with regard to modernization and its impacts. Attempts have been made to find out the nature of religious, social, economic and occupational adoption between the communities. It has been tried to find out the static and dynamic basis of both the communities and their perceptions regarding the supreme power of God. The concerns regarding tradition of both the communities are also the focal point of the study. The interactional exchange approach has been adopted for this empirical study. In this study, the tension between these two communities has not been taken for the study, but the only concern is to find out the religious tolerance and reciprocal relations between both the communities with regard to modernization.

REFERENCES

Aktar, J., 1992, 'Muslims in Varanasi City: A Study in Cultural Geography', Ph.D. Thesis, Banaras Hindu University (unpublished manuscript).

Almond, G.A. and J.S. Coleman, 1960, *The Politics of Developing Areas*. Princeton, NJ: Princeton University Press.

Anderson, Nels, 1959, *The Urban Community*. New York: Holt, Rienhart and Winston.

Barber, B., 1968, 'Social Mobility in Hindu India'. In *Social Mobility in Caste System in India*, edited by James Silverberg, The Hague: Moutan.

Becker, H. and Alvin Boskoff, 1957, *Modern Sociological Theories: In Continuity and Change*. London: Holt Reinehart and Winston.

Berger, P.L., 1967, *The Sacred Canopy: Elements of Sociological Theory of Religion*. Garden City, NY: Anchor Books.

Blau, Peter M., 1964, *Exchange and Power in Social Life*. New York: Wiley.

Bryant, Clinton D. and Dennis L. Peck, 2008, *21st Century Sociology: A Reference Book*. Vol. 1. New Delhi: Sage Publication.

Buch, M.A., 1939, *Rise and Growth of Indian Nationalism*. Bombay: Popular Prakashan.

Cohn, B.S., 1955, 'Changing Status of a Depressed Caste'. In *Village India*, edited by Mckim Marriot, Chicago, IL: University of Chicago Press.

Damle, Y.B., 1976, 'Educated Youth as Promoters of Modernization'. In *Tradition and Modernization*, edited by S.K. Srivstava, Allahabad: Indian International Publication.

Desai, A.R., 1959, *Social Background of Indian Nationalism*. Bombay: Popular Book Depot.

———, 1984, *India's Path of Development*. Bombay: Popular Prakashan.

Dube, S.C., 1965, 'Study of Complex Culture'. In *Towards a Sociology of Culture in India*, edited by T.K.N. Unnithan, Indra Deva and Yogendra Singh, New Delhi: PHI.

Dumont, Louis, 1964, 'Change, Interaction and Comparison', *Contribution to Indian Sociology*, No. VII.

———, 1970, *Homo Hierarchicus*. New Delhi: Vikas Publication.

Durkheim, Emile, 1965, *The Elementary Forms of Religious Life*. London: Allen & Unwin.

Eisenstadt, S.N., 1969, *Modernization: Protest and Change*. New Delhi: PHI.

Friedl, E., 1964, 'Lagging Emulation in Post Peasant Society', *American Anthropologists*, 66(3) (Part I).

Frisby, David, 1992, *Simmel and Since: Essays on Georg Simmel's Social Theory*. London: Routledge.

Ghurye, G.S., 1961, *Caste, Class and Occupation*. Bombay: Popular Prakashan.

Giddens, Anthony, 1991, *Modernity and Self Identity: Self and Society in the Let Modern Age*. Stanford, CA: Stanford University Press.

———, 2007, *Sociology*. Cambridge: Polity Press.

Glock, C.Y. and R.N. Bellah, 1976, *The New Religious Consciousness*. Berkeley, CA: University of California Press.

Gould, Harold, 1963 (1961), 'The Adaptive Function of Caste in Contemporary India', *Asian Survey*, 3(9) and 1961, *Weekly*, 13(25).

Hatt, Paul K. and A.J. Reiss, 1963, *Cities and Societies*. Berkeley: University of California Press.

Homans, George C., (1961, 1974), *Social Behaviour: Its Elementary Forms*. New York: Harcourt Brace and World.

Inkeles, A. and D.J. Smith, 1974, *Becoming Modern*. Cambridge, MA: Harvard University Press.

Jan dt, Fred E., 2006, *An Introduction to Intercultural Communication*. New Delhi: SAGE Publication.

Koshambi, D.D., 1956, *Indian History*. Bombay: Popular Book Depot.

Learner, D., 1962, *The Passing of Traditional Society*. Glencoe, IL: The Free Press of Glencoe.

Lynch, O.M., 1969, *The Politics of Untouchability*. New York: Columbia University Press.

MacIver, R.M. and C.H. Page, 2000 (1950), *Society*. Basingstoke, UK: MacMillan.

Majumdar, D.N., 1958, *Caste and Communication in an Indian Village*. Bombay: Asia Publishing House.

———, 1960, *Social Contours of an Industrial City*. Bombay: Asia Publishing House.

Malinowski, B., 1954, *Magic, Science and Religion and other Essays*. New York: Anchor Books.

Marriott, McKim (Ed.), 1955, 'Little Communities in an Indigenous Civilization'. In *Village India*, Chicago, IL: Chicago University Press.

McClelland, D.C., 1961, *The Achieving Society*. Princeton, NJ: Van Nostrand Co.

Mead, George, 1934, *Mind, Self and Society*. Chicago, IL: University of Chicago Press.

Merton, R.K., 1957, *Social Theory and Social Structure*. New York: The Free Press.

Moore, Wilbert, 1963, *Social Change*. New Jersey: Prentice Hall.

Mukherjee, D.P., 1942, *Modern Indian Culture*. Bombay: Hind Kitab.

Nehru, J.L., 1960, *Discovery of India*. London: Meridian Books.

Pandey, P.N., 1987, 'Approaches to Social Change in India', *Journal of Social and Economic Studies*, 4(1).

———, 1988, *Education and Social Mobility*. New Delhi: Daya Publishing House.

Park, Robert, E.W. Burgess and R.D. McKenzie, 1925, *The City*. Chicago, IL: Chicago University Press.

Parsons, Talcott, 1951, *The Social System*. Glencoe, IL: Free Press.

Pocock, D., 1957, 'Inclusion and Exclusion: A Process in the Caste System in Gujarat', *South Western Journal of Anthropology*, 13.

Pool, Ethiel, 1963, 'The Role of Communication in the Process of Modernization and Technological Change'. In *Industrialization and Society*, edited by B.F. Hoselitz and W.E. Moore, UNESCO.

Rao, M.S.A., 1970, *Social Movement in India*. New Delhi: Manohar Publishers.

Redfield, Robert, 1955, 'Social Organization of Traditions', *Eastern Quarterly*, 15(1): 13–22.

Ritzer, George, 1996, *Sociological Theory*. New Delhi: TMH, Inc.

Rose, Arnold M., 1962, *Human Behaviour and Social Process*. Boston, MA: Houghton Miffin Comp.

Rostow, W.W., 1990 (1960), *The Stages of Economic Growth: A Noncommunist Manifesto*. Cambridge: Cambridge University Press.

Sarvacs, Jon (Ed.), 2008, *Communication for Development and Social Change*, New Delhi: Sage Publication.

Schramm, W., 1964, *Mass Media and National Development*, Stanford, CA: Stanford University Press.

Schwartz, G., 1970, *Sect Ideologies and Social Status*. Chicago, IL: University of Chicago Press.

Shah, A.M., 1964, 'Basic Terms of Concepts in the Study of Family in India', *Indian Economic and Social History Review*, 1(3).

Silverberg, J. (Ed.), 1968, *The New Chauhans: A Caste Mobility Movement In North India*. The Hague: Mouton.

Simmel, Georg, 1971 (1903), 'The Metropolis and Mental Life'. In *Georg Simmel On Individuality and Social Forms*, edited by D. Levine, Chicago: University of Chicago Press.

———, 1978 (1907), *The Philosophy of Money*. London: Routledge & Kegan Paul.

Singer, Milton, 1961, 'Changing Level of Cultural Transmission in India'. In *Aspects of Religions in Indian Society*, edited by L.P. Vidyarthi, Meerut: Kedarnath Ramnath.

———, 1964, 'Social Organization of Indian Tradition', *Diogenes*, Spring.

Singh, Yogendra, 1999 (1977), *Modernization of Indian Tradition*. Jaipur: Rawat.

Smith, W.C., 1957, *Islam in Modern History*. New York: Mentor Books.

Srinivas, M.N., 1952, *Religion and Society among the Coorgs of South India*. Oxford: Clarendon Press.

———, 1956 'A Note on Sanskritization and Westernization', *The Far Eastern Quarterly*, 15(4): 481–96.

———, 1962, *Caste in Modern India and Other Essays*. Bombay: Asia.

———, 1966, *Social Change in Modern India*. Berkeley, CA: University of California Press.

Srivastava, S.K., 1959, 'The Process of Identification and Desanskritization'. Paper presented at *The Fourth All India Conference in Sociology*, Calcutta.

Stark, R. and W.S. Baindbridge, 1980, 'Towards a Theory of Religious Commitment', *Journal for the Scientific Study of Religion*, 19.

The Times of India, New Delhi, 7 October 2007.

Tonnies, Ferdinand, 1963 (1887), *Community and Society*. New York: Harper and Row.

Weber, Max, 1921, *The Sociology of Religion*. Boston, MA: Beacon Press.

———, 1976, *The Protestant Ethic and Spirit of Capitalism*. London: Allen and Unwin.

Williams, Philippa, 2007, 'Hindu Muslim Brotherhood: Exploring the Dynamics of Communal Relations in Varanasi, North India'. Google search, www.hindu-muslimrelationship.org

Wuthnow, R., 1988, 'Sociology of Religion'. In *Handbook of Sociology*, edited by N.J. Smelsor, Newbury Park, CA: Sage.

Young, Jock, 2007, *The Vertigo of Late Modernity*. New Delhi: Sage Publication.

CHAPTER 2

Locale of the Study and Strategy of Investigation

VARANASI: THE METROPOLIS

'Benares is older than history, older than tradition, older even than legend, and looks twice as old as all of them put together.'

—Mark Twain, 1897

Benares, Kashi or Varanasi—an illustrious place of pilgrimage and an idealized nucleus of faith—has been likened to Jerusalem and Mecca. It is acknowledged throughout the world as a core of the Hindu tradition and a seat of ancient learning. It is a city where infinity and continuity, the past and the present live together. There are few cities in the world of greater antiquity, and none of the cities that have so uninterruptedly maintained their ancient celebrity and distinction. Varanasi is a traditional centre and one of the oldest cultures in the world. It can be termed as an orthogenetic city (Singer, 1957; Bier, 1967). Hoselitz (1960) divided the cities of Asia into two categories. Varanasi can be cauterized as a generative city according to his categorization.

Varanasi epitomizes all that is India. Through all that has befallen her, she continues to thrive as the chief centre of religious and cultural traditions of this ancient land. This colourful city, with its mystical ethos and majestic riverfront, has captivated long and enthralled visitors at first sight. The city is situated on a high semi-circular bank, and reaches down to the water's edge.

Mosques, pagodas, temples, houses of different sorts, long flights of steps leading to places of worship—the river, magnificently extended, the stream rapid, the opposite shore beautiful—in short nothing can be more striking and imposing than the first view of Benares. All the buildings are of stone and seem likely to stand the ravages of time. The tridents and crescents, on the tops of the different Hindu temples and Muslim mosques, are all of brass, or gilt, and in the Sun make a magnificent appearance.

Here is another account of the glory and greatness of the city as presented by Sister Nivedita, one of the greatest exponents of Indian culture:

> As the new-comer is rowed down the river (Ganga), past the long line of temples and bathing ghats, while the history of each is told to him in turn, he feels, catching his breath at each fresh revelation of builded beauty, that all roads in India must always have led to Benares. The City is full of places of historical interest not only for Indians but for the people of foreign also. The city is the center of Parshvanath, the twenty-third Jaina Tirthankar and it is the place where Tulsidas, immersed in meditation on Rama, composed the Ramacharitmanas; where Kabir sang his famous sakhis; where Guru Nanak lived as a wandering monk; where Sri Ramakrishna met Trailanga Swami during his pilgrimage; where Raja Chet Singh lived and challenged the British; where Bharatendu Harishchandra produced his literary masterpieces; and where Sheikh Ali Hazi, the renowned saint and poet from Persia, slept never to rise again.' Besides these, the city is concerned with Gautama Buddha, Shankaracharya, Ramanuja, Ramananda, Kabir, Sri Ramakrishna and other religious preachers and leaders. (Nivedita, 2001)

Therefore, it is that almost every temple, every monastery, every house, every lane and every ghat of any antiquity in Varanasi is pregnant with precious history. Each one is associated with the hallowed and loving memories of a saint, a scholar, a monarch or an artiste. Each one has innumerable stories to tell, but very few have been told thus far. They lie just hidden from view, eager to be discovered, to divulge their treasures of the ages to the seeker. Therefore, it is always worthwhile for such seekers to roam meditatively through the narrow, mysterious and whispering lanes of the city, bordered by grey, time-worn mansions, oblivious to the squalor and clamour around them. To do so is a thrilling and unforgettable experience, one which can hardly be evoked from any city other than Varanasi.

The ancient scriptures of the Hindus have eulogized Varanasi in terms that one could not imagine with regard to a mere city. They have proclaimed again and again that Varanasi stands in comparison with no other—either in this world or in worlds beyond. The historian of Vienna H. Vacci has mentioned that Varanasi is the unique place in the world. In his own words,

> As a historian, I am in a position to assert that the citizens of Varanasi are privileged to be placed in a divine atmosphere by having taken birth in the lap of Indian civilization, the greatness of which cannot be compared with the history of any other place in the world.

Sherring (1869) mentioned that 'Benares represents India religiously and intellectually just as Paris represents the political sentiment of France. There are few cities in the world of greater antiquity, and none that have so uninterruptedly maintained their ancient celebrity and distinction.'

Varanasi having evolved in the pre-Christian era was first referred to in the Vedas, the Upanishads and the Puranas. Through the centuries, with its pluralistic character, this 'Golden City' has drawn multitudes of people from far and wide. Some have been enchanted by the majestic beauty and cultural richness, others by the material prosperity and many, of course, have been moved by her spiritual appeal. Devout Hindus believe that the city has a transcendental character and that both living and dying here is a matter of great fortune. According to Hindu scriptures, death in Kashi assures one of emancipation from the painful cycle of birth and death and passing one's last days and, especially, to take one's last breath on the holy ground of Kashi is a cherished dream (Sherring, 1975; Eck, 1983).

The city of Varanasi is located in the middle Ganga valley of North India, in the Eastern part of the state of Uttar Pradesh, along the left crescent-shaped bank of the River Ganga. The land can be very much called plain. Due to yearly low-level floods in the Ganga River, the soil is repeatedly replenished, and hence most part of the city is very productive for agriculture (Singh, 2003). Varanasi is the capital of all knowledge. It attracted people from ancient times here to obtain and share knowledge. The world famous *Shri Ramacharitamanasa* of Tulsidas was completed here. Kabirdas and Shankaracharya also made the city popular by their works. Educational capital or Sarva Vidya Ki Rajdhani, as Varanasi is now described in the song (Kulgeet) of Banaras Hindu University. Millennia-old Varanasi is asserted as an important seat of learning and education from the ancient times. The city has three full-fledged universities, namely Banaras Hindu University, Mahatma Gandhi Kashi Vidyapeeth and Sampurnanand Sanskrit University. Besides these, Varanasi has two deemed universities, namely Safia Islamia and Central Institute for Tibetan Studies at Sarnath, two autonomous colleges, Udai Pratap College and Agrasen Girls P.G. College, along with several post-graduate and degree colleges, imparting higher education to thousands of students from across the country as well as to international scholars. Foreign students from 32 countries such as the United States, the United Kingdom, Europe, Africa, Middle East, Asia and Australia lend an international aura to this great seat of learning. Banaras Hindu University established since 1916 by Mahamana Pandit Madan Mohan Malaviya is the largest residential university in Asia, being a living embodiment of such visionaries such as Pt Malaviya, Dr Annie Besant an Dr S. Radhakrishnan. Varanasi, the millennia-old city, has not only been a glorious seat of oriental learning and spiritual wisdom from times immemorial, but today in the changing scenario of 'global nexus', it also offers modern education in almost all fields through its prestigious academic institutions (Sherring, 1975).

Some tried to understand Banaras by comparison with something 'comparable' in the West. Francois Bernier called it the 'Athens of India', and Edwin Arnold called it 'the Oxford and Canterbury of India is one', referring to its pre-eminence as a seat of learning and religious authority. Being a citadel of spiritual wisdom, the city has several Vedic schools run by different mutts and institutions, famous for rendering education in Vedic Karma Kanda (www.bhu.ac.in).

One may think from various descriptions of its countless old monuments that the city is simply living in the past, but this would be a mistake as it is very much alive and vibrant in the present as well. This is evident from the following facts concerning modern Varanasi. As a matter of fact, it is the living embodiment of tradition and modernity.

Varanasi is the headquarters of Varanasi district and Varanasi division. It is 1,550 sq km in area and stretches between 82°56'E and 83°03'E with a population of 31,47,927 according to the 2001 census. People of all descriptions from India and abroad may be found in its crowded streets. The common tongue of the local people is the Varanasi version of western 'Bhojpuri', while 'Khadiboli' is also used for official purposes, business and publications. Other languages, such as Urdu and Bengali, in particular, are also quite common in Muslim and Bengali neighbourhoods. Varanasi has under its jurisdiction a municipal corporation. New buildings and new streets have been constructed, especially in the outskirts, giving it a modern look; yet the age-old mansions with their countless narrow lanes and by-lanes still preserve Varanasi's appearance of antiquity.

Varanasi is connected with the rest of the world through a vast network of river-traffic, highways, railways and services. In addition to these connections to far-off places, the vast hinterland is also linked for the import of necessary provisions and merchandise and export of the city's products to the rest of the country and abroad (www.varanasi.nic.in).

Varanasi enjoys a magnificent religious mix consisting of innumerable places of worship and monasteries. Devotees of almost all major religious faiths of the world, such as Hinduism, Jainism, Buddhism, Christianity, Islam and Sikhism, can be found here. Its educational spectrum is also notable with four universities and many colleges, high schools, primary schools, traditional seminaries of classical learning and public libraries.

The cultural character of the city has various dimensions with numerous fairs and festivals throughout the year with large numbers of musicians and artistes devoted to instrumental and vocal music and dance and with elaborate arrangements of food and drink, sports and other pastimes. The print media is prolific, with newspapers and journals of different languages, especially Hindi and English, published regularly. Publication of scholastic works in various branches of literature, science and technology and fine arts in different languages has also added to the city's glory and lustre. Public services such as sewerage and sanitation, health centres, hospitals and nursing homes with physicians of both Eastern and Western schools of medicine, water works, electricity, post offices and telecommunication services are all available in Varanasi.

Large- and small-scale industries, cottage industries, banking services, large and small market places and countless shops offering all kinds of merchandise are to be found—almost everything that any modern city provides in addition to the classical, small and cottage industrial enterprise such as silk, jewellery, wooden toys, handicrafts, crackers and artificial lighting arrangements along with the pottery, clayworks, embroidery and so on.

Law and order is maintained by police stations located throughout the city, and there is also a military base, or cantonment, on the outskirts.

This, in short, is an outline of modern Varanasi, a city that may appear like any other modern metropolis. It may, however, induce the reader to ask why then has this city been described as 'Swarna (Golden) Kashi' or why has it been held in such sacred and high esteem by the Hindus as a city of light and an illustrious city with spiritual lustre.

UNIQUENESS OF VARANASI

The fundamental difference between Varanasi and other modern cities, both in character and in tradition, will, however, become evident to anyone who carefully studies Varanasi's history and observes the daily life here with a positive and reverential attitude. Only then can one be convinced that here is a city with a unique ethos.

As it had been in the past, the greatness of Varanasi has also been recognized by the spiritual luminaries of modern India like Sri Ramakrishna and Swami Vivekananda, as well as such illustrious champions of Indian culture as Rabindranath Tagore, Mahatma Gandhi, Pt. Malaviya and others.

In the Western continent, we find that Paris is the intellectual heartland of France, Rome of Italy and Athens of ancient Greece. Likewise in the history of Hindu India, we find that the streams of all centres of learning that developed in places distant from Kashi had always, on some occasion or the other, conjoined in Kashi. In fact, Kashi does not belong to any Indian province in particular; it belongs to all the provinces of India. The chief function of all the places of pilgrimage of India is to see that people of all provinces may feel there the presence of a soul greater than their own. It is at these places of pilgrimage where the great unity of the entire Hindu

India can clearly be realized. The special feature of Kashi, as distinct from those of Puri and other places of pilgrimage, is that it is not only a place where streams of devotion have met but it is also a place where all the different branches of Indian learning have united.

Even among Muslims, who held no special regard for Varanasi, there were those for whom the city was fascinating. Sheikh Ali Hazi, the great saint-poet of Persia, who migrated here around 1750, and Mirza Ghalib, the celebrated poet of Urdu who visited in 1827 from Delhi, were enchanted by the beauty of Varanasi and recognized its greatness. Mirza Ghalib's tribute to the city in Urdu is equally remarkable. Ghalib wrote thus:

> There is also no dearth of Western scholars who, despite their totally different background, have succeeded to a considerable extent in identifying the singularity of Varanasi.

Rev. M.A. Sherring (1869), a scholar and member of the London Missionary Society, who lived here for many years around the mid-nineteenth century and observed the city with the critical eye of a Christian Missionary, wrote thus:

> Not only is Benares remarkable for her venerable age, but also for the vitality and vigour which, so far as we know, she has constantly exhibited. While many cities and nations have fallen into decay and perished, her sun has never gone down; on the contrary, for long ages past it had shone with almost meridian splendour.

And now after the lapses of so many ages, this magnificent city still maintains most of the freshness, and all the beauty of her early youth Calcutta, Madras and Bombay are commercial centres of India, directing to a large extent, the trade of the country. But they do not speak to the masses .... Benares is the living oracle of the nation, and governs the Hindu with despotic hands, in all his sacred rites and practices.

The most striking features of this city, in contrast to the other ancient cities of the world, such as Peking, Jerusalem, Mecca, Athens and Rome, are its comprehensive coverage of human life and its unbroken continuity. Varanasi offers a pattern of life providing scope to all aspects of human life: *dharma, artha, kama* and *moksha*; and this pattern of life, which thrived here at the dawn of human civilization, is still thriving.

THE NAMES: VARANASI, KASHI AND BENARES

There are at least three other cities, Uttar Kashi in the Himalayas, Dakshin Kashi and Shiva Kashi in South India, which have adopted the name Kashi.

The city has been known by various names throughout its long history, but the oldest and most common of these are still Varanasi and Kashi. In the remote past, it was generally held that Kashi and Varanasi had different connotations. While Kashi was the name of the kingdom, Varanasi was its capital, as we find during the age of Shodasha Mahajanapada. In the present day, the names Kashi and Varanasi are interchangeable (Sukul, 2000).

According to one school, the name Varanasi originated from its location between Varuna and Nashi, which was later called Asi. Another suggests that the city took its name from the Varuna River, which was formerly called Varunasi or Varanasi. In the absence of definite historical documents, it is impossible to ascertain the facts today. Nevertheless, most people subscribe to the view that Varanasi derived its name from Varuna and Asi. But even the name *Varanasi* had different versions at different periods and in different places. While the Chinese descriptions of Varanasi are *Pho-lo-nai* and *Po-lo-nisse*, as set by Fa Hien and Hiuen Tsang, respectively, the Muslim name from the time of their occupation of the city was *Banaras*, which continues today. *Benares* is the British variation that has been handed down to the present generation and is still frequently used by many.

According to some, Kashi comes from Kasha, the name of an ancient Hindu King who ruled the city. Others believe that the name simply comes from a kind of tall grass, *kasha*, which once grew abundantly along the riverbank. Then again, according to the *Kashi Khandam*, the name has been derived from the Sanskrit root '*kas*', meaning 'to shine', 'to look brilliant' or 'beautiful'. Hence, Kashi, or what is sometimes called Kashika, is a place where the light, signifying Shiva himself, shines. This City of Light then is essentially 'the city of the enlightenment which liberates souls'.

Varanasi has also been called by various other names in the Hindu scriptures, for example, Avimukta (the never-forsaken), Anandavana (the forest of bliss), Rudravasa (the City of Shiva), Mahashmashana (the great cremation ground) and Jitwari (a place where business is highly profitable).

The *Jatakas* also record various names for the city including Surundhana, Sudarshana, Brahmavardhana, Pushpavati, Ramnagar, Molini and others.

The Mughal Emperor Aurangzeb changed the name to Muhammadabad and also set up a mint from which coins were issued with the intent to disgrace both Hinduism and this centre of Hinduism. This new name remained confined to government documents, however, and this too only for a short time—till the demise of Aurangzeb.

HISTORICAL SOURCES

Sources for the early history of the city are mainly literary. It has been already mentioned that references to Varanasi and Kashi first appear in Vedic literature and also in the *Ramayana* and the *Mahabharata*. Jain literature also has various references to the city, whereas references to it in the Buddhist *Jatakas*, written in Pali, are abundant. Yet, it is *Pauranik* literature that has given special importance to holy places such as Kashi, wherein separate monographs on Kashi are written. The obvious reason is that the Puranas are a mixture of myth and reality. Coins, inscriptions, monuments, architecture and relics that have been discovered in Raj Ghat, Sarnath and elsewhere are often more reliable sources for an ancient history of Varanasi (Basham, 1999).

In addition to Sanskrit and Persian literature, official records and correspondence are important for the medieval history of the city, whereas corpora of government records and various other publications in Indian and European languages are valuable as source material for a modern history. Travel accounts left by ancient, medieval and modem travellers from within the country and abroad are additional sources of information. For example, the travel accounts of Fa Hien (fifth century) and Hiuen Tsang (seventh century) of China, Al-Biruni (eleventh century) of Arabia, Ralph Fitch (sixteenth century) and Reginald Heber (nineteenth century) of England, Jean-Baptiste Tavernier (seventeenth century) and François Bernier (seventeenth century) of France, Nicola Manucci (seventeenth century) of Italy, Malachowski (nineteenth century) of Poland, John B. Ireland (nineteenth century), Mark Twain (nineteenth century) of America, Vijayram Sen (eighteenth century) and Enugula Veeraswamy (nineteenth century) of India throw light on the Varanasi of their respective times. The records preserved by the city's *pandas*, pandits, *rais* and hereditary bankers are also valuable for this study.

HISTORICITY

Conventionally and politically, the history of India has been divided into four major divisions, namely pre-historic, Hindu, Muslim and British. From the viewpoint of time, however, these categories are now justifiably termed pre-historic, ancient, medieval and modern. For our purpose, since the history of Varanasi deals more with religion and culture than politics, the following divisions would perhaps be more appropriate for a better appreciation of the city's history: (1) The Pre-Vedic Age, (2) The Vedic Age, (3) The Age of Jaina and Buddhist Influence, (4) The Puranic Age, (5) The Age of Reformation, (6) The Age of Ascendancy, (7) The Age of Struggle for Existence, (8) The Age of Hindu Revivalism and (9) The Age of the Western Challenge. These milestones of great cultural and religious significance in the setting of political events have been outlined briefly.

The Pre-Vedic Age

Opinions of Indologists differ as to whether the Aryans migrated to India from outside or were the original inhabitants of this land, with the latter view gaining more support in recent years. Whatever the facts may be, Aryans spread into different parts of the country, some of which were already inhabited by Dravidians, Austroloids and other indigenous peoples. It is speculated that a branch of Aryans followed the Ganga–Yamuna tract and proceeded to the south-east. Finally, they reached a place with a beautiful landscape: a ridge with a big river flowing to the east of it and a large, open grass field with canals, lakes and ponds. This land best suited a people who chiefly earned their livelihood by agriculture, and it was this place that would later develop and become known to posterity as Varanasi.

It is not at all unlikely that prior to the settlement of the Aryans there were native peoples here, such as Dravidians, Colarians or some other group, and that these peoples had their own cultures too—but history is silent about them. Nevertheless, the gradual inclusion of many non-Vedic gods and goddesses such as *Yakshas, Nagas, Ganas* and *Matrikas* within the fold of the Vedic gods of Varanasi is a positive indication of the existence of an indigenous population having a distinct religion and culture even before the advent of the Aryans in the area.

Aryans took possession of the area presumably without uprooting either the natives or their culture. Instead, the local people and their culture were gradually assimilated, as assimilation rather than annihilation has been one of the chief traits of Aryan civilization in India since its very inception. With the Aryan settlement here, the naming of places, rivers, lakes and the like started on a large scale, as this is referred in the early scriptures and literature.

The Vedic Age

According to the mythical Puranas, Kashi is a very ancient place—older than what we can conceive of in terms of history. Kasha, the seventh king of the Manu dynasty, was supposedly the first king of Kashi, and hence 'Kashi' possibly derived its name from him. After a few generations, Dhanvantari, the founder of Indian Medical Science, according to this tradition, became the king. Divodasa, another king of Kashi, was engaged in war with the Haihaya king ruling a territory near Jabbalpura and vanquished the latter. This is all, however, part of mythology.

Historically, the probable date of settlement of Varanasi by the Aryans was sometime between 2000 BC and 1800 BC. The city has been referred to profusely in various branches of Sanskrit literature. The Vedas and Upanishads, for example, the *Shatapatha Brahmana* of the *Shukla Yajurveda*, the *Kaushitaki* and the *Brihadaranyaka Upanishads*, have referred to Kashi/Varanasi as an affluent kingdom, a land of sacrifice and also a centre of learning. Such references in the Brahmanas and Upanishads, probably compiled in the second millennium BC, prove that the city must have flourished as one of the centres of the Vedic civilization. About a century before the *Mahabharata War*, the city was subdued by Jarasandha, the Magadha king whose capital was Pataliputra (modern Patna). Kashi soon became independent after the fall of Jarasandha and its king participated in the *Mahabharata War* in around 1400 BC as an ally of the Pandavas, ultimately to be killed in that great war.

During the early centuries of the first millennium BC, the kingdoms of Magadha in Bihar, Kaushambi in central Uttar Pradesh and Koshala in Oudh flourished along with Kashi. Gradually, a rivalry grew between Kashi and Koshala. According to the *Jatakas*, Kansa, the king of Koshala, seized the Kashi *Janapada* and annexed it to his own kingdom, thus earning the title of 'Varanasiggaho'; here we find a reference to this time and to the term *Kashi–Koshala* as one of the pairs of the Shorhasha Mahajanapadas (16 political divisions) that were current in India shortly before the advent of the Buddha (Jha and Shrimali, 1995).

During the Vedic period, the citizens of Varanasi specialized in various professions in pursuit of the *Varnashrama Dharma*, and Varanasi became a prosperous city with skilled persons in all walks of life. Learned preceptors living in ashramas taught the Vedas and other sister disciplines to students who lived with them and led a life of purity and austerity. Thus, since the very foundation of Varanasi under the Aryans, it developed as a centre of learning, where thinkers and scholars of repute were nurtured. In the beginning, Vedic lore was the subject of special study, and the *Vedangas* must have also received special attention. Some educational institutions of Varanasi were older than those of Taxila, which also developed as a famous centre of learning. A free exchange of pupils between the academic institutions of these two places took place over the centuries. Owing to Greek and Scythian invasions later on, Taxila deteriorated as an academic centre, whereas Varanasi, being free from such depredations, not only upheld its former position, but progressed further and reached the dominating position as a centre of learning.

Among various occupations, agriculture and cattle rearing and animal husbandry were prominent. Trade, commerce, arts and crafts were all known to the people. Soft and thin muslins, perfumes, scented oils, silks and silken fabrics, ivory and other forms of art and craft and architecture developed. Among the Vaishyas, or trading castes, members renowned for their wealth were known as *shreshthis*, or business magnates, and with this Varanasi's fame in commerce and arts and crafts grew. The city also had a well-organized army. During this period, Varanasi grew as one of the chief centres of Aryan settlement and developed into one of the most prosperous cities of India.

JAIN AND BUDDHIST INFLUENCE

Suparshvanath, the seventh Tirthankara of the Jainas, was born in Varanasi. Again, Parshvanath, the twenty-third Tirthankara, was born in Bhelupura Ward in the eighth century BC. Mahavira, the twenty-fourth and last Tirthankara, visited the city during his itinerant teaching in the sixth century BC. These holy associations with the Tirthankaras in Varanasi, where Jainism had taken root, especially since the period of Parshvanath, made the city one of the major *Tirthas*, or holy places, of the Jains.

Gautama Buddha came to Ishipattan or Rishipattana (present day Sarnath) in 535 BC, from where he first turned the wheel of Dharma. It is here that he started preaching his sermons on the Four Noble Truths and the Eightfold Path. He also visited Varanasi a number of times during the period from 535 BC to 485 BC, where he preached his message and brought some of its important citizens into the fold.

During the Buddhist period, Sarnath, because of its association with the Buddha, formed the nucleus of a large habitation. During the reign of Ashoka, the great Maurya emperor, Sarnath flourished greatly. During this time, royal patronage brought Sarnath into the limelight, the glory of which had so long been overshadowed by the brilliance of Varanasi. Hundreds of viharas and stupas, numerous statues of the Buddha and beautiful reservoirs were observed by Hiuen Tsang when he visited Sarnath towards the middle of seventh century AD.

The political history of Kashi during the period of Jain–Buddhist influence was somewhat tumultuous. Towards the end of the sixth century BC, when Bimbisara, the king of Magadha, married Koshala Devi, the daughter of King Mahakoshala of Koshala, he was given Kashi as a sort of dowry for the bride. After Bimbisara's murder at the hands of his son, Ajatashatru, and the demise of his queen, Koshala Devi, who died of grief at the king's death, Prasenjit, the eldest son and new king of Koshala, caused a series of wars in reclaiming Kashi. This king of Koshala eventually became victorious in reconquering Kashi. Later on, a peace treaty was concluded between Magadha and Koshala. Prasenjit married off his daughter, Vajira Devi, to Ajatashatru; and once again, Kashi was given to the bride as dowry.

Thus, the kingdom of Kashi lost its independent status and was under the hegemony of the Koshala kings for a time. Prasenjit had placed his brother on the throne of Kashi as an auxiliary king, but Kashi did not remain under the Koshala kings for long and towards the end of Ajatashatru's reign Kashi was incorporated into the kingdom of Magadha.

In the fourth century BC, the Kashi–Koshala territory was ruled by Chandragupta Maurya from Pataliputra and after him by Ashoka (260–222 BC). It was in the third quarter of the first century AD that the city was invaded and conquered by Kanishka, the Kushana ruler. But this occupation of the city by the Kushanas was short lived, as they were driven out towards the end of the second century AD. At this time, the Bharashivas came to the city and performed the *Dashashwamedha Yajna* (the sacrifice of 10 horses) on the banks of the Ganga at a site that is perhaps the present site of the Dashashwamedh Ghat.

Varanasi was ruled by the Guptas during the fourth and fifth century AD and was included in the kingdom of Kanauj in the sixth century AD. It formed part of Harshavardhan's kingdom (AD 610–650) during the first half of the seventh century: During this time, King Shashanka of Gaurh (Bengal) occupied Varanasi; but when he left for Gaurh, Harshavardhan reconquered the city.

THE AGE OF THE PURANAS

Having been associated with the Tirthankaras of the Jainas and the Buddha himself, the city attracted many Jaina and Buddhist devotees, and it came under considerable Jaina–Buddhist influence. This influence, however, was not so great as to overshadow that of Hinduism. In the seventh century AD, Hiuen Tsang observed that the greater portion of the kingdom of Varanasi 'believes in the heretical doctrines, and few revere the Law (religion) of the Buddha'. The time of the initiation of the worship of the Puranic Gods in Varanasi almost synchronized with the Buddhist period of its history. In the Vedic tradition, there was no worship of images. During this period, however, the worship of demigods and goddesses, and the worship of images of both the Vedic and Puranic gods and goddesses were prevalent. Hiuen Tsang notes:

> The statue of the God (Maheshwara Deva) in Teou-Chi (brass) is a little less than a hundred feet in height. Its aspect is Wave and majestic and, at the sight of it, one is filled with respectful awe, as if it were indeed alive!

It was during this period that there was 'the rise to prominence of Shiva, Vishnu, Krishna and the goddess; the emergence of the temple cults; the crafting of *murtis*, which came to be worshipped in the temples; and the development of the popular rites of puja and pilgrimage!'

Scriptures, mainly the Puranas, were written in praise of gods, goddesses and pilgrim centres. The emergence of popular Hinduism took place in the city during this time. Varanasi now emerged as the premier religious centre of India and was considered the holiest of the holy, attracting multitudes of pilgrims not only from every corner of India but also from abroad for its association with Hinduism, as well as Jainism and Buddhism. Thus, Varanasi, according to the *Jatakas*, became famous not only in India but also in the greater part of Asia during this time.

THE AGE OF REFORMATION AND SHANKARACHARYA

The rise of Buddhism was an indication that Hinduism needed reforms. Excessive animal killings in the name of sacrifice, too much emphasis on ritualism and dissension and intolerance among its followers were some of the unhappy developments of Hinduism during this period. Although, the influence of Buddhism checked some of these developments, the exigency of reform of Hinduism and coordination between Hindus was still keenly felt. This exigency was met by Shankaracharya (AD 788–820), the great scholar-monk and religious reformer from South India. Shankaracharya visited North India on a mission to reform Hinduism and bring cohesion, on the one hand, and to counteract the Buddhist influence, on the other hand. Although Buddhism had already started declining around 500 years after the passing away of Buddha, the city now felt the impact of Shankaracharya's presence and preaching, which led to the infusion of a new spirit into its religious and cultural life.

Politically, the Pala emperor of Gaud (Bengal), Rashtrakutas of Deccan and Pratiharas of Rajputana were the main contestants for the possession of Varanasi from the middle of the eighth century AD to the first quarter of the ninth century. Ultimately, the Pratiharas kept it annexed to their territory till the tenth century. The Chedis of Jabbalpore then occupied the city for but a few decades. It was during the rule of the Chedis that the city witnessed the first Muslim invasion in AD 1035 in the person of Nialtagin, a general of the son of Mahmud of Ghazni, and though Nialtagin ransacked the city, he did not remain to rule it.

THE MUSLIM THREAT AND THE STRUGGLE FOR EXISTENCE

The Muslim occupation of the city in the middle ages was marked by intolerance and atrocities committed against the vanquished, threatening the very existence of this old and reputed centre of Indian culture and religion. The people had to face incessant religious persecution and forced conversion by the Muslims.

We have noted that Nialtagin ransacked the city in AD 1035, but left it soon afterwards. Syed Salar Masud, the son of the sister of Mahmud Ghazni, started from Ajmer and went towards Gonda with a passion to spread Islam. One of his followers, Malika Afzal Alvi, proceeded to the city and reached its northeastern boundary. A fierce battle followed, but the invasion was successfully resisted by the Hindus.

In the past quarter of the twelfth century, the Hindu rulers of northern and western India continually vied with one another in extending their respective kingdoms, thereby weakening themselves. Their lack of political and military wisdom and farsightedness played right into the hands of their common enemy, the Muslim invaders. The Muslims took advantage of this internal dissension and disunity among the Indian chiefs, resulting in the defeat of Prithviraj Chauhan of western India at the hands of Muhammad Ghori. Thereafter, Qutbuddin Aibak, Ghori's commander-in-chief, beheaded Prithviraj and invaded Varanasi in 1194; with the fall of Rajghat Fort, the city became exposed to the invaders who exhaustively looted it. Muslim historians have recorded that 1,000 temples were demolished and the booty, loaded on 1,400 camels, was dispatched to the Muslim overlord.

A Muslim governor was appointed to look after the administration of the vanquished land but was soon driven out and

Qutbuddin had to recapture the city in 1197. This time stringent steps were taken to put the new administration on a strong footing.

Except during the rule of Akbar, the great Mughal who not only permitted, but in some cases even sponsored the rebuilding of temples, religious persecution continued during the whole of Muslim rule. Temples were demolished and icons were broken during at least seven separate invasions. Nialtagin, as previously mentioned, devastated the city in 1035; Qutbuddin in 1194; Firoz Shah Tughlaq in 1300; the Sharqi kings of Jaunpur in the 1400s; Sikandar Lodi in the 1400s; and Shahjahan and Aurangzeb in the seventeenth century. During Aurangzeb's rule, in particular, most of the more famous temples, such as the Vishwanatha Temple, the gigantic Bindumadhava Temple and the Krittivasa Temple, were either completely or partially demolished and mosques were built on the sites.

During this Dark Age in Varanasi's history, the light of Hinduism was kept burning by undaunted Hindu residents and also by devout Rajput chiefs, who maintained comparatively close relations with the Mughal emperors (Gandhi, 1986). The role of the champions of the *Bhakti* movement, like Shri Chaitanya, Tulsidas, Kabir, Ramananda, Vallabhacharya and their disciples, who either visited or lived in the city, was also no less remarkable in this respect. Some of these religious personalities, especially Kabirdas and his followers, also advocated a catholic and universal approach to religion. For their part, the Rajputs patronized Hinduism by constructing temples, ghats and mansions and also by maintaining Sanskrit academies, alms-houses and the like.

THE AGE OF REVIVALISM

When the Mughal Empire disintegrated after the passing away of Aurangzeb, lawlessness erupted throughout the empire. The fall of the Mughals coincided with the rise of the Marathas. The militant Marathas, being greatly devoted to Hinduism, were advocates of a Hindu empire and had a special attachment to Varanasi. They cherished a desire to restore the prestige and glory of the city, which had suffered terribly at the hands of the Muslims. With this idea in view, they wanted the Nawab of Oudh to cede Varanasi to them, as one of the conditions of their helping the Nawab against the Rohillas, rulers of the province of Rohillakhand, lying at the base of the Himalayas to the north-west of Oudh. Although the Marathas never gained possession, they poured wealth into Varanasi for various types of religious works, such as the construction of temples and ghats, the running of *satras* and the patronization of scholars and saints, to earn religious merit, as they had done in the Middle Ages on a much smaller scale.

Even in the early part of the eighteenth century, Varanasi was under the Nawab of Oudh who appointed Muslim governors. One such governor was Mir Rustam Ali (1730–1738) who became popular among both the Hindu and the Muslim residents for his sympathetic gestures towards all communities and also for his active interest in the city's culture. In 1738, Varanasi was cunningly seized from Mir Rustam Ali by Mansaram, the *zamindar* of Gangapore, who was the founder of the present Hindu line of the Kashi Raj. Mansaram died in 1740 and was succeeded by his son, Balwant Singh, who was young, active and intelligent and became the first formal Raja of this line. Thus, after more than five centuries of foreign rule, Varanasi got a Hindu ruler. Balwant joined Shah Alam, the Emperor of Delhi and Shuja-ud-Dowlah, the Nawab of Oudh, in their invasion of Bengal in 1763. He also joined the British camp with the Emperor after the Battle of Buxar; and in terms of the arrangement made with the Emperor in 1764, his *zamindari* was transferred from Oudh to the British Government. But these arrangements were not approved by the higher authority of the Government, therefore when the Treaty of 1765 was concluded with Shuja-ud-Dowlah, the estate of Raja Balwant Singh was restored to Oudh. The Nawab, however, allowed Balwant Singh to continue in possession of the estate on condition that he should pay the same amount of revenue as before.

In 1770, Raja Balwant Singh passed away after a busy and chequered life. The Nawab of Oudh had intended to dispose his family of the estate left by him; but at the insistence of the British Government, the Nawab had to recognize the succession of Chet Singh, son of Balwant Singh, to the throne of Varanasi and also grant him a *sunnud* under the guarantee of the British Government. By a treaty concluded between the Nawab and the English in 1775, the sovereignty of the districts dependent upon Raja Chet Singh was transferred, in perpetuity, to the British Government, thereby placing the province under the control of a

British Resident. Thus, 1775 was an important year in the history of the province of Varanasi, for it was in this year that the Muslim hegemony of about 578 years was replaced by yet another foreign rule for 172 more years. A sunnud was granted to Raja Chet Singh confirming him in his zamindari with civil and criminal administrations thereof subject to the following conditions: he should pay a tribute of *Sicca* Rupees 22,66,180; he should adopt appropriate measures for the interest and security of the country; and he should maintain peace. The Raja was also granted the power to coin money in his own name.

In 1778, Warren Hastings, the Governor General, ruled that the Raja should pay a subsidy of five lakhs (5,00,000) of rupees as a war contribution to the British due to Anglo-French hostilities at the time. Chet Singh was compelled to agree to that unjust demand for one year. Hastings exerted this financial pressure again in 1779 and 1780, as he was suspected by the British of being secretly disaffected and of having correspondence with enemies of the British Government.

Over and above this, in 1780 Hastings ordered Chet Singh to furnish 2,000 cavalry, which was later reduced to 1,000 at the latter's request. Obviously, the Raja was reluctant to meet these totally unjust demands from Hastings and to fulfil these feudal obligations to the British Government; nevertheless, he did mobilize 500 cavalry and an additional 500 infantry to meet the quota. Although Hastings was informed by Chet Singh that the sepoys had been gathered and were ready to serve the British Government, he was not pacified.

Hastings was determined 'to make him (the Raja) pay largely for his pardon, or to exact a severe vengeance for his past delinquency,' and himself came to Varanasi to carry out this plan, placing Chet Singh under house arrest. And although Hastings' conduct in this affair was 'cruel, unjust and oppressive' the Raja submitted quietly. The humiliation with which the Raja was treated on the occasion of his arrest, however, caused great indignation among his soldiers, who suddenly rose up against the British and killed a number of English sepoys and three officers. All this happened without any instigation from Chet Singh.

The uprising of the Raja's soldiers and supporters and the consequent massacre of the English officers and sepoys frightened Hastings so much that he fled to Chunar for his life. Soon reinforcements from the British Army strengthened his hand, and he managed to suppress the outbreak in Varanasi. Chet Singh's military guard was cut down and the Raja had to withdraw from the city. He collected his troops and made an appeal for aid to some Indian princes for the recovery of his kingdom but with no result. His troops were defeated in several petty skirmishes with the British and, finally, Chet Singh took refuge under Sindhia, the Maratha Chief, but nothing was ever achieved by this action. Being frustrated at every turn, the indomitable Raja passed away in relative obscurity in Gwalior in 1810.

The period from the downfall of the Mughals to the rise of the British was a period of revivalism for the position Varanasi had lost during the Middle Ages. The Hindu rulers of the city, as well as the chiefs and landlords of other provinces, especially of Maharashtra and Bengal, were instrumental in such a revival. A virtual architectural reconstruction of the city was made during this period and also during the British occupation that followed, and the patronization of Hindu religious traditions was revived in as liberal and extensive a manner as was possible.

THE WESTERN CHALLENGES

The British occupation of the city from 1781 to 1947, the year of India's independence, ushered in a new age in the history of the city. Chet Singh was formally deprived of his estate, which was given to Mahip Narain, grandson (daughter's son) of Raja Balwant Singh, subject to the payment of an annual tribute of forty lakhs of rupees to the Government. This expensive demand made by the British caused much hardship and affliction for the Raja's subjects. The criminal administration of the zamindari and the civil and criminal administration of Varanasi, together with the powers of the mint, were taken out of the hands of the new Raja.

The year 1781 was, thus, a landmark in the history of Varanasi, for it was in this year that the city witnessed another change of masters; henceforth, it would be under the direct administration of a power that was materially advanced, militarily strong and tactically shrewd; a suzerain from a far-away country with which it had absolutely no previous acquaintance. This change brought both immediate and far-reaching consequences that would become evident in the course of time.

In 1794, an agreement was concluded between the British and Raja Mahip Narain for the purpose of introducing the same system of judicial and revenue administration into the province of Varanasi that had been established in the provinces of Bengal, Bihar and Orissa the year before. The Raja agreed to accept one lakh of rupees a year in commutation of his zamindari rights in the provinces, exclusive of his jageers and altumhga grants, which were left to the absolute management of the Raja. Later on, the relation of the Raja with the British was further defined by Regulation VII of 1828, which curtailed more powers of the Raja. According to this Regulation, in the management of his family domains the Raja exercised the power of the Collector of Land Revenue; but in other respects, he was subordinate to the Superintendent appointed by the British to supervise the general administration of his domains. The Raja remonstrated by writing a letter to the British Government requesting them to repeal this Regulation, but to no avail.

Raja Mahip Narain passed away in 1795 and was succeeded by his son, Udit Narain, who was succeeded in 1835 by his nephew and adopted son, Ishwari Prasad Narayan Singh. In March 1862, Raja Ishwari Prasad received the assurance by a sunnud that in the absence of natural heirs, the Government would permit and confirm the adoption of any successor made by himself or by any future chief of his state and that such would be in accordance with Hindu law and the customs of his race. It is interesting to note here that this Raja would receive 13-gun salutes from British Government troops.

Ishwari Pratap Narayan Singh continued to be the Raja of Varanasi for a fairly long time, from 1835 to 1889. He was one of the most remarkable rulers of his line, respected for his strong personality, keen interest in academic and cultural affairs and also for his patronization of distinguished persons in the fields of fine arts, education and literature. Truly the leading proponent of Varanasi culture in the nineteenth century, he exercised a tremendous influence over the people there.

In 1889, Ishwari Prasad was succeeded by Prabhu Narayan Singh, who, in 1912, was vested by the Government with ruling powers over his zamindari. Aditya Narayan Singh succeeded Prabhu Narayan in 1931, but his tenure was very short, as he passed away in 1939. He was succeeded by his adopted son, Vibhuti Narayan Singh, that same year, while he was still very young. Vibhuti Narayan Singh was the last Raja of Varanasi, and he handed over most of his territory to the new government of an independent India in 1947 under a merger agreement. The Zamindari Abolition Act reduced his property holdings even further.

Vibhuti Narayan, himself a scholar and a passionate promoter of Indian culture and classical learning, was also called by the conventional title of Maharaja or Kashi Naresh by the people of the city, who loved him and held him in high esteem.

The challenges faced by Varanasi under British rule were qualitatively different from those under the Muslims, and notwithstanding the fact that life, property and institutions appeared to be more secure than had been the case during the preceding six centuries; these new challenges to this traditional city were also of great magnitude.

In addition to articles written in different magazines, separate monographs were also written on Varanasi by European authors. Among these are Rev. M.A. Sherring's *Benares: The Sacred City of the Hindus*, in 1968 a pioneering work being the first such monograph on the city's history and culture ever published in a European language; J. Murdoch's *Kashi or Benares*, in 1894; A. Parker's *A Handbook of Benares*, in 1895; E.B. Havel's *Benares: the Sacred City*, in 1933; C.P. Cape's *Benares: The Stronghold of Hinduism*, in 1908; and E. Greave's *Kashi*, in 1909.

From the very ancient to this technetronic age, Varanasi has experienced various structural changes due to invasions and incidents of violence. But its traditional character and religiosity are still prevalent and the people of various communities are enjoying a better and healthy social set-up. People from far and wide like to come over here and want to settle permanently. The specific character of the city moulds the people to form a healthy social set-up.

RELIGIOGRAPHY OF THE CITY

This empirical study is based on two different communities, that is, Hindus and Muslims. Both the communities are the nourishers of their religious values apart from the adoptability of modernizing factors. The distribution of the population based on the religion is as follows:

Religiographic Structure

Community	*India*	*Uttar Pradesh*	*Varanasi*
Hindu	82,77,58,868	13,39,79,263	26,27,565
Muslim	13,81,88,240	3,07,40,158	4,97,516
Christian	24,08,006	2,12,578	4,499
Sikh	1,92,15,730	6,78,059	4,496
Buddhist	79,55,207	3,02,031	985
Jains	42,25,053	2,07,111	1,747

Census of India, 2001; 'Religiographic Census of Uttar Pradesh, 2005'; *Dainik Jagran*, Varanasi, 11 July 2006

Despite the presence of various religions, Varanasi is a prime centre of Hinduism. Various temples in Varanasi such as Kashi Vishwanath, Durga Temple, Sankat Mochan Temple and others prove of the continuity of the Vedic Hindu religion. The discussion of *linga* is found in *Agnipurana*. The Shivling is composed of the combination of trios, that is, Brahma, Vishnu and Shiva. The various temples in the city have their classical importance that may be described as follows:

Temple	*Numbers*
Shiva	513
Vishnu	49
Brahma	01
Goddess Durga	75
Vinayaka	71
Skandha	03
Surya	13
Bhairava	11
Vaital	01
Yogini	64
Sivaganga	08
Naga	03

All the temples and pilgrim centres are not of much significance. *Linga Purana* counts this number up to 462, whereas *Kashi Khandam* mentions that the 383 temples and pilgrim centres are of much significance.

REVIEW OF LITERATURE

The relations between Hindu and Muslim communities are much important in the contemporary Indian society. Both the communities are heavily influenced by modernization, urbanization, industrialization and global development. Different social scientists, social activists and NGOs have performed various studies, but there are fewer studies that can exhibit the religious tolerance, social reciprocity and participation of the communities. This study is an attempt to explore the inter-religious social reciprocity, religious tolerant behaviour of both the communities. M.N. Srinivas (1966) used the concept of Sanskritization and Westernization to explain social, economic, religious and cultural changes in contemporary Indian society. The studies of Srinivas reveal that low Hindu castes, or tribal or other group, have a tendency to enhance their social status by imitating higher castes or twice-born. McKim Marriott (1955), a disciple of Redfield, conducted some important studies in India. He applied some of the concepts of Redfield in India's rural society to understand the process of interaction between little and great traditions of Hindu society and how little traditions are transforming into great traditions and accepted universality. He regarded this process as universalization and parochialization. The upward journey of little traditions to become a part of great traditions is universalization. Parochialization is a process of ruralization.

Milton Singer (1964) also studied the changes in modern Indian society keeping in mind the continuity and impact of little and great traditions. He concludes that due to modernization, only superstitions of religion have been narrowed. Singer accepted the continuity of little and great traditions of both Hindu and Muslim communities. Singer has focused on the interrelationships and mutual reciprocity of both the communities. Similar studies have also been presented by Yogendra Singh (1977). He concluded that the communities, namely Hindus and Muslims, have maintained their great traditions despite the influences of modernization and Westernization. He advocated the modernization of Indian tradition by arguing that the religious beliefs and traditions of both the communities are adopting new vision and beliefs. Different studies in Indian context are of much significance, such as the studies by Dumont (1965), Edward Shills (1961), Harper (1959), Ishwaran (1970), Bhattacharya (1999), Hasnain (2008), Sikand (2008), Ali (2006), Madan (1981), Robert Redfield (1955), Ashraf (1959) and Brass (2003).

Sunthar Visuvalingam (1995) presented in detail a history of Hindu–Muslim relations in colonial Banaras. It is an attempt to explore and explain the relationship from the Lat Bhairo Riots of 1809 to the Gandhian civil disobedience of 1811.

Asghar Ali Engineer (1995, 2002) discussed in detail about resolution of Hindu–Muslim problems and strategies for the enhancement of social reciprocity and religious tolerance. He added that the separation between these two communities is in politics, not in religion. Robinson (1974) and Menon (1981) found in their studies that political participation and lifestyle have been changed due to modernization. Smith (1957) presented the explanations of modern Muslim society in regard to the forces of modernization. Aziz Ahmad (1967) discussed elaborately the impact of modernization on the Islamic tradition.

Wright (1983) in his studies of Indian Muslims observed that there are some errors in the communitarian values of Muslims due to traditional, cultural and religious values intermingling with modern values. There are fewer studies concerning the Muslims in urban social set-up. In this regard, the studies of Ansari (1960), Mujeeb (1967), Ahmad (1973) and Madan (1976) are of worth importance. The studies of Masselos (1973) on the Muslims of Mumbai, Siddiqui (1973) on the study of Muslims of Kolkata and Goodfriend (1983) on the study of Delhi are of immense significance in this regard. Madan (1981) conducted his study on the Hindu and Muslim communities in Kashmir and found that there are various similarities despite dissimilarities and differences between both the communities. Saiyid (1981) concluded that the Muslim festival and festivities are somehow affected by the Hindu values. Eade (1983) explained with the help of the study conducted on the educated middle- class Bengali Muslim communities that these people are adopting the various behavioural patterns, cultural values and lifestyles of the Hindu Bengalis. Ghose and Kumar (1991) analysed the socio-psychological prospective of Hindu–Muslim intergroup relations.

Ashutosh Varshney (2004) studied the role of civil society in ethnic conflicts and concluded that both the communities are transforming their social structure in the wave of modernization.

THE PRESENT STUDY

This empirical study is aimed to furnish a descriptive and analytical account of the relations between Hindu and Muslim communities. The relations between these two communities have been seen in different aspects. The first aspect is during the foundation of British rule by the British East India Company; and second, the closure of the final chapter of that rule when the British Parliament directly took over the reins of administration of the city and, for that matter, all of India, after the Indian Revolt of 1857, known as the Sepoy Mutiny. The history of Varanasi during this period is essentially a history of religion and culture and not of politics, although some incidents did occur here, which had political implications as well. Different dimensions of that religious and cultural history, for which this city is so famous, will be taken up for the study. Other important aspects, including its physical layout, society, economy, education, law and order and so on, will also be dealt with to present a total picture of Varanasi.

The British imported new ideas and institutions from the West in an imperialist strategy to consolidate their Indian Empire and to complete the political conquest of this land by cultural conquest as well. Christian missionaries, unwitting accomplices in this design, also aspired to conquer Varanasi for Christ. To what extent these designs were successful and how the city reacted to these challenges of Western culture and civilization will be examined.

As suggested at the outset, there are also certain fundamental queries that must be raised. If Varanasi is truly the great city that many of them claim, what makes it great? If Varanasi is truly unique among the cities of the world, what gives it its uniqueness? Answers to these and other relevant questions will also be attempted in this study. *The interreligious tolerance and social reciprocity in the wave of modernization is the focal theme of this empirical study.*

Culture is the creation of collectivity, which is borne out from the collective efforts of a society and is nourished by behaviour, values, habits, concepts, art, philosophy, ideology and mode of thinking. Culture has the capacity of self-immunization. As such, the appearance of various communities in Varanasi city has created the amazing culture, lifestyle, creativity and religious structure that has not been affected by various invasions or intruders. *The contemporary society is experiencing a new pattern of behavioural exchange and interactions, which is a sociological reality.*

The proposed universe of the study is Varanasi city, which, from time immemorial was the stronghold of Hindu culture and religion. The city of Varanasi reflects a peculiar blend of Hindu–Muslim population.

The present study is concerned with the explanation of socio-religious participation and sharing of values in an urban social structure. To maintain a sociological objectivity, the religiographic morphology of the city is taken into account and the study area is divided as follows:

1. The major Hindu settlement areas
2. The major Muslim settlement areas
3. The Hindu–Muslim conglomeration areas

Major Hindu settlement areas are Assi (Number of Houses – 2005), Bhadaini (Houses – 1100), Bhelupura (Houses – 550), Gurudham-Ravindrapuri (Houses – 1200), Birdopur (Houses – 850), Sonia (Houses – 1900), whereas major Muslim settlement areas are Lallapura (Houses – 1100), Madanpura (Houses – 1900), Rewari Talab (Houses – 500), Alaipura (Houses – 900) and Chowkaghat (Houses – 700). On the other hand, major Hindu–Muslim agglomeration areas are Godowlia (Houses – 4400), Chowk (Houses – 2000), Sonarpura (Houses – 550), Aurangabad (Houses – 1100), Sunderpur (Houses – 1050), Samneghat (Houses – 478) and Ravindrapuri (Houses – 987).

Sampling is taking any portion of a population or universe as representative of that population or universe. This definition does not say that the sample taken or drawn, as researchers say, is representative. It says rather taking a portion of the population and considering it to be representative. Further, on the basis of *purposive random sampling* 100 households from each location have been sorted out where the heads of the families of the aforesaid households are to be selected for collecting the data with the help of diverse questions set in an interview schedule. In order to maintain the *raison d'être*, attempts have been made to have equal representation from each area.

Research design is the plan, structure and strategy of investigation conceived so as to obtain answers to research question and to control variance (Kerlinger, 1998). The plan is the overall scheme or programme of the research. It includes an outline of what the investigator will do from writing the hypotheses and their operational implication to the final analysis of the data. The structure of the research is more specific. It is the outline, the scheme and the paradigm of the operation of variables. The research design has two basic purposes:

1. provide answers to research question
2. control variance

The design of the research is *descriptive cum exploratory*. Description involves the experiences of mutual cooperation and religiosity. The major goal of a descriptive research is to describe events, phenomena and situation (Ahuja, 2003). Generally, in a descriptive research data are collected in a single situation pertaining to single time period. This is called a one-cell design. Exploratory research is qualitative. It involves the new trends, dimension, causes and consequences as compared to older events. This design is used when there is not sufficient information available about the issues to be studied; or in other words, the researcher has either no knowledge or a limited knowledge. The study is based on two types of variables, independent and dependent. The depth of urban residence, age, income, caste, religion and education has been conceived as independent variables, whereas social reciprocity and tolerance are the dependent variables.

HYPOTHETICAL POSTULATES

The following major hypotheses have been formulated whose authenticity has been tested on the basis of the findings:

1. The more the involvement and active orientation of the people in the urban community in regard to modernized means and mode, the greater the communitarian discriminations to erosion.

2. The greater the social, cultural and religious heterogeneity in the urban set-up, the more multidimensional and interactional reciprocity accelerates in an urban social milieu leading to the growth of urbanized life style (Louis Wirth's postulate).
3. The more the increase of modern social values in terms of rational outlook and objective mind-set will increase the greater the boundaries of religious separation and the loyalties of narrow communalism are contested.
4. Urbanism as a way of life proceeds with the demunition of superstitious and irrational social sanctions, while the rationally organized systems of faith increase with much celebrity in both the communities. The perspective of modernity includes the accessibility to material well-being, social privilege and social security. Therefore, the religion and the tradition are also subjected to sophistication.
5. The greater the involvement of social heterogeneity in occupational sector, the more the people of different communities and subcultures come to interact and socially exchange with one another (K. Davis' postulate).
6. Modernity, urbanity and industrial development have not crossed over the boundaries of religious traditions but they have emerged as behaviour friendly in heterogeneous situations (McKim Marriot and Milton Singer).
7. The greater the population of younger generation as against the older generation of both the communities comes into active urban social life, the greater the social arena of reciprocation, accommodation and participation.
8. The greater an urban community involves multiple occupational specialization and dependence on scientific, technological and mechanical equipments such as system of cybernetics and informatics, the more there shall occur changes in the traditional communal and religious practices, the more the regulative forces of tradition get attenuated leading at length to differences in regard to values, ideas and behaviour pattern between the older generation and younger ones.

OBJECTIVES AND LIMITATIONS OF THE STUDY

The study attempts to empirically analyse and highlight the dimensions of social reciprocity and emerging patterns of tolerance as a peculiar feature of urban behaviour in Varanasi. The following objectives as points of reference are taken to proceed in this empirical study:

1. To analyse the interreligious interactions, social cooperation and reciprocity in the context of modernization among the Hindu and Muslim communities in Varanasi city.
2. To analyse the nature of mutual cooperation and participation of people of both the communities with regard to their religious places, ritual performances, observance of festivity, worship and pray.
3. To explore the religious practices occurring in the changes and emerging process of revitalization and continuity in religious practices among the Hindu Muslim religion as a result of the forces of modernization.
4. To discuss the emerging patterns of behaviour and nature of attitudes among both communities with regard to trade, business, occupation, professional networking and contemporary urban life style.
5. To project the perception of the mindset of urban individual (Hindu and Muslim) about the conception of religion and god.
6. To analyse the social profile and personality patterns of people of Hindu–Muslim communities who have uplifted themselves, above the narrow sinks of communal boundaries religious separations and irrational sanctions.
7. To analyse the values, ideas and practices of traditional relations of both the communities which can be differentiable/different/discriminatory.
8. To critically examine and evaluate the dimensions of social reciprocity and quantum of religious toleration and their emerging dimensions.

In the light of the above objectives, the proposed study is to be conducted on the basis of the fact and data collected from two major communities.

The issues that are conflictual and have no correlation with the theme have been discarded. It is not possible to take the opportunity of all the concerned issues. Thus, specific issues have been sorted out. The factors that are responsible for the conflict and tension between both the communities have not been taken for granted, because these are issues for the independent study. Basically, these are the limitations of the study.

The proposed study is based on the following two types of sources for data collection:

1. Primary sources
2. Historical and secondary sources

In the primary sources, the main tool of the data collection is an interview schedule consisting of a number of questions related to social reciprocity, religious tolerance and urban social structure.

Under secondary sources, the district gazetteer, the census report of the city as well as state, the demographic report, the previous research documents, clippings of newspapers, websites and articles published in various journals have been surveyed out.

The facts and the data collected based on the above tools and techniques are classified in terms of independent and dependent variables. Cross-table analysis of the data is also formulated. The independent variables are age, depth of urban dwelling, education, native placipheny, occupation, level of income and so on. The dependent variables are a variety of questions concerning social participation and reciprocity. Statistical devices have been used to trace out the differences interdependent and the nature of relativity between different variables. A common device in this regard is the *Chi-square test: It* is used for analysing contingency tables. It finds out whether two variables are independent of each other. If they are independent of each other, they will not go hard in hand. If they are dependent upon one another, the presence of one of them can be predicted from the presence of the other.

SUMMARY

The Vedic tradition of been borne out from the appearance of Aryans at the Gandak River (then known as Sadanira) located in the East of Kurukshetra. The religious importance of Kashi is supposed to have started from here. Manusmriti has some illustrations regarding the religious importance of Kashi (Manusmriti, 2/17). The appearance of Kashi is also predominant in Upanishadic literature. According to Govinda Sutta of Dighnikaya, Brahmin minister Mahagovind of Emperor Renu had established the city of Varanasi and Dhritrastra became the first king. This was much prior to the appearance of Buddha. According to 'Aitray Brahman' and 'Sankhyayan Shrotsutra', Renu was the son of Vishwamitra. The illustration of Raja Dhritrastra is also found in 'Shatpath Brahman'. The appearance of Divodass, the King of Kashi, was also justified by all the Puranas. Jabali Upanishad and Mahabharat have also the mentions of Varanasi as a pilgrim centre. Maharshi Valmiki has also prayed the Ganga and Varanasi. The appearance of Varanasi as a pilgrimage first appears in Mahabharat (Mahabharat, Van. 84/18). *Skanda Purana* has also descriptions of Varanasi.

Varanasi is one of the oldest cultural centres in the world. Different names have been assigned to it. Puranas have a lot of verses on different aspects of Kasi or Varanasi. *Skanda Purana* (*Kashi Khandam*) has the maximum number of verses (1,500) followed by *Matsya* (411), *Kurana* (226), *Linga* (190), *Padma* (170), *Agni* (112) and *Narada Purana* (400). The Vedas, the Brahmanas, the Upanishads, the Epics, Bhagavata, Harivamsa and Buddhist and Jain text also have a number of references to Kashi. Mythological stories in Saiva or Vaishnava or Sakta Puranas serve mainly two purposes. Outwardly, they satisfy the ordinary man's appetite for the mysterious, the unusual and the horrible. Inwardly, they emphasize the religious or philosophical dogma or moral values and standards and clothe them in a supernatural garb to make them striking and effective.

Varanasi in terms of traditional perception is an *orthogenetic city* and as such is the '*sanctum sanctorum*' of Indian culture and identity. Some scholars of urban studies have classified the cities of Asia mainly into two types: generative cities and parasitic cities. Varanasi is one of the former ones and has the perennial existence from times immemorial. The oldest testaments of history especially the *Atharva Ved Samhita, Mahabharat, Padma Purana* and *Skand Purana* have references of Kashi and Varanasi. The historical survey reveals that Kashi refers to the political and territorial entity and Varanasi to its capital city. Dr. A.S. Altekar (1943) has denoted territorial limits of Kashi up to Ballia in the east, Kanpur in the west, Vindhyan range in the south and Gorakhpur in the north.

The traditional territory of Kashi has dwindled for a long time between the state of Koshal (Awadh) and the state of Magadh. The references of Mahabharat indicate that Varanasi alludes to the area between River Varuna and the rivulet of Assi. Varanasi became victim of foreign invasions for more than five and six times starting before Gazanavi to the times of Aurangzeb. But these invasions and settlements of Muslim populations ultimately gave birth to a specific bond of social reciprocity between Hindus and Muslims whose instances are rare in the cities of Asia. The ancient configuration of the city of Varanasi can be traced from 3000 BC to AD 700 according to the archaeological exploration of Rajghat Plateau. It denotes the existence of large and small households, narrow streets and founded temples bedecked with gardens, playgrounds, ponds, wells and public amenities. Historians like Greaves, Hawell and Sherring all have described Varanasi as a sacred city, a city illustrious, a city of light and a cradle of Indian culture and civilization.

The specific features of civil and urban life style, art, handicraft, silk work, embroidery, cut work, patch work and so on, what I mean to say is that the age-old traditional features of human dexterity, can be seen in the Pucca Mohal and its narrow streets. These streets and narrow lanes still continue to spread the smell of curd, ghee, cream, on the one hand, and the perfumes and scents of flowers, on the other hand. These streets inside the Pucca Mohal create fascination and attract the visitors. The Vishwanath Temple situated in the heartland of the city and the morning scenario with the crack of dawn at Dashashwamedh Ghat present a celestial pleasure with all sublimity beyond imagination. In addition to above, Durga Kund Temple, Sankat Mochan Temple and Manas Mandir are the most celebrated religious places. Sarnath in the north as a place of first sermon by Buddha attracts thousands of pilgrims from Thailand, Japan, Myanmar and China. Varanasi is situated on the left side of the Ganga River and its overall structure manifests a feature of crescent or that of a conch.

The religiographic structure of the city indicates that it has been an eminent centre of almost all religions of the world. Hinduism, Islam, Christianity, Jainism, Buddhism and Sikhism all have flourished and added to the glory of the city. The prayers, hymns and recitation of mantras in temples, mosques, churches and gurudwaras every morning and evening create an atmosphere as if heaven has descended on earth with its celestial bliss. The origin and immigration of the great saints, ascetics, yogis, sanyasis, astrologists, palmists, philosophers, social reformers, scientists, magicians, thinkers, statesmen, patriots and nation builders are a beggar's description. Mention may be made of a few personalities as rare species of humanity. They are Adi Shankaracharya, Chaitanya Mahaprabhu, Swami Ramanand, Kabirdas, Tulsidas, Ravidas, Ramakrishna, Vivekananda, Tailang Swami, Gopinath kaviraj and numerous others. Among the political statesmen, Sheo Prasad Gupta, Sampurnanand, Bhagwandas, Pt. Kamlapati and several others of equal stature added to the glory of Varanasi. The sacred character of the water of Ganga and its perennial flow has been synonymous with the perenniality of Varanasi, a city situated on the trident of lord Shiva. The Manikarnika and Harishchandra Ghats as cremation grounds attract the Hindu sentiments as emancipation grounds. Manikarnika as 'Mahashmashana' is a place where from lord Shiva himself started the creation. The modern city of Varanasi embodies the elements of tradition and modernity in a peculiar fashion. On the one hand, one can witness the age-old traditional localities, markets, shops and commercial social transaction centres in the heartland, whereas on the outskirt and on the fringe the new establishments, multi-storied complexes, plaza, markets, insurance and banking companies along with new colonies and extended settlements with towers, malls, ever growing buildings, hotels, government offices, hospitals, schools and colleges are the additional features in the process of urbanization of the city.

Banaras Hindu University, M.G. Kashi Vidyapeeth and Sampurnanand Sanskrit University are the major institutions of higher learning and researches. In addition to that, the Central Tibetan Institute, Gandhian Institute of Studies and Arabic

University are also here. Nearly, a dozen degree colleges and more than two dozen higher secondary schools and intermediate colleges are actively engaged in enhancing the cause of education.

The traditional localities in the city are occupied by Bengali, Punjabi, Gujarati, Sindhi and South Indian population. On the open areas and the outskirt of the city, regional migrants from neighbouring states and districts have emerged. It is because of the ever-growing economy, cultural, educational and health facilities in the city. The traditional food articles of refreshment are Kachori-Jalebi, Thandai (cold milk with dry fruits) along with Pan Shops and Bhang shops sometimes attract the natives, the visitors and outsiders. On the other hand, the tea stalls, toast-butter, fast food restaurants, cold drinks, Chinese and Manchurian dishes add to the taste of modernity.

The social morphology of the city manifests a peculiar scenario. While moving in the city, one comes across the boiling cauldrons of milk along with curd and cream at every furlong of the city in all directions.

The traditional costumes, dresses and linguistic expressions denote a peculiar continuity of tradition with modern western dresses and dietary manners. All these have made Varanasi a peculiar city on the world map and attracts lakhs of visitors from South and Southeast Asian countries. Europe and America are no more exceptions as thousands of visitors, scholars, diplomats and artists from France, Germany, Italy, the United Kingdom and the United States visit Varanasi every year. As such Varanasi has emerged as one of the most attractive centres of tourism, indeed a cultural capital of India. It is really a peculiar blend, a melting pot of races and cultures, a specific seat of synthesis of orient and occident, ascription and achievement, particularism and universalism, orthogeneity and heterogeneity, reason and rationalization, spiritualism and materialism and is a lively embodiment of tradition and modernity in attitudes, habits and expressions, style of life, customs and manners. The native personality of Varanasi can be characterized not with aggressiveness and burst of emotions but with persistence of attitude, perseverance of will and forbearance of mind.

Pt. Malaviya Ji by establishing Banaras Hindu University in 1916 emerged as a real architect, of course a crusader of intellectual revolution, who has given a wider coverage of modernity to the city of Varanasi and to the whole nation as a greatest centre of higher learning and researches in Asia in the areas of Arts, Literature, Philosophy, Humanities, Science, Technology, Social Sciences, Law, Business Management, Fine Arts, Visual and Performing Arts, Agriculture, Medicine and Surgery and a number of allied disciplines that have produced ever rich galaxy of scientists, technologists, social scientists, medical scientists along with political statesmen, politicians, parliamentarians, business tycoons and entrepreneurs of national and international repute who are indeed the intellectual ornaments of the city and the county.

No doubt, during the past four decades the enormous growth of population has shattered the economic and commercial nerve centres of the city and the unprecedented migration of population from the neighbouring states and the settlements in Varanasi have caused serious problems of overcrowding in the city resulting in the degradation of quality of life, decline in the health and hygiene status of the city and producing a bazar of the unemployed, unwanted and surplus labour force.

The overcrowded crossroads, congestion and jams on the roads creating regular traffic problems, the huddling together of people in the market and ever-growing rush, the short supply of electricity, the insufficient supply of water and the broken conditions of roads and encroachments altogether present a sick picture of the city. The government, Varanasi Development Authority and corporation have to work a lot to provide alternative measures such as restructuring and renovation along with flyover in and outside the city to solve the problems. Most of the urban problems are the outcome of the laxity of bureaucracy as it is with other cities and metropolis of India. As a social scientist, I am unable to check my emotions and would like to utter a parody that '*Varanasi! with all thy faults I love thee still*', because there is no city in the world, neither the city of London in the United Kingdom nor Chicago, New York, Washington in the United States, nor Venice, Rome or Vatican in France and Italy, nor Athens and Sparta in Greece, nor Shanghai or Beijing in China, nor Sydney or Perth in Australia and not even Tokyo in Japan, which have such a rich heritage of the past that still glorifies and adds lustre to the city of Varanasi placing it today as a peculiar blend of tradition and modernity par excellence.

REFERENCES

Ahmad, Aziz, 1967, *Islamic Modernism in India and Pakistan*. London: Oxford University Press.

Ahmad, I., 1973, 'Endogamy and Status Mobility among Siddiqui Sheikhs of Allahabad, U.P.' In *Caste and Social Stratifications among Muslims in India*. New Delhi: Manohar Books.

Ahuja, Ram, 2003, *Research Methods*. Jaipur: Rawat.

Altekar, A.S., 1943, *Banaras: Past and Present*. Banaras: Nawal Kishore & Bros.

Ansari, G., 1960, *Muslim Caste in Uttar Pradesh: A Study in Culture Contact*. Lucknow: Ethnographic and Folk Culture Society.

Ashraf, K.M., 1959, *Life and Condition of the People of Hindustan*. New Delhi.

Basham, A.L., 1999, *The Wonder That Was India*. Agra: Shiv Lal Agrawal.

Bhattacharya, B., 1999, *Varanasi Rediscovered*. New Delhi: Munshiram Manoharlal.

Bier, A.G., 1967, 'Migration Trends and Migrant's Characteristics', *The Cornell Journal of Social Relations*, Spain.

Brass, Paul R., 2003, *The Production of Hindu-Muslim Violence in Contemporary India*. Seattle, WA: University of Washington Press.

Cabe, C.D., 1905, *Benares: The Stronghold of Hinduism*. Calcutta.

Dumont, Louis, 1965, 'The Modern Conception of the Individual', *Contribution to Indian Sociology*, No. VIII.

Eade, John, 1983, 'Modernization and Islamization among Members of Calcutta's Educational Bengali Muslim Middle Class'. In *Modernization and Social Change among Muslims in India*, edited by I. Ahmad, New Delhi: Manohar Books.

Eck, D., 1983, *Banaras: A City of Light*. New Delhi: Penguin Books.

Engineer, Asgar Ali, 1995, *Lifting the Veil: Communal Violence and Communal Harmony in Contemporary India*. Sangam Books.

———, 2002, *Islam in India: The Impact of Civilizations*. New Delhi: Shipra.

Gandhi, Raj Mohan, 1986, *Eight Lines: A Study of Hindu-Muslims Encounter*. Albany, NY: State University of New York Press, Chapter 1, p. 1.

Ghosh, Emmanuel S.K. and Rashmi Kumar, 1991, 'Hindu-Muslim Intergroup Relations in India: Applying Socio-Psychological Perspectives', *Psychology & Developing Societies*, 3(1): 93–112.

Goodfriend, D.E., 1983, 'Changing Concepts of Caste and Status among Old Delhi Muslims'. In *Modernization and Social Change among Muslims in India*, edited by I. Ahmad, New Delhi: Manohar Books.

Greaves, E., 1909, *Kashi*. Allahabad.

Harper, E.B., 1959, 'A Hindu Village Pantheon', *South Western Journal of Anthropology*, XV.

Hasnain, Nadeem, 2008, *Beyond Textual Islam*. New Delhi: Serials.

Havell, E.B., 1933, *Benaras: The Sacred City*. Calcutta.

Hoselitz, B.F., 1960, *Sociological Aspects of Economic Growth*. Glencoe, IL: The Free Press of Glencoe.

Ishwaran, K., 1970, *Change and Continuity in India's Village*. New York: Columbia University Press.

Jha, D.N. and K.M. Shrimali, 1995, *History of Ancient India*. New Delhi: Delhi University.

Kerlinger, Fred H., 2007, *Foundation of Behavioural Research*. New Delhi: Surjeet Publication.

Madan, T.N., 1976, *Muslim Communities of South Asia*. New Delhi: Vikas Publishing House.

———, 1981, 'Religious Ideology and Social Structure: The Muslims and Hindus of Kashmir'. In *Ritual and Religion among Muslims in India*, edited by I. Ahmad, New Delhi: Manohar Publications.

Marriott, McKim (Ed.), 1955, 'Little Communities in an Indigenous Civilization'. In *Village India*, Chicago, IL: Chicago University Press.

Masselos, J.C., 1973, 'The Khojas of Bombay – The Defining of Formal Membership Criteria during the 19th Century'. In *Caste and Social Stratification among Muslims in India*, edited by I. Ahmad, New Delhi: Manohar Book Service.

Menon, Indu, 1981, *Status of Muslim Women in India*. New Delhi: Uppal Publications.

Mujeeb, M., 1967, *The Indian Muslims*. London: Allen and Unwin.

Nivedita, Sister, 2001, *Luminous Kashi*. New Delhi: Ramakrishna Mission.

Panker, A., 1895, *A Handbook of Benares*. Calcutta.

Redfield, R., 1955, 'Social Organization of Traditions', *The Far Eastern Quarteriy*, 15.

Robinson, M., 1974, *Islam and Capitalism*. London: Allen Lane.

Saiyid, A.R., 1981, 'Ideal and Reality in the Observance of Moharram – A Behavioural Interpretation'. In *Ritual Religion among Muslims India*, edited by I. Ahmad, New Delhi: Manohar Publications.

Sherring, M.A., 1869, *The Sacred Cities of the Hindus*. London.

———, 1975, *Benares: The Sacred City of the Hindus*. New Delhi: B. R. Publishing Cooperation.

Shills, Edward, 1961, *The Intellectuals between Tradition and Modernity*. The Hague: Mouton and Co.

Siddiqui, M.K.A., 1973, 'Caste among the Muslims of Calcutta'. In *Caste and Social Stratifications among Muslims in India*. New Delhi: Manohar Books.

Singer, M., 1957, *Traditional India: Structure and Change in Folk Society*. Philadelphia, PA: American Folklore Society.

———, 1964, 'Social Organization of Indian Traditions', *Diogenes*, Spring.

Singh, Rana P.B., 2003, *Varanasi as Heritage City*. UNESCO.

Singh, Yogendra, 1977, *Modernization of Indian Tradition*. The Hague: Mounton Press.

Smith, W.C., 1957, *Islam in Modern History*. New York: Mentor Books.

Srinivas, M.N., 1966, *Social Change in Modern India*. Berkeley, CA: University of California Press.

Sukul, K.N., 2000, *Varanasi Vaibhav*. Patna: Rajbhasha.

Twain, Mark, 1897, *Following the Equator: A Journey around the World*. Hartford, CT: American Pub. Co.

———, 2002, *Civic Life: Hindus & Muslims in India*. New Delhi: Oxford University Press.

Varshney, Ashutosh, 2002, *Ethnic Conflict and Civic Life: Hindus and Muslims in India*. New Delhi: Oxford University Press.

———, 2004, *Ethnic Conflict and Civil Society: India and Beyond*. John Hopkins University Press.

Visuvalingam, Sunthar, 1995, Hindu-Muslim Relations in Colonial Banaras: From the Lat-Bhairo Riots of 1809 to the 'Gandhian' Civil Disobedience of 1911.

Wright, Theodore P., 1983, 'Inadvertent Modernization of Indian Muslims by Revivalists'. In *Modernization and Social Change among Muslims in India*, edited by I. Ahmad, New Delhi: Manohar Books.

Yusuf Ali, A., 1941, 'Muslim Culture and Religious Thought'. In *Modern India and the West*, edited by L.S.S. O'Malley. Oxford University Press.

www.bhu.ac.in

www.censusofindia.gov

www.varanasi.nic.in

www.varanasitourism.com

CHAPTER 3

The Community Under the Empirical Test

The adolescent period of any individual is the period of personality development. Through personality development, an individual enters into the social arena. In this age, he or she assimilates as well as participates actively in cultural activities. Social and cultural factors, thus, are important in the life of an individual. These factors determine the life opportunities and value orientations. Family, as a primary unit of social structure, basically contributes in socialization, personality development and determines the aspirations. According to Cooley (1962), family is a primary group, where social life and ideals of a child are formed. Family is a universal, permanent and pervasive institution characterized by socially approved sexual access and reproduction, common residence, domestic services and economic cooperation (Dube, 1990).

Urbanization, industrialization and modernization have affected the traditional joint family system in India. Different scholars such as Panikkar (1955), Kapadia (1955), Desai (1964), Srinivas (1942), Dube (1958, 1997), Ross (1967), Shah (1999), Raju (1998) and Uberoi (1993) have presented different causal factors underlying in the changes in the joint family system. The presence of hotels, clubs, restaurants, hospitals and recreational centres has shattered the nerves of traditional society, but they cannot change the primary functions of family and its importance in the stability of social life. Industrial development, women education, entry of women into trade, changing patterns of marriages and priority of materialistic ideology have, somehow, narrowed the values and importance of family in the life of an individual (Oommen, 2005).

Systems of family and marriage have also been affected by industrialization, urbanization, migration and global development. Due to the involvement of women in occupations, the form and structure of family and marital life have also changed. Inter-caste marriages have been promoted in place of traditional and religious marriages.

These trends of changes have been observed in both Hindu and Muslim communities. The changes in social, cultural and religious aspects of Hindu social structure have been explained by various sociologists. On the other hand, Muslim community needs some more attention in this regard. Some scholars, such as Madan (1981), Fruzetti (1981), Syed (1981), Ahmad (1983), Eade (1983), Goodfriend (1983) and Lateef (1983), have emphasized their studies towards Muslim family system.

Every individual in his or her life wants to perform certain deeds and activities that, according to his or her own view, are helpful to provide a better life in heaven, that is, the life in ultra mundane. Religion is an important institution to attain the goals of ultra mundane life. Religion may be used to refer to particular aspects of India's cultural tradition. Religion is such an important institution whose adoption is very useful to organize our personality, social control and give a new insight to understand the situations.

Caste is an important factor affecting social life of an individual in the Indian society. Casteism is being perceived as a threat in national development. Caste system in India, from ancient periods, has divided the society into various structural parts. According to Hutton (1959), the system of castes by its thousands of orders and taboos has affected the Indian society for years. Caste not only decides the deeds of the individual but also determines the daily activities. Due to social changes in different perspectives, caste system has also been affected. Besides this, caste has an important place in the determination of values, orientations and lifestyle of young generation in the arena of traditional societies and its changing patterns.

Marriage is an institution, which admits men and women to family life. It is a stable relationship in which men and women are socially permitted to have children implying the right to sexual relations. Edward Westermark (1925) observed marriage as the more or less durable connection between male and female, lasting beyond the mere act of propagation till after the birth of offspring. Malinowski (1926) defined marriage as a contract for the production and maintenance of children.

According to Horton and Hunt (1981), 'Marriage is the approved social pattern whereby two or more persons establish a family.' A sociologist, while studying marriage, analyses not only the primary relationship involved in it but also how marriage involves performing new and varied roles and whether the persons involved are capable of performing those new roles or not, and how the inadequacy of performing these roles leads to family disorganization. What is important in marriage is how the role enactment of one partner corresponds to the role expectations of the other (Blook, 1960: 189).

According to Koos (1953: 44), marriage is a dividing line between the family of orientation and family of procreation in terms of the nature of roles one performs in the two families. Marriage is a miniature social system, which must be kept in equilibrium if it is not to fall apart. Equilibrium requires adjustment, which in turn requires give and take or some sacrifice on the part of both husband and wife. It is a dyad system.

For young generation, marriage is an important *Sanskar*. According to Bogardus (1950), marriage provides status by five ways as follows:

1. Enhancement of status in family
2. Enhancement of status in trade or occupation
3. Providing status in community
4. Providing status in peer group
5. Providing new insights regarding problems in life

According to Bowman (1960), the basic objectives of marriage are sex gratification, desire for home and children, companionship, social position and prestige and economic security and protection. Bowman has rejected the fulfilment of personality as the object of marriage.

Today, as traditional society is changing into a modern one, these reasons for marriage have been relegated to a minor position. The main motivations of marriage now are believed to escape from the feelings of loneliness and for the purpose of living through others. In simple words, we may say that the main object of marriage today appears to be companionship or comradeship. This does not exclude the object of sex gratification from its scope.

Education occupies an important place in Indian society. It plays a vital role in socialization of individuals. In industrial societies, education is provided by the state as a matter of right for all its citizens. Formal institutions, schools, colleges and universities are organized for this purpose. In India, for the past one decade, our government is continuously trying to enhance literacy rate. For this very purpose, education for the children up to 14 years of age is made compulsory by the Constitution of India.

The communities under the empirical test have been analysed with special reference to age, education, caste, family and marital structure, religion, occupation, monthly income, depth of urban residence and nature of their social transactions. This analysis presents a social profile of the respondents from both the communities, which is of immense significance, while analysing the various aspects concerning reciprocity and tolerance.

With regard to age of the respondents under the empirical test, the findings reveal that the majority of the respondents belong to the age group of 26–55 years (70 per cent), whereas 16.67 per cent of the respondents belong to the age group of 25 years and 13.33 per cent of the respondents are more than 55 years of age. The respondents ralling in the age group of 26–55 years have an equal percentage, that is, 23.33 per cent.

The data with regard to the classification of the community based on their religious structure reveal that an equal number (150) has been selected from both the communities for the study.

The findings, concerning the Hindu respondents, reveal that 33.33 per cent of the respondents are Brahmin, 33.33 per cent are Kshatriya, 16 per cent Backward Caste and 17.34 per cent are Scheduled Caste.

The findings with regard to Muslim respondents reveal that 46.67 per cent are Sheikh, 33.33 per cent are Syed, 10.67 per cent are Pathan and 9.33 per cent are Ansari.

The analytical interpretation of the data reveals that 73.33 per cent of the respondents are married, 16.67 per cent are unmarried and 10 per cent are divorcee. Thus, it can be concluded that the majority of the respondents are married (73.33 per cent) (see Tables 3.1–3.5).

Table 3.1 *Distribution of the Respondents Based on Age*

Age (in years)	*Frequency*	*Percentage*
Up to 25	50	16.67
26–35	70	23.33
36–45	70	23.33
46–55	70	23.33
55 and above	40	13.33
Total	**300**	**100.00**

Table 3.2 *Religious Structure of the Respondents*

Religion	*Frequency*	*Percentage*
Hindu	150	50.00
Muslim	150	50.00
Total	**300**	**100.00**

Table 3.3 *Analysis of the Hindu Respondents*

Caste	*Frequency*	*Percentage*
Brahmin	50	33.33
Kshatriya	50	33.33
Backward Caste	24	16.00
Scheduled Caste	26	17.34
Total	**150**	**100.00**

Table 3.4 *Analysis of the Muslim Respondents*

Caste	*Frequency*	*Percentage*
Sheikh	70	46.67
Syed	50	33.33
Pathan	16	10.67
Ansari	14	9.33
Total	**150**	**100.00**

Table 3.5 *Marital Structure of the Respondents*

Marital status	*Frequency*	*Percentage*
Married	220	73.33
Unmarried	50	16.67
Divorce	30	10.00
Total	**300**	**100.00**

With regard to education of the respondents, the findings denote that the majority of the respondents are educated up to primary level (41.33 per cent). A total of 28.67 per cent of the respondents are educated up to graduate and postgraduate levels, whereas 15.33 per cent are educated up to intermediate and 14.67 per cent are educated in vocational or technical stream.

The empirical facts enable us to furnish that the majority of the respondents are engaged in business (46.67 per cent), 36.67 per cent of the respondents belong to service class, whereas 16.66 per cent have established their own industry work, that is, refill making, bulb-making, printing on saree, silk, patch and jari work, toy-making, polish work and carpet-knitting. Thus, it can be concluded that the majority of the respondents have engaged themselves in business.

The facts analysed with regard to the income of the respondents reveal that the majority of the respondents (42 per cent) are earning ₹5,000 per month, whereas 28.67 per cent of the respondents are earning up to ₹10,000 per month, 16 per cent of the respondents are earning up to ₹15,000 and 13.33 per cent of the respondents belong to the income group of ₹15,000 and more.

The empirical facts analysed with regard to the residential structure of the respondents reveal that the majority of the respondents have settled here and migrated from rural areas (56.67 per cent), whereas 43.33 per cent of the respondents hail from urban areas.

Thus far as the depth of urban residence is concerned, it can be concluded that 40 per cent of the respondents are settled in urban life for the last 10 years, 19.33 per cent are living for 11–20 years, 16 per cent are staying in the urban settlement for the last 21–30 years and 24.67 per cent respondents are living in the urban structure for more than 30 years (see Tables 3.6–3.10).

Table 3.6 *Educational Structure of the Respondents*

Education	*Frequency*	*Percentage*
Literate	124	41.33
Up to intermediate	46	15.33
Graduate/ postgraduate	86	28.67
Vocational/technical	44	14.67
Total	**300**	**100.00**

Table 3.7 *Respondents and Occupational Structure*

Occupation	*Frequency*	*Percentage*
Service	110	36.67
Business	140	46.67
Industry	50	16.66
Total	**300**	**100.00**

Table 3.8 *Distribution of Respondents Based on Income*

Income (p.m.)	*Frequency*	*Percentage*
Up to 5000	126	42.00
5001–10,000	86	28.67
10,001–15,000	48	16.00
15,001 and above	40	13.33
Total	**300**	**100.00**

Table 3.9 *Locality of the Respondents*

Locality	*Frequency*	*Percentage*
Urban	130	46.33
Rural	170	56.67
Total	**300**	**100.00**

Table 3.10 *Depth of Urban Residence of the Respondents*

Depth of residence (in years)	*Frequency*	*Percentage*
1–10	120	40.00
11–20	58	19.33
21–30	48	16.00
31 and above	74	24.67
Total	300	100.00

SUMMARY

The chapter is concerned with the socio-economic profile of the community under the empirical testing. A social profile of the respondents has been prepared and analysed to explain age, religious background, caste, family, marital structure and occupational structure, income and depth of urban residence. Findings reveal that the majority of the respondents belong to the age group of 26–55 years and that an equal number from both the communities, Hindus and Muslims, has been selected. With regard to the classification of the Hindu respondents, the majority of the Hindu respondents are Brahmin and Kshatriya, whereas the Muslim community has the majority of the married respondents, literate and 28.67 per cent respondents are graduate and postgraduate. The majority of the respondents are engaged in business and 36.67 per cent of the respondents are engaged in service and jobs. The majority of the respondents are earning ₹ 5000 per month. The majority of the respondents belong to rural areas and are living in Varanasi for the past 10 years.

REFERENCES

Ahmad, Imtiaz, 1983, *Modernization and Social Change among Muslims in India*. New Delhi: Manohar Publications.

Blook, Robert O', 1960, *The Marriage*. Glencoe, IL: The Free Press.

Bogardus, E.S., 1950, *Sociology*. New York: The Macmillan Company.

Bowman, Henery A., 1960, *Marriage for Moderns*. New York: McGraw Hill Co.

Cooley, Charles, 1962, *Social Organization*. New York: Schocken Books.

Desai, I.P., 1964, *Some Aspects of Family in Mahuva*. Bombay: Asia Publishing House.

Dube, Leela, 1997, *Women and Kinship: Comparative Perspectives on Gender in South and South East Asia*. New Delhi: Vistaar Publishing.

Dube, S.C., 1958, *India's Changing Villages: Human Factors in Community Development*. Ithaca, NY: Cornell University Press.

———, 1990, *Indian Society*. New Delhi: NBT.

Eade, John, 1983, 'Modernization and Islamization among Members of Calcutta's Educational Bengali Muslim Middle Class'. In *Modernization and Social Change among Muslims in India*, edited by I. Ahmad, New Delhi: Manohar Books.

Fruzetti, L.M., 1981, 'Muslim Ritual'. In *Ritual and Religion among Muslims in India*, edited by I. Ahmad, New Delhi: Manohar Publications.

Goodfriend, D.E., 1983, 'Changing Concepts of Caste and Status among Old Delhi Muslims'. In *Modernization and Social Change among Muslims in India*, edited by I. Ahmad, New Delhi: Manohar Books.

Horton, P.B. and C. Hunt, 1981, *Sociology*. New York: McGraw Hill Book Inc.

Hutton, J.H., 1959, *Caste in India*. London: Oxford University Press.

Kapadia, K.M., 1955, *Marriage and Family in India*. London: Oxford University Press.

Koos, E.L., 1953, *Marriage*. Glencoe, IL: The Free Press.

Lateef, Shahida, 1983, 'Modernization in India and the Status of Muslim Women'. In *Modernization and Social Change among Muslims in India*, edited by I. Ahmad, New Delhi: Manohar Publications.

Madan, T.N., 1981, 'Religious Ideology and Social Structure: The Muslims and Hindus of Kashmir'. In *Ritual and Religion among Muslims in India*, edited by I. Ahmad, New Delhi: Manohar Publications.

Malinowski, B., 1926, *Crime and Custom in Savage Society*. Stanford: Stanford University Press.

Oommen, T.K., 2005, *Crisis and Contention in Indian Society*, New Delhi: Sage Publication.

Panikkar, K.M., 1955, *Hindu Society at Cross Roads*. Bombay: Asia Publishing House.

Raju, K.N.M., 1998, *Family and Household Functions: A Demographic Study*. Bangalore: Sunrise Publications.

Ross, A.D., 1967, *The Hindu Family in its Urban Setting*. Toronto: University of Toronto Press.

Shah, A.M., 1999, 'The Family in the Census of India', *Sociological Bulletin*, 48(1–2): 235–37.

Srinivas, M.N., 1942, *Marriage and Family in Mysore*. Bombay: The New Book Co.

Syed, A.R., 1981, 'Ideal and Reality in the Observations of Mohurram'. In *Ritual and Religion among Muslim in India*, edited by I. Ahmad, New Delhi: Manohar Publications.

Uberoi, Patricia (Ed.), 1993, *Family, Kinship and Marriage in India*. New Delhi: Oxford University Press.

Westermark, Edward, 1925, *The History of Human Marriage*. London: Macmillan.

CHAPTER 4

Social Institutions and Emerging Attitude

The development in science and technology, industrialization, globalization, modernization, communicative devices, new values, ideas, beliefs, rational attitudes regarding life and marketization of social relations have hampered the social institution and their structure. Family, marriage, religion and caste have been considered as basic institutions; but in the flow of current developments and cultural contacts, these institutions have seriously been injured and wounded. The changes in attitudes, beliefs and behavioural patterns of the people due to modernization have led the communities and sects associated with these institutions towards serious changes.

Novel tools and techniques of science and technology, especially industrial revolution, have brought about global changes. The emerging attributes in the society due to modern science and technology have shattered the nerves of the old traditions by replacing them with new values, systems and institutions (Bryant and Peck, 2008). These new values, ideas and patterns of behaviour are responsible for the emergence of modern lifestyle. These changes in the traditions are mainly due to the ever-growing necessities of the human society. One may perceive it as transformations in the texture of institutions. Although Panikkar (1955) observed that whenever the system of society is subjected to modification according to social needs, the preexisting institutions and mores are revitalized and renovated, and this view is also supported by the traditional *dharmashastra* and epics. By this way, the institutions that have got strong support of the traditional and orthodox epic writers and that have been proliferating are still strongly rooted in the womb of society and culture despite certain circumstantial modifications. Imtiaz Ahmad (1973a) in this regard, especially in the context of the study of Muslim community of Allahabad, concluded that in contemporary society, the endogamous marriages, especially within the family, between the cousins are in the process of erosion and the practice of exogamy and marriages among different families of Muslims and more especially between the Muslim family of different places are increasing. This may be regarded as adaptational changes in the Muslim community emerging as an impact of Hindu society.

Ansari (1960), in his study of Muslim community of Lucknow, observed that the traditional sanctions of differences based on caste stratification among the Muslims are reducing gradually and their relations with other communities and subcultural groups are in the process of increase, which includes kinship and marital relations also. In the process of development of relations, a reciprocal exchange is taking place with regard to inter-cultural values, ideas and life style. Siddique (1973) conducted a study on the Muslim community of Kolkata for the study of the relations to its social institutions and concluded that some radical changes have occurred in Muslim social institutions and values attached with the life style as a result of modern technology and urban values. In other words, it can be concluded that the emergence of modern technology, communicative devices, exposure of media and Western cultural contacts either through direct means or by indirect affiliation have given a new paradigm and insight into both the communities.

The Muslim orthodox and complex social sanctions and traditions are in the way of transformation towards humanism, liberalism, associativism and social tolerance. GottSchalk (2000) and Vreede-de-Steurs (1969) conducted a study of Muslim women and concluded that the custom of *Purdah* (*Burkah*) and religious superstitions among the Muslim women are gradually diminishing due to the spread of modern education, political consciousness and orientation towards economic and material values among them. Gottschalk also added that the participation of Muslim women in various social, cultural, political and economic activities has led them to rubbing their shoulders with men by putting themselves above the confinement of *Purdah*. Vreede-de-Steurs has also made a thorough study of Muslim women of North India and observed the declining practice of *Purdah* among them. In this regard, the present scenario indicates that the declining tendency of the practice of custom of *Purdah* is found at two levels among Muslim women: first, among those Muslim women who are embracing the modern values and ideas of society and correspond to the new generation. Second, there are old Muslim women who are engaged in daily wages works and small business with their counterparts to assist their family. But at the same time, it has also been witnessed that the adult and old women of upper middle and middle classes are still practising the custom of *Purdah* according to old prescriptions. Ahmad (1964), in his studies, found that the origin and development of Islamic culture in India is entirely different than other Muslim nations. Here, the Islamic culture has been proliferated and developed in the form of a *synthesis culture* in which there is assimilation of cultural element of Arabic, Persian, Hindu, Christian and other different sects and communities. In other words, it can be explained sociologically that Islamic culture is an indispensible part in the 'cultural whole' of India. Imtiaz Ahmad (1975), in his study of Muslims of Delhi, observed that the family structure and types of kinship and patterns of marriages among the Muslims have gone through various changes because of the impact of urban culture and values of urbanity. These changes are liberal in nature and above the complex traditions and beliefs of Islamic culture. Baig (1974), in his study, attempted to see the Muslims on an alternative point of crossroads. According to Baig, the contemporary Muslim attitudes are observing themselves between tradition and modernity. Neither they live complacently with prescribed traditions of Islam nor have they fully assimilated with modern democratic, liberal, rational and techno-industrial values of Western society in their life style. In such a state of affairs, the Indian Muslims are standing on a crossroad, confused with the traditional values and attractions of the modern aspirations, motivations and values of life.

In the context of Hindu communities, some fundamental sociological studies have been conducted to highlight the Hindu social system, structure of family and marriages, which focuses on the nature of emerging changes in these social structures. Despite urbanization, industrialization, modernization, global development and Western cultural contacts, basic and fundamental traditions of Hindu family and marriage, sentiments and institutional beliefs are still effective. Kapadia (1966) made a comprehensive study of Hindu marriage and family, and concluded that Hindu sentiments are still in favour of joint family, and therefore, any change proposed by constitution or law has not been adopted properly. Ross (1967), in his study of Hindu family; found that modern education, urbanization, industrialization and Western life style have seriously shattered different superstitions and mores; on the other hand, strong traditions related with the Hindu marriages and beliefs are still in practice. Agrawal (1971), in his study of Hindu family, has found a similar conclusion. As a result, most of the sanctions related with joint family system have been broken. Hindu communities are facing a severe problem of role conflict and role adjustment with regard to women engaged in occupations. Besides these, both the communities are experiencing an extreme change in social structure, attitude, tradition, trade and commerce and above all in the arena of social exchange.

This chapter is concerned with the social institutions and emerging attitudes among the two communities. The structure of family, ideas regarding marriage, nature of marriage, dominant factors in marital relations, attitude concerning caste system and new trends assimilated in urban life style have been analysed, and attempts have been made to interpret the perceived changes in the social institutions.

Family has an important place as a primary agency of socialization and social control. Family is a commonly used word and, in a general sense, it is well understood. It refers to universal, permanent and pervasive institution characterized by socially approved sexual access and reproduction, common residence, domestic service and economic cooperation (Dube, 2005).

The structure of family in traditional India was joint in nature. In contemporary societies, the joint family system is being replaced by nuclear family. The concept of jointness in the term *joint family* has arrived with different scholars. Some scholars such as Karve (1953) regarded co-residentiality as important in jointness; others such as Cohn (1968), Dube (2005 [1990]), Gould

(1968), Kolenda (1968) and Mukherjee (1975) regarded co-residentiality and commensality as essential ingredients of a joint family system; yet others such as Bailey (1960) and Madan (1962) gave importance to joint ownership to property or co-parcenary, irrespective of type of residence and commensality; and a few of them, such as Desai (1964), have given importance to fulfilment of obligation.

According to Iravati Karve (1953: 21), the ancient family in India was joint in terms of residence, property and functions.

Due to modernization, urbanization, industrialization, globalization and social change, the traditional joint family system is deteriorating. In this regard, some scholars such as Desai (1964), Kapadia (1966) and Shah (1964) mentioned that joint and nuclear family is a process of developmental cycle. On the other hand, Gore (1968) and Ross (1967) considered the changes in the joint family system.

Desai (1956: 154–56) gave three conclusions pertaining to the change in urban community:

1. Nuclearity is increasing and jointness is decreasing, and the husband–wife–children group is predominant in the residential and compositional pattern of the families.
2. Spirit of individualism is not growing, as of the households that are residentially and compositionally nuclear, little less than 50per cent are actively joint with other households in the same town or district.
3. The radius of kinship relations within the circle of jointness is becoming smaller.

On the other hand, Ross (1967: 303) studied the pattern of change in the middle- and upper-class families in an urban area. Ross concluded that the pattern of family structure in India is moving towards a far journey from the traditional joint family by adopting the nuclear family in majority.

Edwin Driver (1962), in his studies, found that in the rural areas, joint families are more in the higher income group than in the lower; whereas in the urban areas, they are less in the higher income groups than in the lower.

The caste system in India has been studied widely. Caste can be viewed as both a unit and a system. It can also be looked upon as a structural and a cultural phenomenon. As a unit, caste can be defined as a closed-rank status group; that is, a group in which the status of the members, their occupation, the field of mate selection and interaction with others is fixed. As a system, it refers to interrelated statuses and patterned interaction among castes in terms of collectivity of restrictions, namely, restrictions on change of membership, occupation, marriage and commensal relations. As a cultural phenomenon, caste may be viewed as a 'set of values, beliefs and practices'. Most of the scholars have viewed caste as solidarity and not as a set of values and attitudes (Ahuja, 2004).

Bailey (1960) and Srinivas (1962) avoided the problem of definition of caste; they view caste as structures. Caste is a closed social stratum that determines its members' prestige, occupation and social relationship. In each caste, social relations between members of different castes are severely limited and formulized. Leach (1960) opined that caste is an organic system. Ghurye (1961) believes that Indian caste system is a product of Indo-Aryans and divided caste system in the Hindu society in different parts. Ghurye accepted the role of inter-caste marriages in national integration. Muslim society also has a caste hierarchy. Imtiaz Ahmad (1983) classified Indian Muslims into Sheikh, Sayyed, Mughal and Pathan. The caste system, as it exists today, has grown and developed through many centuries.

The British did little to modify India's religious and social customs. During the Muslim period (AD1200–1757), Hindu society realized many difficulties. Muslims led a religious crusade upon India and tried to convert Hindu people to Islam. But during the British regime, Indian society underwent some drastic changes. They adopted hands-off policy to produce planned social change. They promised complete religious neutrality and freedom of worship to the people. Due to industrialization too Indian society underwent many changes.

In the era of global developments, modernization and western cultural contacts, the caste system in India realized the following broad changes:

(a) Caste system is not in the process of abolition but is trying to make adequate adjustment with modern changes.

(b) The religious bases of caste have been cramped and shattered.
(c) Old social practices of imposing restrictions of varied types have dwindled.
(d) Caste, no longer, is the determining factor in the occupational career of an individual.
(e) Inter-caste strifes are increasing.
(f) The Jajmani system in the villages has been weakened by affecting inter-caste relations.
(g) Caste and politics have come to affect each other.
(h) Caste, no longer, acts as a barrier to social progress and to the nation's development.

Besides the changes in traditional caste system, both the communities, namely Hindu and Muslims, have unchangeable mental set with regard to hierarchy. Theoretically, people from both the communities express a negative attitude regarding casteism, but behaviourally, both communities express an immense interest in caste hierarchy.

URBAN LIFE STYLE AND PERSONALITY PATTERNS

Urban community is a combination of social heterogeneity, multiculturalism and religio-economic complexities (Wirth, 1938). Urban social structure has the extent of closure or openness and the nature of deprivations and gratifications, attributional criteria, mobility and individual ranking. Urban structure holds excessive secondary relations, anonymity, instability, industries, trade and commerce and so on. In the wave of modernization, urban life style has adopted humanitarian and rational view of life and enhanced mutual social relations.

The empirical facts enable us to furnish that the majority of the respondents belong to the nuclear family system composed of three to eight members (63.33 per cent), whereas 36.67 per cent of the respondents belong to joint family system having more than nine members.

The findings reveal that 58.76 per cent of the respondents are in favour of traditional patterns of marriages, whereas 41.33 per cent are in favour of modern system of marriages. Due to the increase in the age of the respondents, their perception regarding the system of marriage is leading to traditional type of marriage. In other words, the older generation is in favour of traditional patterns, and the younger generation likes modern system and modalities. The chi-square value is highly significant, which rejects the null hypothesis that there is no difference between ideas regarding patterns of marriage and the age of the respondents, and justifies the interdependencies between these two variables.

The facts analysed with regard to the education and ideas regarding marriage reveal that the majority of the respondents from all the educational levels are in favour of traditional pattern of marriages (58.67 per cent), whereas 41.33 per cent of the respondents are in favour of modern marriage systems. A total of 72.73 per cent of the respondents educated vocationally or technically have expressed that they are in favour of modern system of marriage.

The chi-square value is highly significant, which reveals that both the variables are extremely interdependent.

Thus far as the opinion of the respondents regarding the mate selection on account of the priority is concerned, the findings reveal that the majority of the respondents up to 45 years of age are in favour of the opinion of bride and groom in marriages (61 per cent), whereas the respondents more than the age of 45 years, in majority, favour the opinion of the parents. Overall, 52 per cent of the respondents are in favour of the opinion as compared to 48 per cent of the respondents who are in favour of the opinion of bride and groom. The chi-square value is highly significant (at 0.01 level), which indicates that both the variables are extremely interdependent.

The data with regard to education and attitude concerning mate selection on account of the priority reveal that the majority of the respondents (52 per cent) have given importance to the opinion of the parents, whereas 42 per cent of the respondents have given importance to the opinion of bride and groom. While analysing the attitude, it has been found that the majority of the literate respondents (62.50 per cent) are in favour of the opinion of the parents in mate selection. The chi-square value proves that both the variables are interdependent (Tables 4.1–4.5).

Table 4.1 *Structure of Family*

Family members	*Nature of family*		*Total*
	Joint	*Nuclear*	
3–8	–	190 (100.00)	190
9–14	60 (54.54)	–	60
14 and above	50 (45.46)	–	50
Total	**110 (36.67)**	**190 (63.33)**	**300**

Table 4.2 *Age and Ideas Regarding Marriage*

Age (in years)	*Ideas regarding patterns of marriage*		*Total*
	Traditional	*Modern*	
Up to 25	10 (20.00)	40 (80.00)	50
26–35	35 (50.00)	35 (50.00)	70
36–45	45 (64.28)	25 (35.72)	70
46–55	50 (71.72)	20 (28.28)	70
56 and above	36 (90.00)	4 (10.00)	40
Total	**176 (58.67)**	**124 (41.33)**	**300**

df = 4, chi-square = 43.63, significant at 0.01 level.

Table 4.3 *Education and Ideas Regarding Pattern of Marriage*

Educational level	*Ideas regarding pattern of marriage*		*Total*
	Traditional	*Modern*	
Literate	82 (66.13)	42 (33.87)	124
Up to Intermediate	22 (47.83)	24 (52.17)	46
Graduate/ Postgraduate	40 (46.51)	46 (53.49)	86
Vocational/ Technical	32 (72.73)	12 (27.27)	44
Total	**176 (58.67)**	**124 (41.33)**	**300**

df = 3, chi-square = 13.89, significant at 0.01 level.

Table 4.4 *Opinion about Mate Selection*

Age (in years)	*Priority must be given to the opinion of*		*Total*
	Parents	*Bridegroom*	
Up to 25	20 (40.00)	30 (60.00)	50
26–35	30 (42.86)	40 (57.14)	70
36–45	34 (48.57)	36 (51.43)	70
46–55	46 (65.71)	24 (34.29)	70
56 and above	26 (65.00)	14 (35.00)	40
Total	**156 (52.00)**	**144 (48.00)**	**300**

df = 4, chi-square = 13.43, significant at 0.01 level.

Table 4.5 *Education and Priority of Opinion in Marriage*

Educational level	*Priority must be given to*		*Total*
	Parent's opinion	*Groom's opinion*	
Literate	75 (62.50)	49 (39.52)	124
Up to intermediate	25 (54.34)	21 (45.66)	46
Graduate/ postgraduate	30 (34.88)	56 (65.12)	86
Vocational/ technical	26 (59.09)	18 (40.91)	44
Total	**156 (52.00)**	**124 (48.00)**	**300**

df = 3, chi-square = 20.86, significant at 0.01 level.

The analytical interpretation of the data reveals that the majority of the respondents from all the age groups are in favour of marriages in their own caste, that is, the endogamy is still prevailing in society; whereas a negligible percentage of the respondent is in favour of the marriages in their subcaste. On the other hand, there are a few respondents who are favouring any caste or religion. These respondents considered themselves as nourisher of modernity, pleader of inter-caste relations and consider themselves as the outcome of Western influences. The chi-square value proves that both the variables are interdependent.

With regard to the education and preference for mate selection, the findings reveal that the majority of the respondents from all the educational levels are in favour of marriages in their own caste (69.33 per cent), whereas 18 per cent of the respondents are in favour of marriages in their subcaste. It is also evident that education had a positive effect and created a caste consciousness among the people of different religious groups and communities. The chi-square value signifies that both the variables are extremely interdependent.

Thus far as the dominant factors in mate selection are concerned, the findings reveal that the majority of the respondents from all educational levels are in favour of the ability of bride and groom in mate selection (49 per cent), whereas 36.67 per cent of the respondents have given importance to religion or caste. A total of 19.33 per cent of the respondents expressed that they are in favour of dowry because it is a status symbol in matrimonial ceremonies. They hold the view that asking for money in marriages is a necessary part according to their own status and hierarchy in society.

The empirical facts analysed with regard to age and attitude concerning caste system reveal that the majority of the respondents from all age groups are not in favour of the prevailing system of caste in social structure. The older generation respondents are in favour of the eradication of this evil system of society. Some of the respondents have advocated that there is a need for slight modification in this system. They expressed that caste is a primary unit that strengthens the bond of interaction. The chi-square value validates that both the variables are interdependent.

The empirical facts enable us to furnish that the majority of the respondents from all the educational levels are in favour of the eradication of the caste system. The respondents up to intermediate level have expressed that the caste system in society is necessary. The chi-square value has statistically proved that both the variables are interdependent, which reveals that the education and the attitude concerning caste system in society is positively correlated (Tables 4.6–4.10).

Table 4.6 *Age and Nature of Marital Relations*

Age (in years)	*Nature of marital relations*			*Total*
	In own caste	*In subcaste*	*In any caste or religion*	
Up to 25	30 (60.00)	10 (20.00)	10 (20.00)	50
26–35	42 (60.00)	18 (25.74)	10 (14.29)	70
36–45	50 (71.43)	12 (17.14)	8 (11.43)	70
46–55	46 (65.71)	14 (20.00)	10 (14.29)	70
56 and above	40 (100.00)	–	–	40
Total	**208 (69.33)**	**54 (18.00)**	**38 (12.67)**	**300**

df = 8, chi-square = 28.74, significant at 0.01 level.

Table 4.7 *Education and Nature of Marital Relations*

Level of education	*Nature of marital relations*			*Total*
	In own subcaste	*In own caste*	*In any caste or religion*	
Literate	30 (24.19)	84 (67.75)	10 (8.06)	124
Up to intermediate	10 (27.74)	24 (52.17)	12 (26.09)	46
Graduate/ postgraduate	8 (9.30)	64 (74.42)	14 (16.28)	86
Vocational/ technical	6 (13.64)	36 (81.82)	38 (12.67)	44
Total	**54 (18.00)**	**208 (69.33)**	**38 (12.67)**	**300**

df = 6, chi-square = 22.18, significant at 0.01 level.

Table 4.8 *Education and Nature of Marital Relations*

Level of education	*Dominant factors in marriages*			*Total*
	Religion/ caste	*Ability of men & women*	*Wealth (dowry), etc.*	
Literate	50 (40.32)	28 (22.59)	46 (37.09)	124
Up to intermediate	16 (34.78)	18 (39.13)	12 (26.09)	46
Graduate/ postgraduate	34 (39.53)	52 (60.47)	–	86

(Continued)

Table 4.8 (Continued)

Level of education	*Dominant factors in marriages*			*Total*
	Religion/ caste	*Ability of men & women*	*Wealth (dowry), etc.*	
Vocational/ technical	10 (22.73)	34 (77.27)	–	44
Total	**110 (36.67)**	**132 (49.00)**	**58(19.33)**	**300**

df = 6, chi-square = 86.04, highly significant (0.01 level).

Table 4.9 *Age and Attitude Regarding Caste System*

Age group (in years)	*Attitude regarding caste system*			*Total*
	Good	*Bad*	*Can't say*	
Up to 25	12 (24.00)	20 (40.00)	18 (36.00)	50
26–35	14 (20.00)	36 (51.43)	20 (28.57)	70
36–45	18 (25.71)	32 (45.71)	20 (28.58)	70
46–55	36 (51.43)	22 (31.43)	12 (17.14)	70
56 and above	24 (60.00)	10 (25.00)	6 (15.00)	40
Total	**104 (34.67)**	**120 (40.00)**	**76 (25.33)**	**400**

df = 8, chi-square = 33.43, highly significant (0.01 level).

Table 4.10 *Education and Attitude Regarding Caste System*

Education	*Attitude regarding caste system*			*Total*
	Good	*Bad*	*Can't say*	
Literate	54 (43.55)	32 (25.81)	38 (30.65)	124
Up to intermediate	24 (52.17)	22 (47.83)	–	46
Graduate/ postgraduate	20 (23.26)	42 (48.84)	24 (27.90)	86
Vocational/ technical	6 (13.64)	24 (54.55)	14 (31.81)	44
Total	**104 (34.67)**	**120 (40.00)**	**76 (25.33)**	**400**

df = 6, chi-square = 40.66, highly significant (0.01 level).

Table 4.11 *Locality of Respondents and Attitude Regarding Caste System*

Locality	*Attitude regarding caste system*			*Total*
	Good	*Bad*	*Can't say*	
Rural	70 (41.18)	70 (41.18)	30 (17.64)	170
Urban	34 (26.16)	50 (38.96)	46 (35.38)	130
Total	**104 (34.67)**	**120 (40.00)**	**76 (25.33)**	**400**

df = 2, chi-square = 14.1, highly significant (0.01 level).

The data with regard to the locality of the respondents and their attitude concerning caste system reveal that an equal percentage of the respondents from rural areas are considering it as a good and bad system, whereas the majority of the respondents (38.96 per cent) from urban areas are not in favour of caste system (Table 4.11).

The findings reveal that the majority of the respondents (44.75 per cent) have accepted that the urban life is a nourisher of equalitarian and egalitarian mode of life. On the other hand, 22.50 per cent of the respondents have accepted the humanitarian approach, and 22.25 per cent of the respondents have advocated the rationalistic approach in urban life. Thus, it can be concluded that the growth of modern education and contacts with various alien cultures have broken the religious orthodoxy and superstitious beliefs, which ultimately led to a positive ideology regarding life and society.

The findings reveal that the majority of the respondents favoured the emergence of equalitarian and egalitarian modes of life residing in the city for either a short period or a long span. *The findings authenticate our first hypothesis that the more the involvement and active orientation of the people in the urban community with regard to modernized means and mode, the greater the communitarian discriminations will come to erosion.*

SUMMARY

This chapter is concerned with the attitude of the respondents regarding social institutions and emerging attitudes, which contain the data related to family, marriage, caste system and urban life style. It has been found that the majority of the respondents belong to the nuclear family system. The attitude of respondents regarding marriage has been analysed in terms of education and age. It has been found that the majority of graduate and postgraduate respondents are in favour of modern system of marriages, whereas the respondents of older generation are in favour of traditional marriage system. It has also been observed that older generation and highly educated respondents are in favour of the opinion of men and women in mate selection.

The majority of the respondents like to marry in their own caste. The dominant factor of marital relations has been analysed in terms of respondents who give importance to the ability of both bride and groom. The attitude of the respondents concerning caste system has been analysed in terms of age, education and native residence. It has been found that mostly all the respondents are in favour of abolition of this system. Among the respondents who are in favour of abolition, the majority falls under old age and are highly educated. Thus, education plays a crucial and important role in diminishing the gap by abolishing the caste system. The majority of the young respondents have adopted the humanitarian approach in life, whereas the respondents of older generation have adopted equalitarian view of life in urban life style.

Tables 4.12 and 4.13 show the empathy as propounded by learner and indicators such as associative individualism, religious tolerance and intercultural relations in the Indian context. Both Hindu and Muslim communities are attached to these indicators. Facts reveal that the young generation of both the communities express disregard concerning orthodoxy beliefs, superstitions and religious narrowness, whereas older generation express an extreme faith in religious beliefs.

Table 4.12 *Age and Attitude Regarding Urban Life Style*

Age group (in years)	*Tendency assimilated in urban life style*				*Total*
	Humanitarian	*Equalitarian*	*Rationality*	*Consciousness regarding same caste/religion*	
Up to 25	10 (20.00)	20 (40.00)	12 (24.00)	8 (16.00)	50
26–35	30 (42.86)	32 (45.71)	8 (11.43)	–	70
36–45	32 (45.71)	18 (25.71)	12 (17.14)	8 (11.43)	70
46–55	–	30 (42.86)	16 (22.86)	24 (34.28)	70
56 and above	14 (35.00)	26 (65.00)	–	–	40
Total	**86 (28.67)**	**126 (42.00)**	**48 (16.00)**	**40 (13.33)**	**300**

Table 4.13 *Depth of Urban Residence and Adoption of Values*

Depth of urban residence (in years)	*Tendency assimilated in urban life style*				*Total*
	Humanitarian	*Equalitarian*	*Rational viewpoint*	*Consciousness regarding same caste/religion*	
1–10	42 (35.00)	36 (31.67)	24 (20.00)	16 (13.33)	120
11–20	18 (31.03)	26 (44.83)	10 (17.24)	4 (4.90)	58
21–30	10 (20.83)	26 (54.17)	8 (16.67)	4 (8.33)	48
31 and above	16 (21.62)	36 (48.65)	6 (8.11)	16 (21.62)	74
Total	**86 (28.67)**	**126 (42.00)**	**48 (16.00)**	**40 (13.33)**	**300**

df = 9, chi-square = 20.76, significant (0.01 level).

REFERENCES

Agrawal, C.P., 1971, *Caste, Religion and Power: An Indian Case Study*. New Delhi: Sri Ram Centre for Industrial Relations.

Ahmad, Aziz, 1964, *Studies in Islamic Culture in the Indian Environment*. London: Clarendon Press.

Ahmad, Imtiaz (Ed.), 1973a, 'Endogamy and Status Mobility among the Siddique Sheikhs of Allahabad (U.P.)'. In *Caste and Social Stratification among Muslims in India*, New Delhi: Manohar Book Service.

———, 1973b, *Caste and Social Stratification among Muslims*. New Delhi: Manohar Book Service.

———, 1975, *Family, Kinship and Marriage among Muslims in India*. New Delhi: Manohar Book Service.

Ahmad, Imtiaz 1983, *Modernization and Social Change Among Muslims in India*, New Delhi, Manohar Publications.

Ahuja, Ram, 2004, *Indian Social System*. Jaipur: Rawat.

Ansari, G., 1960, *Muslim Caste in Uttar Pradesh: A Study in Culture Contact*. Lucknow: Ethnographic and Folk Culture Society.

Baig, M.R.A., 1974, *The Muslim Dilemma in India*. New Delhi: Vikas Publishing House.

Bailey, F.G., 1960, 'The Joint Family in India: A Framework for Discussion', *The Economic Weekly*, 12(8): 345–53.

Bryant, Clinton D. and Denis L. Peck, 2008, *21st Century Sociology: A Reference Book*. Vol. 1. New Delhi: Sage Publication.

Cohn, Bernard S., 1968, 'Notes on the History of the Study of Indian Society and Culture'. In *Structure and Change in Indian Society*, edited by Milton Singer and Bernard Cohn. Chicago, IL: Aldine Press.

Desai, I.P., 1956, 'The Joint Family in India: An Analysis', *Sociological Bulletin*, 5(2).

———, 1964, 'Some Aspects of Family in Mahuva: A Sociological Study of Jointness in a Small Town', *Indian Economic and Social History Review*, 1(3).

Driver, Edwin, 1962, 'Family Structure and Socioeconomic Status in Central India', *Sociological Bulletin*, 2(1–2).

Dube, S.C., 2005 (1990), *Indian Society*. New Delhi: NBT India.

Ghurye, G.S., 1961, *Caste, Class and Occupation*. Bombay: Popular Prakashan.

Gore, N.S., 1968, *Urbanization and Family Change*. Bombay: Popular Prakashan.

Gottschalk, P., 2000, *Beyond Hindu-Muslim: Multiple Identity in Narratives from Village India*. New Delhi: Oxford University Press.

Gould, Harold, 1968, 'Time Dimension and Structural Change in an Indian Kinship System'. In *Structure and Change in Indian Society*, edited by Milton Singer and Bernard Cohn. Chicago, IL: Aldine Press.

Kapadia, K.M., 1966, *Marriage and Family in India*. London: Oxford University Press.

Karve, Irawati, 1953, *Kinship Organization in India*. Pune: Deccan College Monographs.

Kolenda, Pauline M., 1968, 'Religion, Caste and Family Structure: A Comparative Study of the Indian Joint Family'. In *Structure and Change in Indian Society*, edited by Milton Singer and Bernard Cohn. Chicago, IL: Aldine Press.

Leach, E.R., 1960, *Aspects of Caste in South India, Ceylon and North West Pakistan*. Cambridge: Cambridge University Press.

Madan, T.N., 1962, 'A Hindu Joint Family', *Man*, 62(145).

Mukherjee, R.K., 1975, *Exploration in the Family and Other Essays*, edited by D. Narain. Bombay: Thakkar & Company.

Panikkar, K.M., 1955, *Hindu Society at Crossroads*. Bombay: Asia Publishing House.

Ross, A.D., 1967, *The Hindu Family in its Urban Setting*. Toronto: University of Toronto Press.

Shah, B.V., 1964, *Social Change and College Students of Gujarat*. Baroda: M. S. University.

Siddique, M.K.A., 1973, 'Caste among the Muslims of Calcutta'. In *Caste and Social Stratification among Muslims in India*, edited by I. Ahmad, New Delhi: Manohar Book Service.

———, 1974, *Muslims of Calcutta: A Study in Aspects of their Social Organization*. Calcutta: Anthropological Survey of India.

Srinivas, M.N., 1962, *Religion and Society among the Coorgs of South India*. Bombay: Oxford University Press.

Vreede-de-Steurs, Cora, 1969, *Parda: A Study of North Indian Muslim Women*. New York: Humanities Press.

Wirth, Louis, 1938, 'Urbanisation as a Way of Life', *American Journal of Sociology*, Vol 44, No 1, July, p. 8.

CHAPTER 5

Urban Social Structure and Patterns of Reciprocity

Scientific development and technological innovations, revolutions and establishment of industries increase in rapid transport and communications, awareness and growth of rationality-based society, humanitarianism, democratic system, equality, secularism, materialism, socio-economic and political consciousness, increase of urban centres and increasing interactions with different subcultural groups have accelerated the process of modernization, and thereby brought about much more unprecedented changes in the society. These modern forces of social structure have brought about radical changes in the urban social structure. These modern forces of changes have brought about much more material prosperity in human society, especially in the utilization of minerals. The increase in rail, roads and waterways has contributed much to the growth of urban centres and human relations are leading towards rational system. Urban centres are supposed to be the basket full of techno-industrial means and mode of productions. Radio, cinema, TV, press and newspapers are the modern sources of changes that affect the urban society. The appearance of the Internet, e-banking, e-ticketing and e-commerce have changed the society. Communication is regarded as the strongest source of change in terms of accessibility and transmission. These means and modes of communication and information transmission play a significant role in introducing the modernity. The process of industrialization and urbanization go side by side in Indian society.

These novel means of changes have brought about much transformations and modifications in the structure and function of the social institutions. The freedom of speech and expression, equality and individual liberty is the outcome of modern civic life. The urban social complex represents a peculiar social heterogeneity of population where transience of social relations, superficiality, anonymity, heterogeneity, interdependence, individuality, high density of population, occupational multiplicity and differentiations are the major attributes of modern urban social structure (Wirth, 1938).

The declining role of primary groups and increasing importance of secondary relations are dominant in urban structure. Urban social structure consists of anonymous formal relations. Also, people in urban structure can easily leave their religious attributes to get material prosperity; that is, material approach is dominant in social life.

One of the important characteristics of urban social structure is social heterogeneity in terms of caste, class, creed and race. People of different castes, class, cultural and religious background constitute a peculiar associative structure, and these peculiar attributes are generally marked with social individualism in which every person tries to satisfy his or her own personal needs, material interests and attempts to develop his or her own personality patterns and attributes. Urbanism represents such a social network that is composed of social, cultural, economic and occupational diversity. The fundamental dimensions of social relations in urban framework are economic activities and rational achievement that provide exchange model of human behaviour.

In George Homans (1958) and Peter Blau's (1964) terminology of exchange theory, urban centres in contemporary societies are the confluence of different religious communities, but the religiographic distinctions do not play a decisive role in regard to participation in economic activities, commercial activities and business engagements. Such socio-economic networks of relationships in sociological sense exist above the 'boundaries of religions' because materialistic approach towards life is the important feature of urban social organization. The rapid growth of transport and communication, application of technical devices and development of industries have served as a motive for modernization in contemporary Indian Society and the process of modernization get accentuated due to Western impacts. During sixteenth century AD, a revolutionary change began in India as a result of the establishment of printing press brought about in India by Portuguese and Christian missionaries. The first press was established by Britishers in Bombay in 1674. Although the newspapers in the form of handwritten scripts were already started during Mughal period, but printed newspaper was the result of Western contacts. The means of communications, transport and postal services, cinemas, establishment of plaza markets, multiplexes and cineplexes were the outcome of press and media. Introduction of railways, motor buses, aeroplanes and intercontinental waterways by ships and so on increased the international and intercontinental alliances and social relations. Journey by public buses and trains reduced the traditional sanctity of caste hierarchy (Srinivas, 1966), because the sitting arrangements in public buses and trains became available to each and every person irrespective of their caste and class but only on the basis of the payment of fare. These new trends of developments not only led to the growth of modernization but also contributed much in renovation and strengthening of Indian traditions. Hotels, restaurants, clubs, cineplexes, libraries, hospitals, schools, banks and other public agencies and formal institutions provided opportunity of equality to each and every person above the frontiers of caste and religion. This opportunity of equality has been reinforced by the establishment of Indian constitution and Secular Democratic Republic of India (Singh, 1999 [1977]).

Modernization has introduced major changes in traditional, social and political framework of society. The first impact of modernization is the change of patterns of relation between the elites and masses (Krug, 2005). The elites have themselves recognized with a view to maintain their existence of political survival. In modern social, economic and political system, the role of achievement has increased as against that of ascription. In pre-modern agrarian societies, there was little participation of masses in political affairs occurring outside their rural community, but modernity has provided opportunity to the people of rural and urban communities for active participation in regional, national and international political affairs, and this has been much more accelerated by the growth of modern education. The use of scientific methods and new tools of agriculture and the growth of industries, trade and commerce have proved themselves as an effective means for the balance of increasing pressure of population in agrarian economy, which is because of migration of rural population to urban and industrial centres. However, at the same time, it can be said that economic specialization and migration to urban and industrial area had led to the growth of a specific ethnic regionalism, which are based on interest group and are represented by political organization (Desai, 1984). There is a strong desire among the nations of Asia and Africa to be free from dependency on West and to move towards modernization from their agrarian social and political structure; but it has been found that in Western developed societies, the forces of modernization have been generated from within the structure while in the countries of the third world, specially, those of Latin America, Asia and Africa, the forces of modernization are exogenous and imposed from outside. These countries are striving to modernize themselves on the patterns of modern societies of the West. The contemporary patterns of modernization are full of the tendency to maximize the outcomes in minimum period, but this is not practically feasible unless all the spheres of social, political, economic and cultural context of society are coordinated under integrated programme for an overall modernization under a proper planning (Dube, 1967). Modern cities, as described earlier, have been emerged as a melting pot or a confluence of different cultures, sub-cultures, groups, castes, classes, races, ethnicity and creeds. This confluence in sociological sense has functional meaning and significant social utility, especially in regard to the growth of a vast interaction circle within different groups and provides the chances for socio-cultural and religious reciprocation in the long run. In contemporary urban structure, social heterogeneity is being perceived as an important attribute of urban life. The cities of India can be divided into two major categories: (1) orthogenetic cities and (2) heterogeneitic cities (Singer, 1961). In other words, these can also be noted as cities of *moral order* and cities of *technical order*. Varanasi city can be placed under the first category. But the contemporary structural characteristics and attributes of the city have denoted it as a confluence of tradition and modernity, that is, a city that represents a peculiar blend of religio-cultural synthesis. On the one hand, we find that it is a stronghold of traditional Hinduism; and on the other hand, it is nourishing ground for Islam, Christianity, Jainism, Buddhism and Sikhism. Due to the presence of various religions, Varanasi represents a unique international characteristic. The anatomy of city of Benares, unlike the Western cities, presents a panorama of synthesis between tradition and modernity, Hinduism and Islam, original inhabitants and immigrants with a specific nature of reciprocity and social participation and religious tolerance in behaviour. The urban life style of Varanasi is entirely peculiar and different. This reciprocity can be observed in urban life especially the field of material resources and manufacturing, consumption and supply of consumer goods. The process of social reciprocity and exchange of behaviour is articulated from residential areas to the work areas. This process of mutual relations and reciprocity can be expressed in terms of feelings, ideas, exchange of behaviour, religious occasions, festivals and marriage ceremonials that bring both the communities near than nearer. It can be observed in occupational settings, for example, the Hindu–Muslim economic activities and social relations in regard to silk industry of Varanasi. The silk industry of Varanasi has a historical fame from ancient periods. This industry has developed in Varanasi with the participation of both Hindu and Muslim hands. Predominantly, Muslims are engaged in production and manufacturing of silk and zari works. While the storage, collection, export and import of the silk clothes have been controlled and regulated by the Hindu merchants. Occasionally, Hindu–Muslim riots have taken place, but the communal harmony and reciprocal relations are still in good health. Hindus and Muslims have also been found at loggerheads during the tense situation of communal conflict, which are generally aggravated and accelerated by local politicians and self-centred groups. But even in such critical moments, the silk industry in terms of economic and commercial enterprises has been a binding force for social alliance and amiability between these two communities. Perhaps, the cementing factors for social relations between these two communities are the economic interests of the persons of both the communities engaged in this business. If they do not cooperate with each other, not only will this business collapse, but the social and cultural standards of these two communities will also decline. Similar other economic activities have appeared as cementing factors of social alliances between these two communities (Showeb, 1994; Varshney, 2002; Blank, 2003; Brass, 2003; Eichler, 2007).

Moreover, similar scenario was seen in plastic industry, toys, furniture goods, aluminium, gold and silver works, tobacco products, lumen industry and goods concerning ceremonial decoration and so on. Here, it can be observed that production and manufacture lie in hands of Muslims whereas, collection, storage, distribution, selling and export of the same are being conducted by Hindu merchants.

On the basis of the emerging trends of social, economic and commercial activities, it appears that economic activities can be perceived as the determinants of social relations and social participation. The economic activities monetarized attitude and material benefits transcend and supersede the frontiers of religious isolation and mores, the superstitious beliefs that have separated these two communities. Such industrial enterprises and economic activities in urban settings are the functional agencies, which promote friendly environment, occupational interdependency, religious tolerance in behaviour and inter-cultural reciprocity between both the communities. Such phenomenon certainly creates a challenge for sociological study.

Modern education, urban trades, commerce and industries, rapid means of transport and communications are the binding forces that encourage social relations on new dimensions between people of different castes, religions, races and nativity. This chapter is an attempt to analyse and interpret the impact of modern education, trade, commerce, industry and other urban activities, on the nature and the form of Hindu–Muslim relations. The main focus of analysis here is to discuss how the traditional social distance and isolation between Hindu–Muslim communities are being mitigated by the modern forces and resources of life, especially trade, commerce recreational agencies, hotels, restaurants, clubs and so on in urban centres. These formal agencies of urban communities have brought about drastic changes in the field of traditional orthodoxy practised by Hindus and

Muslims. The increasing growth of technology and specialization and application of technological equipments and instruments have created much scope for persons with specialized skills and efficiency to engage in technological and economic arrangement irrespective of religious and cultural discriminations. It is the phenomena that has transformed the Hindu–Muslim social distance into social closeness. The economic interests, attached with the silk industry, as discussed earlier, have worked as a cementing factor for both the communities. In the production of silk clothes, the handlooms and power looms have played an significant role. These are the mean of livelihood for Muslims on the one hand; whereas on the other hand, it is economic incentive for Hindus who handle its trades on national and international level. Consequentially, the religious and commercial discriminations are becoming gradually inactive and dormant at the coast of occupational incentive attached with loom and silk textile industries (Showeb, 1994). Because the achievement of economic benefits of both the sections is based on this business, the very phenomena of Hindu–Muslim interdependence and interrelations authenticate the theory of interactional exchange in an urban setting. In the context of intercultural religious reciprocity occurring in social and occupational life and creating mutual interdependence between, the two produce a mark of historicity in the urban life of Varanasi. Although the theorization of social exchange in sociological literature has been authentically made by contemporary American and European social scientists, historical analysis of social relations in regard to present empirical study indicates that the historicity and practice of the interactional theory of social exchange or the process of interactional exchange have been chiefly originated and continued in India. Therefore, the genetics source of the phenomena and theory of interactional exchange is Indian society but not the European, American or any other society in the world. The ultimate credit for this approach goes to the works of Homans (1958) and Blau (1964) in contemporary sociological literature. The social literature that deals with the historical life style of India, no doubt, narrates the existence of this interactional exchange phenomenon. On the other hand, there are occupations concerning the work of dexterity, embroidery, cut and patchwork, dyeing and printing on the clothes that consist of large population of Muslim; and at the same time ,the storage and export is controlled and governed by Hindus.

The sociological survey of Varanasi reveals that it has the specific features of civil and urban life style, art, handicraft, silk work, embroidery, cut work, patch work and so on what I mean to say that age old traditional features of human dexterity can be seen in the Pucca Mohal and its narrow streets. These streets and narrow lanes still continue to spread the smell of curd, ghee, cream on the one hand and the perfumes and scents of flowers on the other. These streets inside the Pucca Mohal create fascination and attract the visitors. The Vishwanath Temple situated in the heartland of the city and the morning scenario with crack of dawn at Dashashwamedh Ghat present a celestial pleasure with all sublimity beyond imagination. In addition, Durga Kund Temple, Sankat Mochan Temple and Manas Mandir are the most celebrated religious places. Sarnath in the north, as a place of first sermon by Buddha, attracts thousands of pilgrims from Thailand, Japan, Myanmar and China. Varanasi is situated on the left side of the river Ganga, and its overall structure manifests a feature of crescent or that of a conch.

The data in regard to occupations and relations with different religious groups reveal that the majority of the respondents from both the communities have expressed cooperative and associative relations with the members of different religious communities.

As regards the depth of urban residence and ideas regarding relations with various religious communities, findings reveal that the majority of the respondents (92.67 per cent) have observed that there is a gradual increase in the relations with the people of other communities. The chi-square value validates the findings. This value is significant at 0.05 levels, which manifests that there is a negligible chance of deviation among the communities regarding the attitude of religious relations.

Analytical interpretation of data reveals that the majority of the respondents engaged in all sorts of occupations have observed an increase in relations with other communities (92.67 per cent) (Tables 5.1–5.3).

Table 5.1 *Occupation and Nature of Relations to Different Religions*

Occupation	*Nature of relations*		*Total*
	Competitive	*Cooperative*	
Service (job)	15 (13.64)	95 (86.36)	110
Business	–	140 (100.00)	140
Self-owned industry	10 (20.00)	40 (80.00)	50
Total	**25 (8.33)**	**275 (91.67)**	**300**

Table 5.2 *Depth of Urban Residence and Ideas Regarding Mutual Relations*

Depth of residence (in years)	*Relations have increased positively*		*Total*
	Yes	*No*	
1–10	104	16	120
11–20	55	3	58
21–30	47	1	48
31 and above	72	2	74
Total	**278 (92.67)**	**22 (7.33)**	**300**

df = 3, chi-square 10.64, significant (0.05 level).

Table 5.3 *Occupation and Ideas Concerning Inter-Religious Relations*

Occupation	*Relations have increased positively*		*Total*
	Yes	*No*	
Service	102	8	110
Business	131	9	140
Own industry	45	5	50
Total	**278 (92.67)**	**22 (7.33)**	**300**

df = 2, chi-square 1.75, not significant.

The findings reveal that the majority of the respondents from all the educational level have realized a gradual increase in relations with other religions.

Table 5.4 *Education and Ideas Regarding Mutual Relations*

Education	*Relations have increased positively*		*Total*
	Yes	*No*	
Literate	109	15	124
Up to intermediate	39	7	46
Graduate/ postgraduate	86	–	86
Occupational/ technical	44	–	44
Total	**278 (92.67)**	**22 (7.33)**	**300**

df = 3, chi-square 18.66, highly significant (0.01 level).

Table 5.5 *Depth of Urban Residence and Relationship to Neighbours*

Period of residence (in years)	*What is appropriate in urban life?*		*Total*
	Yes	*No*	
1–10	–	120 (100.00)	120
11–20	–	58 (100.00)	58
21–30	–	48 (100.00)	48
31 and above	–	74 (100.00)	74
Total	–	**300 (100.00)**	**300**

The empirical facts enable us to furnish that the respondents from all the residential groups have observed a cooperative and friendliness relations with their counterparts in urban life (Tables 5.4 and 5.5).

As regards the the role of modern education in context of social relations, the findings denote that the majority of the respondents from all the educational level have observed a positive outcome of modern education. Modern education has increased the social consciousness and reciprocity among the communities.

The majority of the respondents educated up to post graduate and of technical education believe in the existence of a universal God, that is, the monotheistic belief in life.

As far as the attitude regarding social adjustment and accommodation with regard to the depth of urban residence is concerned, it can be concluded that the majority of the respondents living in the city have observed radical changes in the mutual relations. They observed accommodative and helping relations rather than conflicts and differentiations. As the depth of residence in the urban settings increases, a high degree of cooperative and associative relations is observed. The chi-square value also proves the interdependency between these two variables. *The findings validate our second hypothesis that the greater the social, cultural and religious heterogeneity in the urban set-up, the more multidimensional and interactional reciprocity accelerates in an urban social milieu, leading to the growth of urbanized life style.*

The facts reveal that the majority of respondents from all group of urban residence expressed a positive change in their attitude, behaviour and trends in the urban settings after engaging in occupations (91 per cent), whereas a negligible percentage of the respondents (9 per cent) have observed no changes. The respondents living in the city over 30 years have observed a drastic change in this regard (100 per cent). The chi-square value is significant which reveals that both the variables are extremely interdependent.

Analytical interpretation of the data reveals that the majority of the respondents engaged in any type of occupations have realized the changes in their attitude after engaging in the jobs or occupations in the city (Tables 5.6–5.8).

Table 5.6 *Depth of Urban Residence and Opinion Regarding Mutual Relations*

Period of urban residence (in years)	*Mutual cooperation is perceived rather than differences and disparities*		*Total*
	Yes	*No*	
1–10	104 (86.67)	16 (13.33)	120
11–20	46 (79.31)	12 (20.69)	58
21–30	48 (100.00)	–	48
31 and above	74 (100.00)	–	74
Total	**272 (90.67)**	**28 (9.33)**	**300**

df = 3, chi-square 23.69, significant (0.01 level).

Table 5.7 *Depth of Urban Residence and Attitudinal Changes*

Depth of urban residence (in years)	*Changes observed in attitude and behaviour*		*Total*
	Yes	*No*	
1–10	104 (86.67)	16 (13.33)	120
11–20	50 (86.21)	8 (13.79)	58
21–30	45 (73.75)	3 (6.25)	48
31 and above	74 (100.00)	–	74
Total	**273 (91.00)**	**27 (9.00)**	**300**

df = 3, chi-square 12.15, significant (0.01 level).

Table 5.8 *Occupation and Change in Attitude and Behaviour of Respondents*

Occupation	*Change in attitude before occupational setting*		*Total*
	Yes	*No*	
Service	93 (84.55)	17 (15.45)	110
Business	134 (95.71)	6 (4.29)	140
Own industry	46 (92.00)	4 (8.00)	50
Total	**273 (91.00)**	**27 (9.00)**	**300**

df = 2, chi-square 9.48, significant (0.01 level).

Table 5.9 *Age and Perception Regarding Visit of Religious Places*

Age (in years)	*Temple or mosque for prayer and worship*		*Total*
	Yes	*No*	
Up to 25	42 (84.00)	8 (16.00)	50
26–35	64 (91.43.00)	6 (8.57)	70
36–45	58 (82.86.00)	12 (17.14)	70
46–55	42 (60.00)	28 (40.00)	70
56 and above	32 (80.00)	8 (20.00)	40
Total	**238 (79.33)**	**62 (20.67)**	**300**

df = 4, chi-square 20.46, significant (0.01 level).

Urban life style is entirely different from rural life. The social, economicandoccupationalrelationsintheruralsocietygetaccelerated due to habitation, occupation and economic activities. The rural society is somehow different from urban structure in regard to identity, interaction and interdependency. This can be termed as I^3 theory of rural society. This loss of personality of an individual, as described by Zimbardo with regard to crowd behaviour, can also be perceived in urban colonial life style. Due to mutual interactions and economic activities, a cooperative and associative personality develops. These mutual interactions are concerned with achievement orientation (Burgess, 1925). In the same manner, reciprocal relations and mutual interactions get accentuated through commensality, habitation, recreation, education and use of public places. The formal organizations in society provide a wider scope for mutual interaction and interpersonal relations. When people engaged themselves in the common activities, they create a reciprocal relations and tolerant behaviour in regard to occupational, social and religious life. These mutual relations emerge as an indispensable character of urban life (Weber, 1962). In urban structure, the presence of various cultures and religions sometimes are unable to develop an associative character and create a conflictual situation along with religious fanaticism (Sellin, 1938). The urban structure has specific personality patterns. A common characteristics of urban life, *core of urban personality* develops, which inherently consists of some basic and relatively permanent attitudes and tendencies that enable the people of various religious backgrounds to interact and associate with each other. These tendencies can be explained psychologically, as *psychogenic attributes* (Burgess and Locke, 1945). The urban life and social structure is full of diversities. As compared to urban contexts, the village is a centre of cooperation as having lesser scope for conflict. It has its own traditional mechanisms of conflict resolution and social mobilization.

The empirical facts reveal that the majority of the respondents from all the educational level and every type of occupations have expressed that the formal organizations such as hotels, clubs, restaurants, recreational centres, availability of better health facilities and hygiene, industries and occupations and modern education have motivated the people of different religions to develop a cooperative and associative relations.

The findings reveal that the majority of the respondent from both the communities have favoured that the religious discriminations and abolition of untouchability must be eradicated for the erosion of the communal conflicts. Some of the respondents (47 per cent) have expressed a need for Muslim reservation in this regard.

As far as the issue of communal riots is concerned, all the respondents from all age groups have found its genesis in political interests and unwanted social elements of the society (Tables 5.10–5.12).

Table 5.10 *Education and Perception Regarding Visit of Religious Places*

Education	*Temple or mosque for prayer and worship*		*Total*
	Yes	*No*	
Literate	102 (82.26)	22 (17.74)	124
Up to intermediate	31 (67.39)	15 (32.61)	46
Graduate/ postgraduate	68 (79.07)	18 (20.93)	86
Occupational/ technical	37 (84.09)	7 (15.91)	44
Total	**238 (79.33)**	**62 (20.67)**	**300**

df = 3, chi-square 32.39, highly significant (0.01 level).

Table 5.11 *Age and Attitude Concerning Worship at Hindu–Muslim Religious Places*

Age (in years)	*Worship of Hindu pilgrimage and Muslim tomb*		*Total*
	Yes	*No*	
Up to 25	50 (100.00)	–	50
26–35	70 (100.00)	–	70
36–45	70 (100.00)	–	70
46–55	70 (100.00)	–	70
56 and above	40 (100.00)	–	40
Total	**300 (100.00)**	–	**300**

Table 5.12 *Education and Attitude Concerning Cooperation and Conflict*

Education	*Attitude of cooperation in religion rather than conflict*		*Total*
	Yes	*No*	
Literate	95	29	124
Up to intermediate	39	7	46
Graduate/ postgraduate	86 (100.00)	–	86
Occupational/ technical	44 (100.00)	–	44
Total	**264 (88.00)**	**36 (12.00)**	**300**

df = 3, chi-square 33.41, highly significant (0.01 level).

Empirical facts enable us to furnish that the majority of the respondents from all the age groups and educational level have expressed that they like all the communities to visit temples and mosques frequently for prayer and worship. A negligible percentage of the respondents (20.67 per cent) have expressed that they are not in favour of the visits. The chi-square value proves the interdependency between these two variables.

The findings reveal that the majority of the respondents from all educational level have expressed a need for humanitarian and equalitarian approach towards others communities and religions. These respondents are not in favour of the discriminations based on caste, class, religion or gender, and they probe the society to be a force from these hurdles (Tables 5.13–5.15).

Table 5.13 *Depth of Urban Residence and Attitude Concerning Cooperation and Conflict*

Depth of residence (in years)	*Attitude of cooperation in religion rather than conflict*		*Total*
	Yes	*No*	
1–10	120 (100.00)	–	120
11–20	50 (100.00)	–	50

(Continued)

Table 5.13 (Continued)

Depth of residence (in years)	*Attitude of cooperation in religion rather than conflict*		*Total*
	Yes	*No*	
21–30	36 (75.00)	12 (25.00)	48
31 and above	50 (67.57)	24 (32.43)	74
Total	**264 (88.00)**	**36 (12.00)**	**300**

df = 3, chi-square 61.2, significant (0.01 level).

Table 5.14 *Age and Attitude Concerning Cooperation and Conflict*

Age (in years)	*Attitude regarding religious cooperation and conflict*		*Total*
	Yes	*No*	
Up to 25	50 (100.00)	–	50
26–35	70 (100.00)	–	70
36–45	54 (77.14)	16 (22.86)	70
46–55	59 (84.29)	11 (15.71)	70
56 and above	31 (77.50)	9 (22.50)	40
Total	**264 (88.00)**	**36 (12.00)**	**300**

df = 4, chi-square 28.92, significant (0.01 level).

Table 5.15 *Age and Ideas Regarding Religion*

Age (in years)	*Each religion must be given respect and faith*			*Total*
	Agree	*Disagree*	*Can't say*	
Up to 25	50 (100.00)	–	–	50
26–35	70 (100.00)	–	–	70
36–45	70 (100.00)	–	–	70
46–55	40 (57.14)	30 (42.86)	–	70
55 and above	22 (55.00)	18 (45.00)	–	40
Total	**252 (84.00)**	**48 (16.00)**	–	**300**

The empirical facts about the perception of the respondents in reference to the attitude regarding the importance of cooperation and assimilation rather than conflict, as per education, depth of urban residence and age reveal that the majority of the respondents is in favour of cooperation rather than conflict (88 per cent), whereas a negligible percentage of the respondents (12 per cent) disagree to produce a cooperative religious structure in society (Tables 5.16 and 5.17)

Table 5.16 *Age and Ideas Regarding Superstitions of Religion*

Age (in years)	*Religion is a hindrance in mutual relations*		*Total*
	Yes	*No*	
Up to 25	50 (100.00)	–	50
26–35	70 (100.00)	–	70
36–45	70 (100.00)	–	70
46–55	70 (100.00)	–	70
56 and above	40 (100.00)	–	40
Total	**300 (100.00)**	–	**300**

Table 5.17 *Education and Ideas Regarding Caste or Religion*

Education	*Caste or religion is social construct*		*Total*
	Yes	*No*	
Literate	94 (75.80)	30 (24.20)	124
Up to intermediate	37 (80.40)	9 (19.60)	46
Graduate/ postgraduate	86 (100.00)	–	86
Occupational/ technical	44 (100.00)		44
Total	**261 (87.00)**	**39 (13.00)**	**300**

Findings from Tables 5.14–5.16 reveal that the people from both the communities like to visit frequently to the temples and mosques, considering these religious places for the well-being of their own. In doing so, they develop a rational and materialistic attitude that is far from the religious fanaticism and sectarian thinking. These facts include interest articulation, interest aggregation and achievement orientation (McClelland) as psychological indicators of modernity. Interpretation of Tables 5.16–5.17 denotes further that the young and highly educated respondents have the tendency to assimilate the humanitarian approach and religious tolerant behaviour. These are the psychological indicators of modernization. The majority of the respondents from both the communities expressed that caste and community are created by human in society. It must be modified and changed. It is a well-known fact that modernization is a process of change and modification. The majority of the respondents from both the communities have expressed that religion and caste are human-generated social environment, and it must be modified and regulated as per contemporary societal demands. Hence, it is evident that modernization is a process of change and modification.

Modernization of social life has changed the scenario of communitarian feelings. Development of science and technology, innovations, industrial revolutions, establishment of industries, political consciousness, democratic values, communicative devices, extremism, humanitarianism and religious consciousness, urbanism and cultural contacts have been considered as the forces of modernization, all of which have narrowed the boundaries of superstitions and religious fanaticism. The process of modernization includes social changes that completely transform the lives of individuals. The urban society has better opportunities and options for industrial development because this society holds all the modern devices of communication, trade and recreations where the access to any information is easy and fast. In Indian context, the availability of markets, communicative devices, establishment of industries and urban development have led the foundations of a developed nation. *It is of worth importance to analyse the religious attitude and feelings of individuals in the wave of modernization.*

In this regard, the findings reveal that the majority of the respondent from all the age groups are in favour of faith and honour to all the religions. These respondents are not in favour of religious discrimination and fanaticism. They hold the view that all the religions are equal and the product of the same God. The young respondents as compared to the the old ones have expressed that the people must be free from religious boundaries and may perceive all the religions equally.

Analytical interpretation of the data reveals that the majority of the respondents from all the age groups and educational level considered that both the communities do not put any hindrance in regard to the visit of saints and preachers, and caste and religion are social construct. In other words, the respondents are in favour of erosion of religious discrimination and separation based on caste or religion.

The various facts in the empirical survey have been proved by rating scale to explain the indicators of modernity. The facts have been discussed in regard to psychological and sociological aspects of the respondents. The findings from Table 5.1 reveal that both the communities have observed associative behaviour, religious tolerance and inter-cultural contacts in urban social setup. As regard the urban depth of residence, occupations and education, it has been observed that religious tolerant behaviour and intercultural contacts have been intermingled in most of the respondents of both the communities (Tables 5.2–5.4). Later on, Tables 5.6–5.8 that are related to the analysis of personality patterns of individuals reveal that their personality is full of associative individualism, social reciprocal behaviour and intercultural contacts. As far as the modification and transformation in behaviour are concerned, the communities have realized that the depth of urban residence and participation in occupation in the urban set-up are the major determinant for this change and transformation. But naturally, the occupational relations between different castes and religions will increase in urban set-up that ultimately creates the achievement orientation among the individuals.

This analysis coincides and approves the notion about the occupational characters in regard to modernization, and it indicates the tendency of social transactions among the respondents. Social transaction has been selected as a sociological indicator in this study. The majority of the respondents in the empirical survey have expressed that the mechanism of erosion of communitarian discriminations, abolition of intolerability and reservation for Muslims in structured organization are the sources for reducing the communal violence and religious fanaticism, which indicates the appearance of rationality, humanitarian and scientific approach. These are the indicators of modernity.

SUMMARY

This chapter concerns the urban social structure and communitarian relations. The inter-communitarian relations, social isolation, changes in behavioural patterns, conflicts, perceptions and feelings regarding communities, reciprocity and exchange in behaviour, motive for reciprocity, perception regarding religion and caste have been analysed and discussed elaboratively in this chapter.

Findings reveal that the respondents from all the occupational groups have observed cooperative relations with their neighbours. The analysis of the findings in regard to the relations with the other community, with reference to the depth of urban residence, occupations and education reveal that the majority of the respondents from both the communities have experienced a growth in mutual relations, and the highly educated respondents have observed a cooperative and friendliness behaviour with their religious counterparts. As far as the role of modern education is concerned, the majority of the respondent from all the educational level has observed an increase in social consciousness, development in mutual relations, and they all have adopted the monotheistic approach regarding the existence of the Almighty.

Analysis of the social isolation and conflicts in regard to urban depth of residence, indicates that the majority of the respondents have developed a reciprocal relations and tolerant behaviour rather than isolation and differentiation. The majority of the respondents expressed that attitude and behaviour have changed after engaging in the jobs in the city. The majority of respondents considered that the appearance of clubs, hotels, Cineplex's recreational centres, urban lifestyle, modern education, health and hygiene and industrial sector has promoted the mutual interaction in urban life. The communal riots and conflicts can be avoided by the elimination of discriminations based on caste and religion, abolition of untouchability and by providing reservations to the Muslims. The majority of the respondents have observed that the riots are the outcome of the political interests. The majority of the respondents have accustomed to visit temples and mosques frequently for the religious prayers and worships and the respondents of all the age groups are in favour of the frequent visit to the Hindu and Muslim religious places as well.

The respondents have accepted that the division of society in terms of caste is the outcome of the society itself; that is, the caste hierarchy is social construct.

The majority of the respondents have favoured cooperation and assimilation in an urban social set-up. The majority of the respondents from both the communities have developed an associative character in behaviour and action both. These respondents believe in super-power of the Almighty. This tendency has increased with the increase in the depth of urban residence.

The findings authenticate and validate the indicators of modernization, especially psychological indicators such as faith in desirably and possibility of change, associative individualism, religious tolerance, rational and humanist approach, materialistic approach and sociological indicators such as intercultural contacts. Findings validate the existence of associative individualism, religious tolerance and intercultural contacts in urban settings. Analysis of Table 5.13, which reveals the attitude and ideas of the respondents in regard to erosion of communitarian discrimination like untouchability, is a representation of rational, humanitarian and scientific approach of the respondents. Tables 5.14 and 5.16 concern the rational materialistic and goal-oriented attitude of the respondents. These facts represent interest articulation, interest aggregation (Almond and Coleman) and achievement orientation (McClelland) as the psychological indicators of modernity.

REFERENCES

Blank, J., 2003, 'Ethnic Conflict and Civic Life: A Review Essay', *India Review*, 2(2): 97–112.

Blau, Peter M., 1964, *Exchange and Power in Social Life*. New York: John Wiley and Sons Inc.

Brass, P., 2003, *Production of Hindu-Muslim Violence in Contemporary India*. New Delhi: Oxford University Press.

Burgess, E.W., 1925, 'The Growth of the City: An Introduction to a Research Project'. In *The City*, edited by Robert E. Park, E.W. Burgers and R.D. Mekenzie, Chicago, IL: University of Chicago Press.

Burgess, E.W. and H.S. Locke, 1945, *The Family, from Institution to Companionship*. New York: American Book Company.

Desai, A.R., 1984, *India's Path of Development*. Bombay: Popular Prakashan.

Dube, S.C., 1967, 'Modernization and its Adaptive Demands on Indian Society'. In *Papers in the Sociology of Education in India*, edited by M.S. Gore, I.P. Desai and Sima Chitnis, New Delhi: NCERT.

Eichler, Mike, 2007, *Consensus Organizing: Building Communities of Mutual Self Interest*. New Delhi: Sage Publication.

Homans, Georges, 1958, *Social Behaviour: Its Elementary Form*. New York: Harcourt Brace and World Inc.

Sellin, Thorsteen, 1938, *Cultural Conflict and Crime*. New York: Social Science Research Council.

Showeb, M., 1994, *Silk Handloom Industry of Varanasi: A Study in Socio-economic Problems of Weaves*. Varanasi: Ganga Kaveri Publishing House.

Singer, Milton, 1961, 'Changing Level of Cultural Transmission in India'. In *Aspects of Religion in Indian Society*, edited by L.P. Vidyarthi, Meerut: Kedarnath Ramnath.

Singh, Yogendra, 1999 (1977), *Modernization of Indian Tradition*. Jaipur: Rawat Publications.

Srinivas, M.N., 1966, *Social Change in Modern India*. Berkeley: University of California Press.

Varshney, A., 2002, *Ethnic Conflict and Civic Life: Hindu and Muslim in India*. New Delhi: Oxford University Press.

Weber, Max, 1962, *The City*, translated by Martindale and New Wirth, Collier Book Edition. Glencoe, IL: The Free Press.

Wirth, L., 1938,'Urbanism as a Way of Life', *American Journal of Sociology*.

CHAPTER 6

Inter-Religious Reciprocity and Social Adjustment

Religion is of immense significance in understanding human behaviour. Various studies in the field of Sociology, Psychology and Anthropology have been conducted from time to time in this regard. Religion has had a stronghold over the lives of human beings for thousands of years. In one form or the other religion is found in all known human societies. Throughout subsequent history, religion has continued to be a central part of human experience, influencing how one perceives and reacts to the environments in which one lives (Giddens, 1984; 2007).

Sociologists define religion as a cultural system of commonly shared beliefs and rituals that provides a sense of ultimate meaning and purpose by creating an idea of reality that is sacred, all encompassing and supernatural (Durkheim, 1961; Berger, 1967; Wuthnow, 1988). Religions are among the most important institutions in society. They are a primary source of most deep-seated norms and values (Warner, 1993). Various social scientists, anthropologists and sociologists have developed various theories and ideologies regarding religion. Most important are Karl Marx, Max Weber and Emile Durkheim. Marx was much influenced by Feuerbach (1957); religion consists of ideas and values produced by human beings in the course of thin cultural development, but mistakenly projected on to divine for us or gods. Feuerbach uses the term 'alienation' to refer to the establishing of Gods or divine forces distinct from human beings. Values and ideas created by humans come to be seen as the product of alien or separate beings—religious forces and Gods. Marx accepted the view that religion represented human self-alienation. It is often believed that Marx was dismissive of religion, but this is far from reality. Religion, he writes, is the 'heart of a heartless world'. Marx declares, in a famous phrase, that religion has been the 'opium of the masses'. On the other hand, Durkheim concentrated himself particularly on religion in small-scale, traditional societies. He discussed religion in terms of sacred and profane. He strongly emphasized that religions are never just a matter of belief. All religions involve regular ceremonial and ritual activities in which a group of believers meet together. In collective ceremonials, a sense of group solidarity is affirmed and heightened. Weber's writings on religion differ from those of Durkheim in that they concentrate on the connection between religion and social change, something to which Durkheim gave little attention.

In traditional India, as Weber pointed out, there was at certain periods a significant development of commerce, manufacture and urbanism, but these did not generate the radical patterns of social change involved in the rise of capitalism in the West. Religion was a major influence in inhibiting such change. For example, Hinduism is what Weber called an 'other-worldly' religion.

In traditional societies, religion usually plays a central part in social life. Religious symbols and rituals are often integrated with the material and artistic culture of the society—music, painting and carving, dance, storytelling and literature. In small cultures, there is no professional priesthood, but there are always certain individuals who specialize in the knowledge of religious practices. Religion is increasingly an individual quest for meaning rather than a collective act of worship (Bellah, 1965). In this way, religion has undergone a process of individuation whereby the individual works out his own salvation and follows his own path to ultimate meaning. The importance of religion has not declined; rather, its form of expression has changed. This changed form has brought about various radical changes in the interaction and interactive processes among various religious groups.

In a study, Lenski (1962) found that membership of religious groups affect the attitudes and behaviour of individual as much as the religious structure itself.

The culture and civilization of India have a historic importance for specific religions, rituals and spiritual considerations. According to S. Radhakrishnan (1947), religion is a regulating force of social relation and routine life. It is inclusive of all the structures and activities that shape and help the continuity and existence of human life. It is religion in society that brings about integration and adjustment between diverse aspirations, desires and requirements (Singh, 1980). It is not only supernatural or super social, but is also very substantial with regard to ethical and existential process of human society. The anthropological outlook of religion itself has been quiet sensational with regard to the change in intellectual and emotional perspectives. A number of social scientists such as Edward Tylor (1871), Radcliff-Brown (1952), Malinowski (1948), Durkheim (1912), Levi-Strauss (1949), Marx (1843) and Thomas F. O'Dea (1969) have devoted to functional and casual analysis of religion in society. Frazer (1996 [1870]) observes religion as an appropriation of power that influences the course of nature as well as society. To Malinowski, it is a system of faith as well as a mode of action, a sociological phenomena as well as a personal experience.

The expression of religion and modernity in Indian context has some fundamental difficulties. Religion is being considered as a barrier to modernization, because it has no sensitivity for scientific developments, innovations and technological developments. Weber (1963) presented his ideas in this regard, especially for Asian countries.

But, it is also true that the religious beliefs have been modernized according to changing situations. Srinivas (1966) observed religion as a source of dynamics of social change and propounded his theory of sanskritization. He found that the lower castes, in order to raise their position in the caste hierarchy, adopted some customs of the Brahmans, especially of twice-born castes. Singer (1956) described the process of compartmentalization that he considers as a process of dynamic continuity.

A conception of religion as interpreted by Weber has been criticized by a number of empirical studies. Robert Bellah (1965) presented a critique of the Weberian notion of religion. Dube (1965) in his studies found that religion in India is not a hindrance in its progress. The notion of unity in India is expressed through a symbolic form of cultural continuity, which is regarded as concerned with the theory of consciousness, and it contributes to the adjustments of its internal structure. This internal structure is primarily based on religious theory and their interpretations. This idea of unity or adjustment was not immutable; rather, it was related with the dynamic aspect, growth of the Indian civilization. Although the value structure, ritual methods and beliefs may have continued long, the urban social relations developed as a result of occupational interactions, urban housing, recreations and interpersonal contacts. The social heterogeneity of urban population provides simple scope for inter-religious exchange and interactions, renovation and discards of old beliefs, and a rebirth of novel morale and ethics exists between Hindus and Muslims of Varanasi city. It appears that the custom of *sati* was prevalent even before Islam and the custom of Zouhar, practised during Islamic period in India, is somewhat of the custom of *sati*. But the popular practice of Zouhar diminished gradually. During the Turkish invasion, the ladies from the family of royal patronage of Rajput Rajas resorted to the custom of Zouhar and sacrificed their lives with a view to maintaining their chastity. During the period of Alauddin's invasion, Maharani Padmini was forced to sacrifice her life by way of Zouhar. Muslim ladies too adopted this custom of Zouhar and maintained their chastity. At the time of Tamur's invasion, Alauddin, then governor of Matner, burnt all his property and wives to save his prestige. These all are influences of Hindu society and customs that Muslims have also adopted from the traditions of Hindus. On the other hand, polygamous marriages in Hindu society have been adopted by Muslims. It can be concluded that both the communities from the ancient periods have influenced each other. These mutual interactions and effect have led to a specific personality pattern of society consisting of adjustive nature and full of reciprocal behaviour. This specific personality pattern can be termed *bowl of sweat and blood* because both the communities despite all the disparities and dissimilarities, riot and differences have worked together for the well-being of all.

There are various methods to analyse the impacts of Hindu practices on the Muslim society. Although polygynous marriage was in practice even before the medieval Muslim rule, as Hindu treatises such as Mahabharat and Ramayan are replete with the example, its popularity got more encouragement during the Islamic rule because there was religious sanction for polygyny confined to four wives. As a result of the establishment of Muslim rule, the social, political and economic systems of society were influenced by the Islamic ideology of life, society and social relations. Most of the Hindus adopted Muslim dressing syle and dietary systems. In the beginning, the Muslims of Arabia were accorded high status and prestige; later in terms of prestige, a distinction emerged between Arabian and non-Arabian Muslims. In Arabian society, the dynastic line of Quraish Muslims related to the Prophet Mohammad was regarded superior. The descendants of Fatima, the daughter of the Prophet, were known as Syad (Gottschalk, 2000; Gustchow, 2006).

They hold the same prestige and status in Muslim society as do the Brahmins in Hindu society. Various Muslim rulers learnt and adopted from native Hindu rajputs, kings and emperors. They adopted the use of valuable royal dresses, glowing sphere and swords, inscribed and engraved with valuable stones as diamond, elephants and horses decorated with silver gold saddles and cups. It is a manifestation of cultural exchange between Hindus and Muslims.

Some specific ornaments such as ring, ear tops, necklace, gold chain and so on were adopted by Hindus from the Muslim society. The use of silk clothes embroidered with gold and silver yarns by the Muslims was also adopted by the Hindu society. By this way, it appears that a social and cultural exchange took place between these two communities and cultures.

The urban social structure is characterized by associative individualism as compared to persistent traditionalism of rural society. Their social relations are made on the basis of selections that emanated from organizational and occupational groupings and specialized native jobs marked with techno-economic specialty and division of labour. The urban people work for the fulfilment of the requirements of urban dwellers. As a consequence, the urban social structure develops wider network of social relation, irrespective of caste, clan, culture and ethnicity. Urbanization represents a common behavioural pattern, the dimensions of which provide scope for social exchange, interaction and cooperation. The city represents a confluence of cultures, creeds, ethnicity and races, and it creates an environment in which numerous religions, moral codes, style of life and ideologies flourished and through which urban dwellers are forced to develop a compromising personality that incorporates the attributes of social tolerance, liberal attitude, humanism and associative character. This chapter attempts at highlighting the emerging dimensions of inter-religious reciprocity contact that are as of social adjustment, impact of urbanism on religious and cultural interaction between the two communities: the Hindus and Muslims.

URBAN RESIDENCE AND RELIGIOUS RECIPROCITY

Social heterogeneity is one of the major characteristics of any urban structure. The social structure and configuration of urban community prima facie represents a picture of the city, which is marked with social diversity. Most of the dwellers in urban settings have rented housings due to their engagement in urban trades, commerce, industry and other remunerative jobs. These people are mainly businessmen, traders and service men. As a result, a mutual reciprocal relation among various religious groups and communities has emerged. This associative and reciprocal form of urban life presents a unique pattern of urban society. In Europe and America, the habitation is based on race and religion whereas in India, the habitation is based on region, language and religion. This is termed as natural area of the study (Zorhaugh, 1926). After all, these separate places of the city have developed gradually and tend to form the web of cultures. The picture of Varanasi city represents a mosaic of social diversities and heterogeneity. One can trace out here the Hindu-dominated areas, the Muslim-dominated areas and the joint areas of Hindus and Muslims despite a number of social discriminations and differences (Dalmia, 1997). Both the Hindus and Muslims in the city are inseparably related with cultural reciprocation and religious participations. This particular inter-religious pattern may sociologically be referred to as an outcome of the social ecology of Varanasi.

OCCUPATION, TRADE AND INTER-RELIGIOUS PARTICIPATION

Urbanization denudes the household of economic function and throws the individual into associated relations determined by the specific interest of work and temperament. The urban dwellers associate themselves with a number of industries, trade and commerce, economic activities in terms of their specialized efficiency, work efficiency and technical know-how. By this way, the urban social structure presents a configuration of class hierarchy and class character of the people engaged in diverse economic activities. To fulfil their common interest, urbanity itself takes the form of a life where the urban dwellers reciprocate and interact with one another transcending all the frontiers of religion and caste. The city of Varanasi too presents a style of life and urban culture like other cities. Although religious and cultural values are still predominant, the modern voluntary organizations such as tradesman association, chamber of commerce, clubs, labour union, trade union, associations of intellectual professionals and manual workers provide a network of urban social structure. For the specific Hindu–Muslim reciprocal relations, the cultural history of Varanasi is more responsible.

The analytical interpretation of data depicts that the majority of the respondents (92 per cent) agree that urban life is based on specification and mutual cooperations. It can be concluded that the interpersonal relations and mutual cooperation are indispensible in urban life.

The data analysed with regard to urban life and occupations reveal that the majority of the respondents (92 per cent) engaged in different occupations agree that urban life is a confluence of mutual cooperation and accommodation, as well as the majority of the respondents, while analysing their response based on their educational level, have also favoured that mutual cooperation and accommodation are basic necessities in urban life. All the respondents educated up to graduate and postgraduate level and expert in vocational or technical streams have expressed their agreement in this regard. The findings reveal that the majority of the respondents from all age groups have expressed an extremely positive condition with regard to religious tolerance and friendly behaviour in urban set-up. The chi-square value is highly significant, which validates that both the variables are interdependent.

As far as the education and opinion of the respondents regarding religious tolerant behaviour and reciprocal relations are concerned, the findings reveal that the majority of the respondents have expressed that modernization in society has provided a positive approach regarding religious tolerance and reciprocity. The chi-square value is highly significant, which validates the interdependency between these two variables. The findings validate our third hypothesis that *the more the increase of modern social values in terms of rational outlook and objective mind set, the greater the boundaries of religious separation and the loyalties of narrow communalism are contested* (Tables 6.1–6.5).

Table 6.1 *Depth of Urban Residence and Views Regarding Urban Life*

Depth of residence (in years)	*Urban life is based on specialization and reciprocity*		*Total*
	Agree	*Disagree*	
1–10	110 (91.67%)	10 (8.33%)	120
11–20	50 (86.21%)	8 (13.79%)	58
21–30	42 (87.50%)	6 (12.50%)	48
31 and above	74 (100.00%)	–	74
Total	**276 (92.00%)**	**24(8.00%)**	**300**

df = 3, chi-square = 12.53, significant (0.01 level).

Table 6.2 *Occupation and Views Regarding Urban Life*

Occupation	*Urban life is based on specialization and reciprocity*		*Total*
	Agree	*Disagree*	
Service	101 (91.82%)	9 (8.18%)	110
Business	130 (92.86%)	10 (7.14%)	140
Self industry	45 (90.00%)	5 (10.00%)	50
Total	**276 (92.00%)**	**24 (8.00%)**	**300**

df = 2, chi-square = 0.48, not significant.

Table 6.3 *Education and Views Regarding Urban Life*

Education	*Urban life is based on specialization and reciprocity*		*Total*
	Agree	*Disagree*	
Literate	108 (87.10%)	16 (12.90%)	124
Intermediate	38 (82.16%)	8 (17.39%)	46

(Continued)

Table 6.3 (Continued)

Graduate/ postgraduate	86 (100.00%)	–	86
Technical/ vocational	44 (100.00%)	–	44
Total	**276 (92.00%)**	**24(8.00%)**	**300**

df = 3, chi-square = 20.87, significant (0.01 level).

Table 6.4 *Age, Religious Tolerance and Social Reciprocity*

Age (in years)	*Religious tolerance and social reciprocity*			*Total*
	Extreme	*Average*	*Uncertain*	
Up to 25	50 (100.00%)	–	–	50
26–35	70 (100.00%)	–	–	70
36–45	70 (100.00%)	–	–	70
46–55	44 (62.86%)	14 (20.00%)	12 (17.14%)	70
56 and above	26 (65.00%)	14 (35.00%)	–	40
Total	**260 (86.67%)**	**28 (9.33%)**	**12 (4.00%)**	**300**

df = 8, chi-square = 105.43, significant (0.01 level).

Table 6.5 *Education and Social Reciprocity and Religious Tolerance*

Education	*Social reciprocity and religious tolerance*			*Total*
	Extreme	*Average*	*Uncertain*	
Literate	94 (75.81%)	21 (16.94%)	9 (7.25%)	124
Intermediate	36 (78.26%)	7 (15.22%)	3 (6.52%)	46
Graduate/ postgraduate	86 (100.00%)	–	–	86
Vocational/ technical	44 (62.86%)	–	–	44
Total	**260 (86.67%)**	**28 (9.33%)**	**12 (4.00%)**	**300**

df = 6, chi-square = 36.89, significant (0.01 level).

The findings reveal that the majority of the respondents engaged in all types of occupations expressed that the occupational life in urban settings has promoted cultural mix-up and religious tolerant behaviour. This cultural mix is a matrix where one cultural trait mixes with another cultural trait.

The empirical facts enable us to furnish that the majority of the respondents are in favour of friendly behaviour and humane relations besides differences in communities and religions (82.67 per cent). In other words, these respondents have given importance to friendship and human relations.

The data, with regard to age of the respondents and their attitude in reference to friendly behaviour and humanitarian approach, reveal that the majority of the respondents (82.67 per cent) have expressed the agreement regarding friendliness behaviour and humanitarian approach. These respondents have expressed that there should be no discrimination besides different religion and community. In other words, these respondents are in favour of social reciprocal relations and religious tolerant behaviour.

As far as the education of the respondents and their attitude regarding religious superstitions and beliefs are concerned, the findings validate that the majority of the respondents (72 per cent) agree that the modernization and cultural contacts have diminished the religious superstitions and misconceptions. A negligible percentage of the respondents (13.67 per cent) disagree, and 14.55 per cent of the respondents are uncertain about the issue. The findings validate that modernization has narrowed the widening of religious misconception and superstitions.

The empirical facts reveal that the majority of the respondents (72 per cent) have shown agreement regarding the decline in religiosity due to modernization. The respondents have expressed that modernization has led to erosion of the religious misconception and superstitions and led to the emergence of a new society based on rationality. This modern society is predominantly governed by rational thinking and mode of behaviour. This agreement increases due to the increase in the depth of urban residence. A negligible percentage of the respondents disagree and show uncertainty (13.67 and 14.33 per cent, respectively). The chi-square value is significant at 0.01 levels, which validates that both the variables are extremely interdependent.

The data analysed with regard to the friendly behaviour due to occupations reveal that the majority of the respondents (91.33 per cent) have expressed that due to occupational relations the friendly relations and cooperation have been increased. Negligible percentage of the respondents

(8.67 per cent) mentioned that the relations are not strengthened. The chi-square value validates the interdependency between these two variables (Tables 6.6–6.11).

Table 6.6 *Occupation and Approach Regarding Religion and Culture*

Occupation	*Occupational life has affected positively to both the communities*		*Total*
	Yes	*No*	
Service	110 (100.00%)	–	110
Business	140 (100.00%)	–	140
Self industry	50 (100.00%)	–	50
Total	**300 (100.00%)**	–	**300**

Table 6.7 *Education and Erosion of Superstitious Beliefs*

Education	*Religious discrimination should be abolished*			*Total*
	Agree	*Disagree*	*Uncertain*	
Literate	64 (51.61%)	28 (22.50%)	32 (25.81%)	124
Intermediate	22 (47.83%)	13 (28.27%)	11 (23.90%)	46
Graduate/ postgraduate	86 (100.00%)	–	–	86
Vocational/ technical	44 (100.00%)	–	–	44
Total	**216 (72.00%)**	**41 (13.67%)**	**43 (14.33%)**	**300**

df = 6, chi-square = 90.13, significant (0.01 level).

Table 6.8 *Depth of Urban Residence, Religion and Modernization*

Depth of urban residence (in years)	*Religiosity due to modernization has been decreased*			*Total*
	Agree	*Disagree*	*Uncertain*	
1–10	74 (61.67%)	26 (21.67%)	20 (16.66%)	120
11–20	42 (72.41%)	10 (17.24%)	6 (10.35%)	58
21–30	32 (66.66%)	5 (10.42%)	11 (22.92%)	48
31 and above	68 (91.89%)	–	6 (8.11%)	74
Total	**216 (72.00%)**	**41 (13.67%)**	**43 (14.23%)**	**300**

df = 6, chi-square = 27.88, significant (0.01 level).

Table 6.9 *Education and Mutual Relations due to Occupations*

Education	*Mutual relations strengthen*		*Total*
	Yes	*No*	
Literate	106 (85.48%)	18 (14.52%)	120
Intermediate	38 (82.61%)	8 (17.39%)	46
Graduate/ postgraduate	86 (100.00%)	–	86
Vocational/ technical	44 (100.00%)	–	44
Total	**274 (91.33%)**	**26 (8.67%)**	**300**

df = 3, chi-square = 23.79, significant at 0.01 level.

Table 6.10 *Occupation and Status of Mutual Relations*

Occupation	*Mutual relations strengthen*		*Total*
	Yes	*No*	
Service	93 (84.55%)	17 (15.55%)	110
Business	140 (100.00%)	–	140
Self industry	41 (82.00%)	9 (18.00%)	50
Total	**274 (91.33%)**	**26 (8.67%)**	**300**

df = 2, chi-square = 25.21, significant (0.01 level).

Table 6.11 *Education and Ideas Regarding Socio-religious Superstitions*

Education	*Change is necessary in social and religious superstitions*			*Total*
	Agree	*Disagree*	*Uncertain*	
Literate	84 (67.74%)	26 (20.96%)	14 (11.30%)	124
Intermediate	35 (76.08%)	9 (19.57%)	2 (4.35%)	46
Graduate/ postgraduate	86 (100.00%)	–	–	86
Vocational/ technical	44 (100.00%)	–	–	44
Total	**249 (83.00%)**	**35 (11.67%)**	**16 (15.33%)**	**300**

The empirical facts enable us to furnish that the majority of the respondents (91.33 per cent) are in favour of increase in mutual relations due to occupational involvement in modern techno-economic set-up.

The data reveal that the majority of the respondents (83 per cent) abandoned superstitious beliefs and religious narrowness and have gone above the narrow attitude to life and society. This attitude is increasing due to increase in education. The postgraduate and technically educated respondents (100 per cent) have expressed that this religious narrowness must be replaced by a harmonious relations. The findings validate our fourth hypothesis that *Urbanism as a way of life proceeds with the diminution of superstitious and irrational social sanctions. While the rationally organized systems of faith increase with much celebrity in both the communities. The perspectives of modernity include the accessibility to material well-being, social privilege and social security. Therefore, the religion and the tradition are also subjected to sophistication* (Tables 6.12 and 6.13).

Table 6.12 *Education and Impact of Science and Technology*

Education	*Equal importance to all human beings*		*Total*
	Yes	*No*	
Literate	86 (69.35%)	38 (30.65%)	124
Intermediate	26 (56.52%)	20 (43.48%)	46
Graduate/ postgraduate	67 (77.91%)	19 (22.09%)	86
Vocational/ technical	39 (88.64%)	5 (11.36%)	44
Total	**218 (72.67%)**	**82 (27.33%)**	**300**

df = 3, chi-square = 13.59, significant (0.01 level).

Table 6.13 *Education and Erosion of Communitarian Discriminations*

Education	*Communitarian discriminations have been diminished*		*Total*
	Yes	*No*	
Literate	87 (70.16%)	37 (29.84%)	124
Intermediate	33 (71.74%)	13 (28.26%)	46

(Continued)

Table 6.13 (Continued)

Education	*Communitarian discriminations have been diminished*		*Total*
	Yes	*No*	
Graduate/ postgraduate	71 (82.50%)	15 (17.44%)	86
Vocational/ technical	37 (84.09%)	7 (15.91%)	44
Total	**228 (76.00%)**	**72 (24.00%)**	**300**

df = 3, chi-square = 5.39, not significant.

Table 6.14 *Occupation and Erosion of Communitarian Discriminations*

Occupation	*Status of communitarian discriminations*		*Total*
	Yes	*No*	
Service	73 (66.36%)	37 (33.64%)	110
Business	111 (79.29%)	29 (20.71%)	140
Self industry	44 (88.00%)	6 (12.00%)	50
Total	**228 (76.00%)**	**72 (24.00%)**	**300**

Analytical interpretation of the data reveals that the majority of the respondents from all educational levels have expressed that all human beings must be given an equal importance based on the knowledge of science and technology (72.67 per cent). There are a few respondents who are not in favour of facilitating this equality (27.33 per cent). The chi-square value is highly significant, which signifies that both the variables are interdependent. In other words, the presence of one variable will affect the other. While analysing the data to assess the opinion of the respondents regarding communal discrimination, the findings reveal that the majority of the respondents from all educational groups and all types of occupation have expressed that the modernizing factors and urban lifestyle have led to the erosion of communal discriminations (Tables 6.14–6.16).

Table 6.15 *Age, Modernization, Religious beliefs and Superstitions*

Age (in years)	*Religious beliefs, values and standards have been changed*			*Total*
	Agree	*Disagree*	*Uncertain*	
Up to 25	40 (80.00%)	6 (12.00%)	4 (8.00%)	50
26–35	62 (88.57%)	–	8 (11.43%)	70
36–45	66 (94.29%)	4 (5.71%)	–	70
46–55	54 (77.14%)	8 (11.43%)	8 (11.43%)	70
56 and above	18 (45.00%)	12 (30.00%)	10 (25.00%)	40
Total	**240 (80.00%)**	**30 (10.00%)**	**30 (10.00%)**	**300**

df = 8, chi-square = 49.79, significant (0.01 level).

Table 6.16 *Occupation, Modernization and Religious Beliefs*

Occupation	*Religious beliefs, values and standards have been changed*			*Total*
	Agree	*Disagree*	*Uncertain*	
Service	93 (84.55%)	8 (7.27%)	9 (3.18%)	110
Business	112 (80.00%)	15 (10.71%)	13 (9.29%)	140
Self-industry	35 (70.00%)	7 (14.00%)	8 (16.00%)	50
Total	**240 (80.00%)**	**30 (10.00%)**	**30 (10.00%)**	**300**

df = 4, chi-square = 4.83, not significant.

The analytical interpretation of the data reveals that the majority of the respondents from all the age groups have shown their agreement regarding the changes in religious values and moral standard due to the influence of science and technology (80 per cent), whereas 20 per cent of the respondents do not agree with this. The chi-square value is significant at 0.01 levels, which is highly significant and rejects our null hypothesis that there is no relation between these two variables. In other words, both the variables are extremely interdependent. The findings validate our fifth hypothesis that *the greater the involvement of social heterogeneity in occupational sector, the more the people of different communities and sub cultures, who come to interact and socially exchange with one another.*

The findings reveal that the majority of the respondents engaged in any type of occupations expressed that modernity has changed the religious values and moral standards (80 per cent), whereas a negligible percentage of the respondents (10 per cent) do not agree, and 10 per cent of the respondents are uncertain about this. The chi-square value is not significant, which accepts our null hypothesis that there is no relation between these two variables.

The empirical facts enable us to furnish that all of the respondents from all the age groups have accepted that modern education, urbanism and industrialization have promoted the cultural and religious contacts. The findings validate our sixth hypothesis that *modernity, urbanity and industrial development have not crossed the boundaries of religious traditions, but they emerged as behaviour-friendly in heterogeneous situations*.

As far as the education of the respondents and their attitude regarding inter-religious participation in the wave of modernization and urbanization are concerned, it can be concluded that the majority of the respondents (88.67 per cent) realized that modernization and urbanization have promoted the inter-religious participations and social reciprocation. The significance of chi-square value depicts that the null hypothesis is rejected, and both the variables are extremely interdependent (Tables 6.17–6.20).

Table 6.17 *Age and Ideas Concerning Culture and Religion due to Modernization*

Age (in years)	*Cultural and religious relations have increased*			*Total*
	Agree	*Disagree*	*Uncertain*	
Up to 25	50 (100.00%)	–	–	50
26–35	70 (100.00%)	–	–	70
36–45	70 (100.00%)	–	–	70
46–55	70 (100.00%)	–	–	70
56 and above	40 (100.00%)	–	–	40
Total	**300 (100.00%)**	–	–	**300**

Table 6.18 *Education, Modernization, Urbanization and Religious Tolerance*

Education	*Modernization and urbanization have strengthened the religious tolerance*			*Total*
	Agree	*Disagree*	*Uncertain*	
Literate	95 (76.61%)	29 (23.39%)	–	124
Intermediate	41 (89.13%)	5 (10.87%)	–	46
Graduate/post graduate	86 (100.00%)	–	–	86
Vocational/ technical	44 (100.00%)	–	–	44
Total	**266 (88.67%)**	**34 (11.33%)**	–	**300**

df = 3, chi-square = 34.49, significant (0.01 level).

Table 6.19 *Depth of Urban Residence, Modernization, Urbanization and Religious Tolerance*

Depth of urban residence (in years)	*Modernization and urbanization have increased the religious tolerance in behaviour*			*Total*
	Agree	*Disagree*	*Uncertain*	
1–10	99 (82.50%)	21 (17.50%)	–	120
11–20	49 (84.48%)	9 (15.52%)	–	58
21–30	44 (91.67%)	4 (8.33%)	–	48
31 and above	74 (100.00%)	–	–	74
Total	**266 (88.67%)**	**34 (11.33%)**	–	**300**

df = 3, chi-square = 15.47, significant (0.01 level).

Table 6.20 *Education and Mutual Cooperation between Communities*

Education	*Urban society is a confluence of heterogeneity and communal harmony*		*Total*
	Yes	*No*	
Literate	94 (75.80%)	30 (24.20%)	124
Intermediate	39 (84.70%)	7 (15.30%)	46

(Continued)

Table 6.20 (Continued)

Education	*Urban society is a confluence of heterogeneity and communal harmony*		*Total*
	Yes	*No*	
Graduate/ postgraduate	86 (100.00%)	–	86
Vocational/ technical	44 (100.00%)	–	44
Total	**273 (87.67%)**	**37 (12.33%)**	**300**

The findings reveal that the majority of the respondents (88.67 per cent) have observed that the mutual religious relations and reciprocal behaviour have increased due to modernization and urbanization. All the respondents (100 per cent) living in the city for over 30 years have expressed and perceived reaction that the relations; social, economic occupational and personal have increased.

The data reveal that the majority of the respondents (88.67 per cent) realized that urban set-up is based on heterogeneity but values of urban life are responsible for the accommodation and reciprocation among various religious groups and communities. The findings validate that urban social structure is providing such an environment where the people from the groups and communities are forming a new social structure (Tables 6.21 and 6.22).

Table 6.21 *Education and Religious Separation*

Education	*Religious separation is a hindrance to urban life*		*Total*
	Agree	*Disagree*	
Literate	93 (75.00%)	31 (25.00%)	124
Intermediate	33 (71.74%)	13 (28.26%)	46
Graduate/ postgraduate	75 (87.21%)	11 (12.79%)	86
Vocational/ technical	44 (100.00%)	–	44
Total	**245 (81.67%)**	**55 (18.33%)**	**300**

df = 3, chi-square = 18.35, significant (0.01 level).

Table 6.22 *Depth of Urban Residence and Religious Separation*

Depth of urban residence (in years)	*Religious separation is a hindrance to urban life*		*Total*
	Agree	*Disagree*	
1–10	83 (69.17%)	37 (30.83%)	120
11–20	49 (84.48%)	9 (15.52%)	58
21–30	39 (81.25%)	9 (18.75%)	48
31 and above	74 (100.00%)	–	74
Total	**245 (81.67%)**	**55 (18.33%)**	

df = 3, chi-square = 29.51, significant (0.01 level).

With regard to education and urban depth of residence and religious separation, the findings reveal that the majority of the respondents from all educational levels accepted that separation is a hindrance in the urban social set-up (81.67 per cent), whereas a negligible percentage (18.33 per cent) of the respondents disagreed in this regard. As far as the age and education are concerned, the findings reveal that the majority of respondents expressed the agreement that modernizing factors have changed the superstitions correlated with religion (Tables 6.23–6.26).

Table 6.23 *Age and Ideas Regarding Religious Superstitions*

Age (in years)	*Regarding changes to religious superstitions*			*Total*
	Agree	*Disagree*	*Uncertain*	
Up to 25	41 (82.00%)	9 (18.00%)	–	50
26–35	58 (82.86%)	7 (10.00%)	5 (7.14%)	70
36–45	54 (77.14%)	9 (12.86%)	7 (10.00%)	70
46–55	61 (87.14%)	6 (8.57%)	3 (4.29%)	70
56 and above	23 (57.50%)	17 (42.50%)	–	40
Total	**237 (79.00%)**	**48 (16.00%)**	**15 (5.00%)**	**300**

df = 8, chi-square = 33.97, significant (0.01 level).

Table 6.24 *Education and Opinion about Changes in Superstitions*

Education	*Opinion regarding changes in religious superstitions*			*Total*
	Agree	*Disagree*	*Uncertain*	
Literate	87 (70.16%)	26 (20.97%)	11 (8.87%)	124
Intermediate	29 (63.04%)	13 (28.26%)	4 (8.70%)	46
Graduate/ postgraduate	77 (89.53%)	9 (10.47%)	–	86
Vocational/ technical	44 (62.86%)	–	–	44
Total	**237 (79.00%)**	**48 (16.00%)**	**15 (5.00%)**	**300**

df = 6, chi-square = 34.20, significant at 0.01 level.

ATTITUDE TESTING

Various facts concerning inter-religious tolerance and social reciprocity have been tested and verified. Tables 6.1 and 6.3 indicate that people from both the communities have developed associative individualism and religious tolerance in their behaviour and Tables 6.4 and 6.5 represent the appearance of intercultural contacts. The high participation as the indicator of modernity as given by D. Learner is also subsumed in Tables 6.6, 6.20 and 6.21. In the same manner, Table 6.9 represents the rational ends–means calculation, which is the indicator of modernization. Tables 6.7, 6.11 and 6.12 symbolize the reality of occupational relations, and Tables 6.6, 6.10, 6.15 and 6.16 indicate rational and humanist attitude in the people of both the communities. Modernization has changed the nature and patterns of religion and humanity.

SUMMARY

In this study, interactional exchange approach has been employed as a major theoretical paradigm. This chapter concerns inter-religious reciprocity and social adjustment. The findings reveal that people from both the communities have developed associative individualism and religious tolerance in their behaviour due to cultural contacts in the urban set-up. This intercultural contact has been nurtured by urban lifestyle, values of urbanism and relations between various occupational groups. Due to social interaction and exchange, both the communities have adopted humanitarian values in religion and morality. In the wave of modernization, the traditions of both the communities have changed and a new pattern of accommodation and adjustment has been observed. The Muslim communities have adopted various values, norms and patterns of Hindus culture. Hindus have also adopted that of Muslim society.

The findings reveal that urban life is based on specialization and mutual dependency. In this regard, the majority from both the communities has favoured that the interpersonal relations and mutual contacts are inevitable. The younger respondents from both the communities have greater attitude of interdependency and associative character. Highly educated respondents from both the communities have developed strong commitments in this regard.

The respondents engaged in any type of occupations have added that occupational life has provided and facilitated the people with friendly behaviour in urban social set-up. The majority of the respondents from both the communities have observed that modernization has decreased the religious fanaticism, superstitious beliefs and orthodoxy in Indian society. The respondents from both the communities are eagerly expecting for the change in social and religious superstitions. The majority of the respondents have observed that all human beings must be given equal importance in the society that is dominated by science and technology.

The respondents in majority from both the communities have expressed that urbanization, modern occupational structure and industrial development have narrowed the superstitious beliefs and communitarian discriminations. The majority of the respondents from both the communities expressed that development in science and technology has changed the standards of moral practices and religious values. The respondents from both the communities have accepted that modernization and urbanization worked as a facilitator for the participation in religious activities and rituals. In this regard, highly educated respondents and those who are residing in the city for a long time have a greater percentage. The respondents in majority from both the communities regarded that urban social structure is based on heterogeneity and the religious structure is based on multiplicity and materialism, and there is no space for spiritualism and religious fear. Depth of urban residence has widened the attitude of the respondents, and they have no space for religious separation and communitarian discriminations. The respondents from both the communities considered that the superstitions overlapped the religious values and the underlying factors in religions are responsible for religious separation. It must be abolished and modified as for existing social values. The respondents from both the communities have observed faith in all religions, and they like visiting the religious places either of any community if they have any benefit from the visit. The spread of modern education has modified the structure of religion and tendencies regarding religious faith.

The study denotes that both the communities in Varanasi city have adopted the values of religious pluralism and heterogeneity in population, and all of them have developed associative individualism, religious tolerance in behaviour and social reciprocal relations.

An overall assessment of social participation and religious tolerance made above provides an integrated picture of urbanism. The depth of urban residence has affected much of the social relations and attitude concerning religions and communities. As such, education and income have a significant correlation with the attitude and perception of the respondents.

REFERENCES

Bellah, Robert (Ed.), 1965, 'Epilogue'. In *Religion and Progress in Modern Asia*, Glencoe, IL: The Free Press of Glencoe.

Berger, P.L., 1967, *The Sacred Canopy: Elements of a Sociological Theory of Religion*. New York: Garden City.

Dalmia, V., 1997, *The Nationalism of Hindu Traditions: Bhartendu Harishchandra and 19th Century Banaras*. New Delhi: Oxford University Press.

Dube, S.C., 1965, 'Cultural Problem in the Economic Development of India'. In *Religion and Progress in Modern Asia*, edited by R.N. Bellah, Glencoe, IL: The Free Press of Glencoe.

Durkheim, Emile, (1912/1961), *The Elementary Forms of Religious Life*, translated by Karen E. Fields, 1961. New York: The Free Press.

Feuerbach, L., 1957, *The Essence of Christianity*. New York: Harper & Row.

Frazer, James, 1996 (1870), *The Golden Bough: A Study in Magic and Religion*. New York: Penguin Classics.

Giddens, Anthony, 1984, *The Constitution of Society: Outline of the Theory of Structuration*. Cambridge: Polity Press.

———, 2007, *Sociology*. Cambridge: Polity Press.

Gottschalk, P., 2000, *Beyond Hindu-Muslim: Multiple Identity in Narratives from Village India*. New Delhi: Oxford University Press.

Gustchow, N., 2006, *Banaras: The Sacred Landscape of Varanasi*. Germany: Buch.

Lenski, G., 1962, *The Sociology of Religion in United States: A Review of Theoretically Oriented Research*. Glencoe, IL: The Free Press.

Levi-Strauss, Claude, 1949, *Les Structures Élémentaires de la Parenté (The Elementary Structures of Kinship)*, translated by J.H. Bell, J.R. von Sturmer, and Rodney Needham, edited by Rodney Needham, 1969.

Malinowski, B., 1948, *Magic, Science, and Religion*. New York: Doubleday.

Marx, K. and F. Engels, 2001 (1848), *The Communist Manifesto*. London: Electric Book Company.

O'Dea, Thomas F., 1969, *The Sociology of Religion*. New Delhi: Prentice Hall.

Radcliff-Brown, A.R., 1952, *Structure and Function in Primitive Society*. Glencoe, IL: The Free Press.

Radhakrishnan, S., 1947, *Religion and Society*. London: Allen & Unwin Ltd.

Singer, M. (Ed.), 1956, 'The Great Traditions and Metropolitan Centre, Madras'. In *Traditional India: Structural Change*, Glencoe, IL: The Free Press of Glencoe.

Singh, H., 1980, *Approach to the Study of Religion*. Patiala: Punjab University.

Srinivas, M.N., 1966, *Social Change in Modern India*. Berkeley, CA: University of California Press.

Tylor, Edward, 1871, *Primitive Culture*. London: John Murray.

Warner, S., 1993, 'Work in Progress Toward a New Paradigm for the Sociological Study of Religion in the United States', *American Journal of Sociology*, 98.

Weber, Max, 1963, *The Sociology of Religion*. Boston, MA: Beacon.

Wuthnow, R., 1988, 'Sociology of Religion'. In *Handbook of Sociology*, edited by N.J. Smelsor, New Delhi: Sage Publication.

Zorbaugh, Harvey, 1926, 'The Natural Areas of Cities'. In *The Urban Community*, edited by E.W. Burgers, Chicago, IL: University of Chicago Press.Ede facidit. Pere ex sus, me publin sent.

CHAPTER 7

Emerging Features of Religion and Faith

Indian society is a confluence of a great historicity of interaction, social reciprocity and religious tolerance among various castes and communities. Sociologists, anthropologists and historians have discussed this very nature from time to time. Indian society has faced the invasions of Muslims from the seventh century AD, but the Muslim empire started during the fourteenth century. Arabic and Turkish emperors came to India, looted the wealth of nation and left their successor to rule over here (Nehru, 1951). Muslim emperors ruled here for years. The Muslim dynasties being started by Aibak and the Mughal dynasty by Babur were the landmark in this regard (Jha and Shrimali, 1995).

The spread of Muslim tradition and assimilation with Hindu tradition was possible only due to elite class of Muslim of that period (Singh, 1999 [1977]). As compared to the structure of the Hindu tradition, the Islamic tradition is being founded on a universal view, which is apparently non-hierarchical and is purely monotheistic and messianic historical in ethos. The Hindu religion provides an important place for priests, saints and religious persons; but in Islam, it is an adverse figure. Islam does not permit any institutionalized role for priests, the Ulemas are in no sense priests; rather, they correspond to the scribes in Judaism. Strictly speaking, Islam has no clergy, as any Muslim may lead a congregation in prayer (Smith, 1972). Similarly, in ideal-typical form, Islam has a more developed orientation towards the holistic principle in its conception of social order than even Hinduism. The holistic principle in Hinduism is derived from the fundamental theory of the normative order (Dharma), which is internally differentiated and hierarchical in socio-cultural manifestations. In Hinduism, in sociological sense, but not in principle, the very ideology of holism can be differentiated from hierarchism; there is a less substantive place for the latter in the tradition.

Islamic holism is based on the unity of the Muslim ummah, the collectivity of the faithful. This unity in principle transcends the boundaries of territory and nation and is derived from the conformity of members of the religio-ethical codes and principles embodied in the Quran and/or Sunna, the hadith (various traditions) and the Shariya (legal codebook of Islam).

The contact of India with Islam is almost a millennium old. It started with Arab conquest during the beginning of the eighth century. Thus, historically as well as in magnitude, Islam is an important and sociologically very meaningful cultural tradition in India. Since both Hinduism and Islam represent the combination of two paradoxical and traditional views, it is a major thrust of the study to find out the patterns and directions that modernized these two communities. Acculturation and endogenous changes in the great tradition of Islam in India have evolved through three major stages. These stages were set by the historical forces and greatly influenced the structure of this tradition. The first stage related to the duration of Islamic regime in India; the second was initiated after the establishment of the British dominion, and finally the last stage can be marked at the beginning of the Indian freedom movement, leading to the country's partition and political independence. Many Muslim scholars and rulers made overt efforts to reconcile some aspects of the Hindu tradition with Islam (Jan dt, 2006). Akbar attempted it through the introduction of a new religion called divine faith (Din-e-Ilahi), which was a mixture of Islam, Jainism, Hinduism and Zoroastrianism. Dara Shikoh pleaded for a synthesis of Upanishadic monotheism with that of Islam and emphasized the similarities between the two traditions. Among the literary figures, Amir Khusro did a great job to interpret the endogenous traditions of Hinduism to the Muslim world. In the sixteenth and seventeenth centuries, various Muslim poets and writers selected Hindi as the language in their writings. The mention may be made of Jayasi, Nabi, Bahri, Chisti, Gangohi and Rahim as representatives in this regard. Kabir played a unique role in unifying both the communities.

'*Purdah* system' is a contribution of Islamic tradition and was accepted by Hindus also. According to Srivastava (1980), 'Akique' and 'Bismillah' of Muslim tradition are equal to 'Mundan' and 'the sacred thread ceremony' and starting of schooling. Id-ul-Fitra, Bak-ra-eid and other Muslim festivals, such as Holy, Deepawali and Dushehara, are equally important to all communities. Shab-e-barat of Muslim and Maha Shivratri of Hindus are equal (Majumdar, 1967). Dr Tara Chand (1954) mentioned that Hinduism adopted not only art, literature and science of Muslim culture but also the soul of Hindu religion has also changed. Islam brought some radical changes in Hindu society. As a result, a new culture named 'Indo-Islamic' culture developed. It is evident from historical surveys that both the communities are living together, and it is impossible to make a separate study while living together. Thus, a unique interaction is evident between these two communities. The origin of 'Hindu' is geographical and is related to those living in the Indian subcontinent. The Sindhu (Indus) river was referred to as 'Hindu' by the Persians and the Greeks. The Arabs referred to it as al-hind. Thus, the inhabitants of al-hind were the Hindus. The term 'Hindu' was first used to mean all those who lived in al-hind but were not Muslim. In terms of the religion of the Hindus, the Persian sources refer to various Hindu religions, the earlier text mentioning forty-two and later ones lasting at least five (Zaehner, 1962).

Both Hindu and Muslim religions have accepted the supreme power of the Almighty and believe that both the communities are the creation of Almighty. The Hindu view of life in Vedic thought is that man is altogether and throughout composed of the elements borne out from the inner needs of the individuals. The salient feature of the Hindu thought is that it believes in unity. In Hindu ideology, the deeds, destiny, desires and decision are closely related. *It can be termed as D-4 theory of the religion.* D-4 implies that the deeds and destiny are correlated. This means that the destiny of an individual is based on his or her deeds or duties performed. If no desires are left, the individual is being supposed to be intermingled with Brahma (God). Thus, karma or deeds are the sources of linkage between desires and rebirth. If any of the wishes in the life of an individual is not fulfilled, he or she cannot attain salvation and is captured in rebirth.

The major characteristics of Hindu religion are the presence of various religious beliefs, faiths and appearance of different Gods. All Hindu devotees believe in various gods and goddess. Hinduism believes in certain theological ideas such as rebirth, soul, sin, merit, deeds, morality and salvation. Hindu religion is secular and tolerant.

The appearance of Buddhism and Jainism has affected the Hindu ideology to a greater extent. Although both developed as separate religions, their roots deeply underlie in the Hindu tradition; Jainism had the patronage of urban-mercantile community, whereas Buddhism had princely patronage. Hindu beliefs and values were further affected by the appearance of Shankaracharya's Advait philosophy (ninth century), Ramanujacharya (1017–1137) and Madhvacharya (fourteenth century AD), all of whom established monasteries in different corners of the country for propagating monotheism.

Various religious schools that emerged between the fifteenth and sixteenth centuries attempted to popularize some new values in the Hindu religion. Saints such as Kabir (1440–1518), Guru Nanak (1469–1538), Ramananda (fourteenth and fifteenth centuries), Chaitnya (1485–1535), Mira Bai (1504–1550), Tulsidas (1532–1623), Tukaram and Ramdas emphasized on equalitarian and non-hierarchical value system in Hinduism. They also made efforts towards liberalization of Hindu tradition and its synthesis with Islam. Islam influenced Hindu religion and ideals in the medieval period. Although invasions by Muslims on India had started during the tenth century, it was more frequently from the fifteenth century onwards that the impact of Islamic culture on Hindu tradition was observed. Islam is so against any form of idol worship. It is monotheistic and non-hierarchical; that is, it believes in equality. Although both Islam and Hinduism are oriented to the principle of holism but in Hinduism, holism is linked with hierarchy; whereas in Islam, holism is differentiated from hierarchism.

Contrary to the structure of the Hindu tradition, the Islamic tradition is based on a universal viewpoint, which is apparently non-hierarchical, is purely monotheistic and messianic-historical in ethos (Singh, 1999 [1977]). Emphasis on the historical nature of the tradition is paramount in all Abrahamanic religions; but in Islam, it is most prominent.

Islamic holism is based on the unity of the Muslim 'Ummah', the collectivity of the faithful. This unity in principle transcends the boundaries of territory and nation and is derived from the conformity of the members of the religio-ethical codes and principles embodied in the Quran and Sunna, the Hadith (various traditions) and the Shariya (legal codebook of Islam).

GENERATION DEPTH AND COMMUNITARIAN RECIPROCAL RELATIONS

The older generation are the proponents and nourishers of religious beliefs, traditions, customs, superstitions, values and religious ethical codes; whereas the younger generation are directly affected by the changes that occur due to modernization, development of science and technology and spread of Western lifestyle. The emerging ideas regarding complex societies have affected much. The process of Westernization, modernization and globalization has implanted a seed in the younger generation that grow in the direction of a nonreligious character and far from superstitions, values, ideology and religious bondage. Thus, naturally, the younger generation is leading towards new orientations and changes. In such a state of affairs, a gap or distance is being perceived between these two generations. The younger generation is the nourisher of novelty, modernity and contemporary changes. Thus, there is an occurrence of qualitative and quantitative differences between these two generations in the urban social structure. Every religion has some symbols to perform their rituals. The statue of God is considered a symbol. Every religion contains some mores, proverbs and stories that evoke the faith in that religion.

TRADITIONS, CUSTOMS AND MORES

Sumner (1906) applied the term *mores* for those folkways that are considered by the group as most important and significant and, therefore, indispensable for the welfare of the group. Mores and traditions are much important for a society to survive. Various scholars are concerned with the study of modernization; Daniel Lerner (1962), Wilbert Moore (1963), S. C. Dube (1965), McClelland (1961), Ethiel Pool (1963) and Yogendra Singh (1999 [1977]) revealed in their studies that due to modernization new values, ideas, norms, ideology, technology and rationality-based social structures have developed: due to this development, various radical changes are found in mores, traditions and customs. Milton Singer (1961) and Mckim Marriot (1955) in their studies found that modernization has narrowed the superstitious beliefs and illogical activities of religion and new structure of traditions and beliefs intermingled with rational social set-up have been developed. They observed that modernization has not replaced the religious beliefs and traditions, but they have been modified, re-established, restructured and spreaded in a new form with a rational approach. New form of modified transformations has also been found in Hindu–Muslim traditions.

In contemporary Indian society, religion, mores, traditions and customs all have a prominent place. Due to the importance of these factors, some sanctions are applicable for the members in reference to social mobility, sexual intercourse and speed of social change is comparatively slow.

FESTIVALS AND FESTIVITY

Every society has certain festivals and festivities for the prayer and worship of the Almighty. Each community organizes the festivals and festivities to pray the Almighty. In this regard, the study of the mutual interactions between the communities, their interest in other communities, their participation in the marriage ceremonies and so on are the central point of the analysis to understand the religious tolerant behaviour and social reciprocation.

The empirical facts enable us to furnish that the majority of the respondents (74 per cent) from all the educational levels have expressed that the reciprocal relations among the young respondents are much better than the older generations. From findings, it can be concluded that as the education of the respondents increases, there occurs a positive attitude regarding the reciprocal relations with the communities.

The findings reveal that the majority of the respondents (81 per cent) expressed that they observed a close relationship with the people of other communities besides the conservative ideology being nurtured by their own family. It is evident that the education has broken the narrow sink of superstitions and communitarian beliefs. The chi-square value is significant at the 0.05 level, which signifies that education and communitarian relations are closely related; that is as the education increases, the orthodox religious beliefs weaken.

As far as the age of respondents and their relations with the other communities are concerned, the findings reveal that the majority of the respondents from all the age groups have observed a close relationship with other communities in urban social set-up besides the conservative family of their own.

The data in regard to education and perception concerning the Almighty reveal that mostly all of the respondents (95.67 per cent) have expressed that the various communities are carrying the same objective to reach God, holding different perspectives. It is evident that the respondents have observed that the Almighty has various forms in the different communitarian beliefs, but all the religious groups and communities are pleading for the existence of one authority that can be ultimately termed *God*.

Findings reveal that the majority of the respondents (84.33 per cent) have accepted that modernization has given a new trend and realization about traditional values, its practices and importance. They have observed that the modernizing factors have not destroyed or diminished but instead changed the mode of practices, importance and experiences of traditional religious beliefs, and helped enormously in spreading and widening the traditional values and ideologies. The chi-square value is significant at the 0.01 level, which signifies that education and perception about traditional values and practices in the lap of modernization are highly interdependent (Tables 7.1–7.5).

Table 7.1 *Social Reciprocity and Education*

Level of education	*Reciprocity is much in younger generation than the older*		*Total*
	Yes	*No*	
Literate	74 (59.68)	50 (40.32)	124
Up to intermediate	30 (60.21)	16 (39.79)	46

(Continued)

Table 7.1 (Continued)

Level of education	*Reciprocity is much in younger generation than the older*		*Total*
	Yes	*No*	
Graduate/ postgraduate	78 (90.70)	8 (9.30)	86
Vocational/ technical	40 (90.90)	4 (9.10)	44
Total	**222 (74.00)**	**78 (26.00)**	**300**

Table 7.2 *Education and Communitarian Relations*

Level of education	*Besides conservative family, you perceive the affinal relations*		*Total*
	Yes	*No*	
Literate	110 (88.71)	14 (11.29)	124
Up to intermediate	38 (82.61)	8 (17.39)	48
Graduate/ postgraduate	81 (94.19)	5 (5.81)	86
Vocational/ technical	44 (100.00)	–	44
Total	**273 (91.00)**	**27 (9.00)**	**300**

df = 3, chi-square = 10.17, significant (0.05 level).

Table 7.3 *Age and Communitarian Relations*

Age (in years)	*Besides conservative family, you perceive the affinal relations*		*Total*
	Yes	*No*	
Up to 25	45 (90.00)	5 (10.00)	50
26–35	63 (90.00)	7 (10.00)	70
36–45	64 (91.43)	6 (8.37)	70
46–55	63 (90.00)	7 (10.00)	70
56 and above	38 (95.00)	2 (5.00)	40
Total	**273 (91.00)**	**27 (9.00)**	**300**

df =4, chi-square = 1.29, not significant.

Table 7.4 *Education and Perception Regarding Almighty*

Education level	*Both communities are different ways of reaching the Almighty*		*Total*
	Yes	*No*	
Literate	111 (89.52)	13	124
Up to intermediate	46 (100.00)	–	46
Graduate/ postgraduate	86 (100.00)	–	86
Vocational/ technical	44 (100.00)	–	44
Total	**287 (95.67)**	**13 (4.33)**	**300**

df = 3, chi-square = 19.43, significant (0.01 level).

Table 7.5 *Education, Modernization and Traditions*

Education level	*Due to modernization, traditions have not been destroyed, but their importance and practice have enhanced*			*Total*
	Agree	*Disagree*	*Can't say*	
Literate	90 (72.58)	23 (18.55)	11 (8.87)	124
Up to intermediate	33 (71.74)	13 (28.26)	–	46
Graduate/ postgraduate	86 (100.00)	–	–	86
Vocational/ technical	44 (100.00)	–	–	44
Total	**253 (84.33)**	**36 (12.00)**	**11 (3.67)**	**300**

df = 6, chi-square = 51.92, significant (0.01 level).

The data in regard to age and ideas concerning religious values and traditions reveal that all the respondents up to 35 years of age have expressed that modernization has spreaded the practice and importance of traditional values rather than abolishing it. On the other hand, the majority of the respondents of the age group of 36 and more years have also expressed the same viewpoint. The respondents have observed that the modernizing factors have presented a new shape to the religious traditions and beliefs. The superstitious religious beliefs have been replaced by the new values and beliefs full of rationality. The chi-square validates that both the variables are interdependent. The value is significant at the 0.01 level, which explains that our null hypothesis is accepted, and both the variables are extremely interdependent on each other; in other words, the presence of one variable will affect the presence of the other.

The empirical facts reveal that the majority of the respondents from all the educational levels (80.67 per cent) have expressed that the value differences are inevitable in the different communities. The postgraduate and technically educated respondents have expressed that the value differences are very much necessary for the consolidation of the social structure. The chi-square value is significant, and this proves that both the variables are extremely interdependent on each other.

Analytical interpretation of the data reveals that the majority of the respondents from all the age groups (80.67 per cent) have observed that the value differences are inevitable among the communities. The least number of respondents (14 per cent) has shown a disagreement in this regard. They hold that the value differences are not necessary. The chi-square value is highly significant (0.01 level), which signifies that both the variables, that is, the age and the perception regarding value differences, are extremely interdependent.

The findings in regard to the festivals and cultural activities of the communities, that is, participation of the Hindus in Muslim festivals and the participation of Muslims in Hindu festivals, reveal that the majority of the Hindu respondents have expressed active participation in the festivals, festivities and cultural activities of the Muslims. The higher educated respondents of both the communities have a high degree of participation as compared to their less-educated counterparts. The majority of the Muslim respondents have observed that they actively participate in the cultural activities, festivals and rituals of the Hindu communities. Both the communities engaged in any type of occupation (service, business or self-industry) mentioned that they, like Hindus, celebrate the festival of candle burning (Deepawali) and the festival of colours (Holi). They prepare special dishes on these occasions and invite their Hindu friends to their residence for lunch or dinner. This provides a unique example of religious tolerant behaviour in an urban setting unaffected by various religious separation movements, riots and personal interests (Tables 7.6–7.11).

Table 7.6 *Age, Modernization and Traditions*

Age (in years)	*Modernization has enhanced the practice and importance of religious traditions rather than abolishing it*			*Total*
	Agree	*Disagree*	*Can't say*	
Up to 25	50 (100.00)	–	–	50
26–35	70 (100.00)	–	–	70
36–45	51 (72.86)	13(18.57)	6 (8.57)	70
46–55	53 (75.71)	14 (20.00)	3 (4.29)	70
55 and above	29 (72.5)	9 (22.5)	2 (5.00)	40
Total	**253 (89.33)**	**36 (12.00)**	**11 (3.67)**	**300**

df = 6, chi-square = 39.43, significant (0.01 level).

Table 7.7 *Education and Perception Concerning Values*

Level of education	*Value differences are inevitable*			*Total*
	Agree	*Disagree*	*Indefinite*	
Literate	80 (64.52)	33 (26.61)	11 (8.87)	124
Up to intermediate	32 (69.57)	9 (19.57)	5 (10.86)	46
Graduate/ postgraduate	86 (100.00)	–	–	86
Vocational/ technical	44 (100.00)	–	–	44
Total	**242 (80.67)**	**42 (14.00)**	**16 (5.33)**	**300**

df = 6, chi-square = 56.56, significant (0.01 level).

Table 7.8 *Age and Perception Concerning Values*

Age (in years)	*Value differences are inevitable*			*Total*
	Agree	*Disagree*	*Can't say*	
Up to 25	28 (56.00)	13 (26.00)	9 (18.00)	50
26–35	51 (72.86)	15 (21.43)	4 (5.71)	70
36–45	56 (80.00)	11 (15.71)	3 (4.29)	70
46–55	67 (95.71)	3 (4.29)	–	70
55 and above	40 (100.00)	–	–	40
Total	**242 (80.67)**	**42 (14.00)**	**16 (5.33)**	**300**

df = 8, chi-square = 47.44, significant (0.01 level).

The findings validate the seventh hypothesis that *the greater the population of younger generation as against the older generation of both the communities that come into active urban social life, the greater the social arena of reciprocation, accommodation and participation.*

The data in regard to the religious faith, respect and importance to the religion reveal that the majority of the respondents from all the educational levels have expressed that all the religions must be given equal importance and respect (92.67 per cent), whereas a negligible percentage of the respondents (7.33 per cent) are not in favour of ideology. All of the postgraduate and vocationally and technically educated respondents have perceived that all the religions are equal and have created the same Almighty, thus it should be given equal importance and honour. The chi-square value is highly significant, which indicates that both the variables, that is, the education and attitude regarding other religions, are extremely interdependent.

Analytical interpretation of the data reveals that the majority of the respondents (92.67 per cent) from all the age groups have expressed that the religion of others must also be given equal importance, faith and respect.

As far as the age of the respondents and their perception in regard to holy books of the communities is concerned, the findings reveal that all of the respondents of both the communities have expressed that both the Gita and Quran are the sermon of the Almighty and must be given equal faith and respect (Tables 7.12–7.14).

Table 7.9 *Education and Participating Relations*

Education	*Hindu participation*				*Muslim participation*				*Total*
	Complete	*Partial*	*No*	*Total*	*Complete*	*Partial*	*No*	*Total*	
Literate	20 (50.00)	12 (30.00)	8 (20.00)	40	40 (97.62)	22 (26.19)	22 (26.19)	84	124
Up to intermediate	15 (57.69)	7 (26.12)	4 (15.39)	26	10 (50.00)	6 (30.00)	4 (20.00)	20	46
Graduate/ postgraduate	35 (63.64)	15 (27.27)	5 (9.09)	55	20 (64.51)	11 (35.49)	–	31	86
Vocational/ technical	20 (68.46)	9 (31.04)	–	29	12 (80.00)	3 (20.00)	–	15	44
Total	90 (60.00)	43 (28.67)	17 (11.33)	150	82 (54.67)	42 (28.00)	26 (17.33)	150	300

Table 7.10 *Occupation and Commensal Relation*

Occupation	*Do you invite your Muslim friends to the festivities and ceremonies at your residence?*		*Total*
	Yes	*No*	
Service (job)	73 (81.11)	17 (18.89)	90
Business	30 (100.00)	–	30
Industry	21 (70.00)	9 (30.00)	30
Total	**124 (82.67)**	**26 (17.33)**	**150**

df = 2, chi-square = 9.81, significant (0.01 level).

Table 7.11 *Occupation and Commensal Relation*

Occupation	*Do you invite your Hindu friends to the festivities and ceremonies at your residence?*		*Total*
	Yes	*No*	
Service (job)	20 (100.00)	–	20
Business	110 (100.00)	–	110
Private industry	20 (100.00)	–	20
Total	**150 (100.00)**	–	**150**

Table 7.12 *Education and Perception Regarding Religions*

Education	*Should equal importance, respect and faith be given to other religions too?*		*Total*
	Yes	*No*	
Literate	107 (86.29)	17 (13.71)	124
Up to intermediate	41 (89.13)	5 (10.87)	46
Graduate/ postgraduate	86 (100.00)	–	86
Vocational/ technical	44 (100.00)	–	44
Total	**278 (92.67)**	**22 (7.33)**	**300**

df = 3, chi-square = 18.61, highly significant (0.01 level).

Table 7.13 *Age and Perception Regarding Religion*

Age (in years)	*Should equal importance, faith and respect be given to other religions too?*		*Total*
	Yes	*No*	
Up to 25	107 (86.29)	17 (12.00)	50
26–35	61 (87.14)	9 (12.86)	70
36–45	65 (92.86)	5 (7.14)	70
46–55	68 (97.14)	2 (2.86)	70
56 and above	40 (100.00)	–	40
Total	**278 (92.67)**	**22 (7.33)**	**300**

df = 4, chi-square = 10.04, highly significant (0.05 level).

Table 7.14 *Education and Perception Regarding Religion*

Education	*Should equal importance, respect and faith be given to religions of each other?*		*Total*
	Yes	*No*	
Literate	103 (83.06)	21 (16.94)	124
Up to intermediate	45 (97.80)	1 (2.20)	46
Graduate/ postgraduate	86 (100.00)	–	86
Vocational/ technical	44 (100.00)	–	44
Total	278 (92.67)	22 (7.33)	300

df = 3, chi-square = 24.91, highly significant (0.01 level).

Table 7.15 *Age and Perception Regarding Holy Books*

Age (in years)	*Are Faith and respect to the holy books of both the communities necessary?*		*Total*
	Yes	*No*	
Up to 25	50 (100.00)	–	50
26–35	70 (100.00)	–	70

(Continued)

Table 7.15 (Continued)

Age (in years)	*Are Faith and respect to the holy books of both the communities necessary?*		*Total*
	Yes	*No*	
36–45	70 (100.00)	–	70
46–55	70 (100.00)	–	70
56 and above	40 (100.00)	–	40
Total	**300 (100.00)**	–	**300**

ATTITUDE TESTING

This chapter concerns the emerging features of religious beliefs, attitude regarding religion of the others and sanctions. Findings reveal that both the communities, Hindus and Muslims, have developed a reciprocal relation and religious tolerant behaviour, faith and empathy regarding religions, festivals, cultural activities and rituals. This attitude is better among the younger generation and highly educated respondents of both the communities. Analytical interpretation of the data reveals that *empathy* (as propounded by D. Learner) and *religious tolerance* (Indian context) have been found as an indicator of modernity among the young and highly educated respondents. They have also expressed a rational and humanist attitude (Tables 7.1–7.4 and 7.10–7.14).

CHANGES IN RELIGIOUS BELIEFS, MORALS, VALUES AND BEHAVIOURAL STANDARDS

The facts reveal that due to modernization, religious beliefs, values and standards of behaviour have also changed. All these are the indicators of modernization (Tables 7.2, 7.3 and 7.5–7.8).

SUMMARY

This chapter concerns the analysis of religious beliefs and emerging features of faith For this generation, depth of both the communities' reciprocity, mores, traditions, customs, festivals and festivities, attitude towards authority of the Almighty have been tested and analysed. The younger generation of both the communities has better reciprocal relations as compared to the older generation. Highly educated respondents have a positive attitude in regard to cooperation and accommodation as compared to the less-educated respondents.

The majority of the respondents are very eager to maintain their friendship with other communities, besides the religious conservative family of their own. It can thus be concluded that education is a major factor that leads the people towards religious tolerance and social reciprocal behaviour.

All the respondents educated up to more than high school conceived that different religions are only different ways to reach the Almighty. In other words, they emphasized the universal existence of a single God, that is monotheistic approach of religion. Different religions have difference means of reaching God. But the final and ultimate goal of all the religions is same. Due to modernization, religious beliefs and moral practices have been somehow changed while holding their traditional values and characters.

It has also been evident that the younger generation is a nourisher of modernity, whereas the older generation is tied with superstitions and traditions. This is the reason why differences in values are found between the two generations. The majority of the respondents like to participate in religious and cultural festivals of other communities; education has played a significant role in minimizing the attitude of the respondents regarding distant attitude towards festivals and festivities of other communities. The majority of the Hindu respondents expressed that they are very keen about making commensal relations with their Muslim friends either in the marriage ceremonies or in the festivals and festivities. It has been observed that the respondents who have engaged in the business or have established their own production and distribution work experience multiple occupational specialization, and appearance of modern techniques has led them towards the demand of specialized hands. The demand of the different people can be fulfilled by various communities. This accelerates the communal harmony and mutual dependency between the people of different communities.

The majority of the respondents have expressed that equal respect and honour must be provided to other religions. It has been observed that highly educated respondents have a high degree of respect and honour. The majority of the respondents mentioned that the critics of religions of others are imbecile and far from the realization and existence of God. Education plays an important role in deteriorating the critical nature of the individual for the other religions. All the respondents from both the communities observed that both the Gita and Quran are two different modes of sermon given by the same Almighty. Both must be given equal respect, honour and faith.

Attitude test analysis shows that both Hindu and Muslim communities have developed religious tolerance, empathy, faith, belief in each other's religious standards, customs, morals, ethics and code of conducts. This tendency is much in younger generation and highly educated respondents. It has been found with the help of empirical survey that the respondents from both the communities have developed social reciprocal relations; religious tolerant behaviour; and participatory behaviour in the religious activities, rituals, festivals and festivities of the other communities as well.

REFERENCES

Chand, Tara, 1954, *Influence of Islam in Indian Culture*. Allahabad: The Indian Press.

Dube, S.C., 1965, 'Cultural Problems in the Economic Development of India'. In *Religion and Progress in Modern Asia*, edited by R.N. Bellah, Glencoe, IL: The Free Press of Glencoe.

Jan dt, Fred E., 2006, *An Introduction to Intercultural Communication*. New Delhi: Sage Publication.

Jha, D.N. and K.M. Shrimali, 1995, *History of Ancient India*. New Delhi: Delhi University.

Lerner, Daniel, 1962, *The Passing of Traditional Society*. Glencoe, IL: The Free Press of Glencoe.

Majumdar, R.C., 1967, *The Delhi Sultanate: The History and Culture of the Indian People*. Bombay.

Marriot, Mckim (Ed.), 1955, 'Little Communities in an Indigenous Civilization'. In *Village India*, Chicago, IL: Chicago University Press.

McClelland, D.C., 1961, *The Achieving Society*. Princeton, NJ: Van Nostrand Co.

Moore, Wilbert, 1963, *Social Change*, Princeton, NJ: Princeton University Press.

Nehru, J., 1951, *Discovery of India*. London: Meridian Books.

Pool, Ethiel, 1963, 'The Role of Communication in the Process of Modernization and Technological Change'. In *Industrialization and Society*, edited by B.F. Hoselitz and Wilhert Moore, UNESCO.

Singer, Milton, 1961, 'Changing Level of Cultural Transmission in India'. In *Aspects of Religions in Indian Society*, edited by L.P. Vidyarthi, Meerut: Kedarnath Ramnath.

Singh, Yogendra, 1999 (1977), *Modernization of Indian Tradition*, Jaipur: Rawat.

Smith, M.G., 1972, *West Indian Family Structure*. Cambridge: University of Washington Press.

Srivastava, A.L., 1980, *Mugal Kaleen Bharat*. New Delhi: Shivlal Agrawal & Co.

Sumner, W.G., 1906, *Folkways: A Study of the Sociological Importance of Usages, Manners, Customs, Mores, and Morals*. Boston: Ginn.

Zaehner, R.C., 1962, *Hinduism*. London: Oxford University Press.

CHAPTER 8

Urban Power Structure and Patterns of Interactions

Urban communities are developing as a centre of political activities (Johnson, 1972). Local political parties, and their power structure along with awareness, have played a significant role in the shaping and structuring of the nation (Houser, 1957). This political dominance and its effective nature are being perceived in all contemporary societies. The concept of dominant caste (Srinivas, 1962) is playing a significant role in the power structure of village India. Cities have a specific personality pattern. Wilkinson (2004) observed that in contemporary Indian social structure, the dominance of caste-based politics has been replaced by the emergence of business class and entrepreneurs. This class consists of the people from occupational structure, trade and business. This class is much active and effective in political arena with strong and rich economic background. They affect the culture of the cities, for example, lifestyle, habitation, housing, accommodation, occupational attitude, habit, behaviour, norms, values and industrial formation. Apart from the dominance over culture of the cities, they also control the various organizations and bodies in the cities such as municipal corporations, development authorities, economic organization and many more. In other words, this section of urban citizenry is dominant and is a determinant of urban lifestyle (Fuller, 2006). They have their influence on administrative bodies, executive units, sanitation and health and educational institutions. The officials expect that these 'dominant class' provide them their suggestions with regard to the complete development of the urban social structure. Thus, they have their influence on the various structures of district, state and national levels. These people are economically strong, but show differences in social and cultural backgrounds. Besides this, they have an important role in coordination and adjustment in the social life in cities, economic and administrative processes in institutions (Weber, 1962). This elite class plays an important role in the selection and manipulation of each and every activity in the urban complex. As far as the nature of urban power structure is concerned, the sociologists and political scientists have diverse opinions. In this reference, mention may be made of the studies of Lynd and Lynd (1937); of middle town in the United States, Hunter (1953); and of Atlanta city in this regard. Some of the scholars of urban power structure have mentioned that urban power structure is unified.

Various studies in India have specified that the nature of the urban political structure is diverse (Bose, 1964; Sovani, 1955; Majumdar, 1960; Zachariah, 1962; Puniyani, 2003).

In contemporary societies, the political structure is influenced and afflicted by various factors. These factors can be summarized as place, time and situation. Due to these factors, the political structure may be simple and unified at one place, and it may be have multiple parties at other places. Various nations in the world such as the United States, the United Kingdom, Pakistan, France and India have multiple political parties. In the Indian context, the political structure can easily be divided in terms of national and regional political structure. Thus, the emergence of regional and national political parties is an integral part and of vital necessity. All the major cities in India have realized the presence of various political parties.

The presence of this elite class in the urban structure is governed by specific value orientation. Much importance is given to influential persons, intellectuals, owners of trade, commerce and mills in Indian political structure also as found in the case of the United States and the United Kingdom (Miller, 1969; Sassen, 2007; Young, 2007). In urban political power structure, the people, on the one hand, are inclined towards better economic affluence. On the other hand, they want to be in touch with various political parties and leaders. The leaders of various political parties are very keen about making relations with the people without identifying their caste and religion. In contemporary Indian society, although some political parties are using caste and religion as the triumph card, their victory is momentary. The voters are now conscious and aware regarding their voting behaviour. The Hindu and Muslim communities have a decisive role and dominant character regarding national politics.

At regional level, in Uttar Pradesh, the Muslim population has been concentrated in the urban agglomeration of Aligarh, Lucknow, Agra, Saharanpur, Varanasi, Akbarpur and Azamgarh. In Varanasi, 4.97 lakh Muslims constitute the population of the distinct. In Azamgarh, the Muslims constitute 5 lakh in a total population of 23 lakh. In Uttar Pradesh, 4 crore Muslims constitute the population of the state in comparison with 14 crore of the Hindu population.

As far as the mutual understanding and interdependence is concerned, both the communities in Varanasi have played a vital role. The Muslim voters in Varanasi have proved their significance in the elections from bottom to top in the urban political power structure of Varanasi city; both the communities have hand-to-hand contributions.

The people from different communities engaged themselves in various business, trade and occupations. For the safety and security of their business and trade, they are attached with their social organizations; on the other hand, they are incorporated with the political parties. Both the communities, Hindus and Muslims, have made contacts with the political leaders for their well-being in regard to trade and commerce.

The need for political power creates a situation of conflict and tension between these two communities. But the interdependency between both the communities in certain respects is indispensable. Thus, the nature of political power structure in Varanasi city is cooperative and mutually interdependent rather than conflictual and competitive. The candidates in elections mutually depend on both the communities. The Hindu candidates have to ask votes from Muslims to get victory in elections and also Muslims from Hindu voters. This creates a reciprocal relation between both the communities. In contemporary politics of the city, various Muslim leaders are highly active and play a decisive role in the political power structure of the state and nation as well.

The data with regard to the relationship of the respondents with political parties reveal that the majority from both the communities have greater sympathetic concern with Congress Party (48 per cent); however, regional parties have also made in roads in the vote banks of both the communities.

The analytical interpretation of data depicts that the majority of the respondents from all the age groups selected for the study are highly active in political activities and elections. The respondents of the age group of 36–45 years are much active as compared to others (78.56 per cent).

The empirical facts analysed with regard to education and activity of the respondent in the political affairs reveal that except for the vocationally and technically educated, all the respondents are highly active and engage in political affairs (73.70 per cent) (Tables 8.1–8.3).

Table 8.1 *Hindu–Muslim Communities and Political Affiliations*

Comm unity	*Political parties*					*Total*
	Congress	*SP*	*BJP*	*CP*	*Others*	
Hindu	73 (48.70%)	43 (28.70%)	17 (11.30%)	11 (7.30%)	6 (4.00%)	150
Muslim	71 (47.4%)	45 (30.00%)	15 (10.00%)	15 (10.00%)	4 (2.60%)	150
Total	**144 (48.00%)**	**88 (29.30%)**	**32 (10.70%)**	**26 (8.90%)**	**10 (3.30%)**	**300**

Table 8.2 *Age and Political Inclination*

Age (in years)	*Political participation*			*Total*
	Highly active	*Average active*	*Less active*	
Up to 25	32 (64.00%)	10 (20.00%)	8 (16.00%)	50
26–35	53 (70.70%)	11 (15.72%)	6 (8.58%)	70
36–45	55 (78.65%)	10 (14.25%)	5 (7.10%)	70
46–55	53 (75.70%)	9 (12.70%)	8 (11.60%)	70
55 and above	28 (70.00%)	7 (17.50%)	5 (12.50%)	40
Total	**221 (73.70%)**	**47 (15.70%)**	**32 (10.60%)**	**300**

Table 8.3 *Education and Political Inclination*

Level of education	*Political involvement*			*Total*
	Highly active	*Average active*	*Less active*	
Literate	95 (76.60%)	14 (11.30%)	15 (12.10%)	124
Up to intermediate	31 (67.30%)	7 (15.20%)	8 (17.50%)	46
Graduate/ postgraduate	75 (87.20%)	6 (6.90%)	5 (5.90%)	70
Vocational/ technical	20 (45.40%)	20 (45.40%)	4 (9.20%)	44
Total	**221 (73.70%)**	**47 (15.70%)**	**32 (10.60%)**	**300**

With regard to the occupation and participation in political affairs, the findings reveal that the majority of the respondents engaging in business are highly active in political affairs and elections (82.20 per cent). Overall, the majority of the respondents (723.70 per cent) are highly active in political activities.

The data with regard to depth of urban residence and nature of participation in political affairs of local organizations, *Vyapar Mandals* and delegacies, reveal that the majority of the respondents (73.70 per cent) are highly active in the political affairs and participation in the election in the local bodies (Tables 8.4–8.6).

Table 8.4 *Income and Political Inclination*

Level of income	*Political involvement*			*Total*
	Highly active	*Average active*	*Less active*	
Up to 5000	86 (68.20%)	24 (19.10%)	16 (12.70%)	126
5001–10,000	66 (76.70%)	11 (12.70%)	9 (10.60%)	86
10,001–15,000	37 (77.10%)	7 (14.50%)	4 (8.40%)	48
15,001 and above	32 (80.00%)	5 (12.50%)	3 (7.50%)	40
Total	**221 (73.70%)**	**47 (15.70%)**	**32 (10.60%)**	**300**

Table 8.5 *Occupation and Political Inclination*

Occupation	*Level of involvement and participation*			*Total*
	Highly active	*Average active*	*Less active*	
Service	78 (70.90%)	23 (20.90%)	9 (8.20%)	110
Business	115 (82.20%)	11 (7.80%)	14 (10.00%)	140
Self-industry	28 (56.00%)	13 (26.00%)	9 (18.00%)	50
Total	**221 (73.70%)**	**47 (15.70%)**	**32 (10.60%)**	**300**

Table 8.6 *Depth of Urban Residence and Participation in Local Politics*

Depth of residence (in years)	*Level of participation*			*Total*
	Highly active	*Average active*	*Less active*	
1–10	83 (69.20%)	25 (20.80%)	12 (10.00%)	120
11–20	45 (77.50%)	7 (12.10%)	6 (10.40%)	58
21–30	36 (75.00%)	7 (14.60%)	5 (10.40%)	48
31 and above	57 (77.10%)	8 (10.80%)	9 (12.10%)	74
Total	**221 (73.70%)**	**47 (15.70%)**	**32 (10.60%)**	**300**

The facts reveal that the majority of the respondents from literate to highly educated have observed an average participation in the elections of *Vyapar Mandals* and delegacy elections (72.70 per cent). Among them, the postgraduate respondents (82.50 per cent) in majority engage at an average level in the local political affairs.

As far as the occupations and nature of political participation are concerned, it can be concluded that the majority of the respondents engaged in their own industry are highly active in local political affairs and elections of *Vyapar Mandals*, delegacies and local administrative units. Overall, the majority of the respondents (72.70 per cent) observe an average participation.

The analytical interpretation of data depicts that the majority of the respondents from all groups of education like to choose better and liable candidates either from any community (47.33 per cent). The majority of the literate respondents (41.90 per cent) wish to choose the candidates from their kin groups. It can be concluded that education has created a vision in the respondents for better thinking and selection (Tables 8.7–8.9).

Table 8.7 *Education and Participation in Local Political Organization*

Level of education	*Political involvement*			*Total*
	Highly active	*Average active*	*Less active*	
Literate	10 (81.10%)	97 (78.40%)	17 (13.50%)	124
Up to intermediate	10 (21.80%)	29 (63.10%)	7 (15.10%)	46
Graduate/ postgraduate	11 (12.80%)	71 (82.50%)	4 (4.70%)	86
Vocational/ technical	19 (43.10%)	21 (47.80%)	4 (9.10%)	44
Total	**50 (16.70%)**	**218 (72.70%)**	**32 (10.60%)**	**300**

Table 8.8 *Occupation and Political Involvement in Local Politics*

Occupation	*Level of participation*			*Total*
	Highly active	*Average active*	*Less active*	
Service	8 (7.30%)	97 (88.10%)	5 (4.60%)	110
Business	23 (16.40%)	103 (73.60%)	14 (10.00%)	140
Self-industry	19 (38.00%)	18 (36.00%)	13 (26.00%)	50
Total	**50 (16.70%)**	**218 (72.60%)**	**32 (10.70%)**	**300**

Table 8.9 *Education and Bases for Nomination of Candidates*

Level of education	*Base of nomination*			*Total*
	Kin group	*Liable persons from any community*	*Native people*	
Literate	52 (41.90%)	42 (33.80%)	30 (24.30%)	124
Up to intermediate	13 (28.20%)	22 (47.90%)	11 (23.90%)	46
Graduate/ postgraduate	8 (9.30%)	51 (59.30%)	27 (31.40%)	86

(Continued)

Table 8.9 (Continued)

Level of education	*Base of nomination*			*Total*
	Kin group	*Liable persons from any community*	*Native people*	
Graduate/ postgraduate	8 (9.30%)	51 (59.30%)	27 (31.40%)	86
Vocational/ technical	8 (18.20%)	27 (61.40%)	9 (20.40%)	44
Total	**81 (27.00%)**	**142 (47.30%)**	**77 (25.70%)**	**300**

The data with regard to the bases of candidate selection and age of the respondents reveal that the majority of the respondents from all age groups are in favour of better and liable candidates. The respondents from 46 to 55 years (30 per cent) are in favour of the candidates from their kin groups. A total of 35 per cent of the respondents from 56 years and above are in favour of the native people in urban political power structure.

As far as the bases of candidate selection are concerned, the findings reveal that the majority of the respondents from both the communities (47.40 per cent) are in favour of the better and liable candidates either from any community (Tables 8.10 and 8.11).

Table 8.10 *Age and Bases for Nomination of Candidates*

Age (in years)	*Base of nomination of candidates*			*Total*
	Kin group	*Liable persons from any community*	*Native people*	
Up to 25	12 (24.00%)	27 (59.00%)	11 (22.00%)	50
26–35	20 (28.60%)	33 (47.10%)	17 (24.30%)	70
36–45	19 (27.10%)	34 (48.60%)	17 (24.30%)	70
46–55	21 (30.00%)	31 (44.30%)	18 (25.70%)	70
55 and above	9 (22.50%)	17 (42.50%)	14 (35.00%)	40
Total	**81 (27.00%)**	**142 (47.40%)**	**77 (25.60%)**	**300**

Table 8.11 *Community and Bases for Nomination of Candidates*

Community	*Base of nomination of candidates*			*Total*
	Kin group	*Liable persons from any community*	*Native people*	
Hindu	41 (27.30%)	79 (52.70%)	30 (20.00%)	150
55 and above	40 (26.70%)	63 (42.00%)	47 (31.30%)	150
Total	**81 (27.00%)**	**142 (47.40%)**	**77 (25.60%)**	**300**

This chapter concerns urban power structure, political interest and inter-religious reciprocity. Findings have been analysed with regard to the indicators of modernizations, and it can be concluded that both the communities have developed religious tolerant behaviour, rational and humanitarian approach and institutionalized political competition, social, economic and political awareness. This tendency is high among highly educated respondents having much income and young respondents. Findings reveal that young and rich respondents of both the communities have expressed the indicators of modernity as propounded by Learner (high participation) and Almond & Coleman (institutionalized political competition). In the Indian context, rational humanist attitude and religious tolerance as an indicator of modernity, as propounded by Inkless, are also found between the respondents of both the communities.

SUMMARY

With regard to the political power structure, political interest and inter-religious tolerance, the attitude of respondents have been analysed. The relations with the political parties, political participation and involvement in elections, bases of candidates' selection, political interests and participation in local body organizations have been analysed. Findings reveal that the majority of the respondents like congress party. The respondents from all age groups are highly active in elections and political affairs. Highly educated respondents are very active in the political arena. Highly active respondents belong to higher income group, where the majority of the respondents are from business class.

The respondents living in the city for more than one decade are highly active in political activities in the city. The respondents having their own industry are active as compared to other occupational groups. *The majority of highly educated respondents select liable and responsible candidates in elections*. The respondents from all age groups are in favour of better and liable candidates either from any community. Highly educated and young respondents from both the communities have observed active participation and institutionalized political competition as indicators of modernity.

The findings enable us to furnish that Varanasi, due to its peculiar blend of tradition and modernity, has changed the mindset of the communities with regard to work participation, attitude regarding religions, trade and commerce. The narrow lanes and streets in the city are the symbol of religious tolerant behaviour and extreme social participation, which is manifested by the gathering of the masses every morning and evening in these narrow lanes and streets, and the discussions regarding their daily routine, religious activities, family, political and business affairs are the symbols of social participation and reciprocation. The people from each community have resided in these streets for generations. The participation of the people in each other's festivals and festivities is the indicator of religious tolerant behaviour.

As far as the political inclination of the city with special reference to Hindu–Muslim communities is concerned, the city has always been a central point in the politics of state and nation as well. Both the communities have played a significant role in this regard. The Muslim businessmen are predominantly dependent on Hindu workers and Hindu businessman play the role of marketing of the products by Muslim workers. During elections, voters from both the communities, that is the Muslim and Hindu, select those who are interested in the welfare of both the communities. Thus, the city is a unique frame of reference in this regard. Thus, it can be concluded that Varanasi city by its very nature has a specific personality pattern, which provides such a place for all the communities to flourish their ideals, values, religions and education. It is the finest example in the world, and no other city has such a specific character that is free from fanaticism in the lack of fanatic character and free from communal violence in the midst of communal differences.

REFERENCES

Bose, N.K., 1964, *Calcutta: A Social Survey*. Bombay: Lalwani.

Fuller, Steve, 2006, *The New Sociological Imagination*. New Delhi: Sage Publication.

Houser, P.N., 1957, *Urbanization in Asia and Far East*. Calcutta: UNESCO Research Centre, On Social Implications of Industrialization in Southern Asia.

Hunter, F., 1953, *Community Power Structure*. Chapel Hill: University of North Carolina Press.

Johnson, J.H., 1972, *Urban Geography*. Oxford: Pregaman Press.

Lynd, R. and Helen Lynd, 1937, *Middle Town in Transition*. New York: Harcourt Bress.

Majumdar, D.N., 1960, *Social Contours of an Industrial City*. Bombay: Asia Publishing House.

Miller, D., 1969, *International Community Power Structure*. Bloomington, IN: Indiana University Press.

Puniyani, Ram, 2003, *Communal Politics*. New Delhi: Sage Publication.

———, 2005, *Religious Power and Violence*. New Delhi: Sage Publication.

Sassen, Saskia, 2007, *Cities in World Economy*. New Delhi: Sage Publication.

Sovani, N.V., 1955, *Poona: A Re-survey*. Poona: Gokhale Institute of Politics and Economics.

Srinivas, M.N., 1962, *Caste in Modern India and Other Essays*. Bombay: Asia.

Weber, Max, 1962, *The City*. Glencoe, IL: The Free Press of Glencoe.

Wilkinson, S., 2004, *Vote and Violence: Electoral Competition and Communal Riots in India*. Cambridge: Cambridge University Press.

Young, Jock, 2007, *The Vertigo of Late Modernity*. New Delhi: Sage Publication.

Zachariah, K.C., 1962, *Migrants in Greater Bombay*. Bombay: Asia Publishing House.

CHAPTER 9

Conclusions

The present study concerns the interactions and interrelations of the two communities, namely Hindu and Muslim, in an urban set-up, and these two have been analysed in the wave of modernization. These two processes gave birth to the reciprocal and tolerant behaviour. The study is an attempt to find out the degree of interactive process in the wave of modernization. The concept of modernization refers to the process in which society passes through industrial development, urbanization and other social changes, which solely transform the lives of individuals. The concept of modernization comes from a view of societies as having a standard evolutionary pattern as described in the social evolutionism theories.

The nature and degree of reciprocal behaviour have been somehow changed due to modernizing factors. Due to modernization, new values, ideas, norms, new structure in society and orientations have become predominant. This very process of modernization has its roots in Western European and North American countries during the seventeenth century and has spread to other European countries, South America, Asia and Africa during the nineteenth and twentieth centuries. Although, it has a single root, the models are various in different nations. The variation is mainly due to modern values, ideals and technological innovations.

The process of modernization has brought about recital changes in society. Due to this process, the socio-economic specialization, division of labour, interdependency, individualistic approach and intercultural contacts have been accelerated, and drastic changes have been observed in values, ideals, behavioural patterns and approaches towards life. Several social scientists have contributed much in explaining modernization. Various social scientists, demographers, sociologists and psychologists have contributed much for the better understanding of modernization and in studying communal relations.

Apart from these studies and indicators, the active indicators of modernization in urban settings have also been selected. All the indicators have been divided into two categories, that is, psychological indicators and sociological indicators. Attempts have been made to analyse the degree of participation of both the communities in the festivals and festivities of their religious counterparts. The focal theme of this empirical study is to find out the attitude of the people regarding religious values of others in the wave of modernization. The mutual interactions of both the communities have their roots deeply in the religious values and ethics. The static and dynamic bases of both the communities are also the major concerns of the study. The great traditions of both the communities have not been elapsed but have got mutual importance. In this empirical study, the 'Interactional Exchange Approach' has been used for observation and measurement of the religious tolerant behaviour and social reciprocity of both the communities. The areas that are somehow concerned with the disseminations and differentiations have not been taken for granted.

The universe of the study is the Varanasi city, which from times immemorial is the stronghold of Hindu religion and belief. The city of Varanasi reflects a peculiar blend of Hindu–Muslim population. The city of Benares, as described by Sherring, is regarded as sacred to Shiva, and as a place over which he exercises divine authority. Varanasi, as denoting a city, has been a name familiar to Brahminical literature. The word is crudely referred by modern inventives, to a combination of *Varana* and *Asi*. The *Kasi-Khanda* of *Skanda-Purana* has the mention of *Kasi*. The Jabala-Upanishad places *Avimukta*—which is Puranik title of Benaras. The expression *Kashipuri Varanasi* in the 'Dasa-Kumara-Charita' means 'Varanasi', 'a city of the Kasis'. In the subjoined verse, from the Ramayan, Uttara-Khand, XXXVIII, VI, 17, Varanasi is qualified by an expression meaning, the commentator says, 'a city in the country of the Kasis'. In the Mahabharata, Adi-Parvan, sl. 4083,

4084, there is the mention of the King of the Kasis as dwelling in the city of Varanasi.

The inter-religious reciprocity and tolerant behaviour are being perceived in a greater extent in Varanasi city. To maintain the sociological objectivity, the religiographic morphology of the city has been taken for the study, and the study, area is divided as,

1. Major Hindu settlement areas
2. Major Muslim settlement areas
3. Hindu–Muslim conglomeration areas

Further, on the basis of *purposive random sampling,* 100 households from each location have been sorted out where the heads of the families of the aforesaid households are to be selected for collecting the data with the help of diverse questions set in an interview schedule. In order to maintain the *raison d'être,* attempts have been made to have equal representation from each area. *Descriptive cum exploratory* research design have been adopted for the present empirical survey.

The majority of the respondents in this empirical study belong to the age group of 26–55 years (70 per cent), equal number from both the communities has been selected, that is 150. The Hindu respondents have been classified as Brahmin, (33.33 per cent), Kshatriya (33.33 per cent), Backward Castes (16 per cent) and Scheduled Castes (17.34 per cent); whereas, Muslim respondents have been distributed as Sheikh (46.67 per cent), Syed (33.33 per cent), Pathan (16.67 per cent) and Ansari (9.33 per cent). The majority of the respondents are married (73.33 per cent) and educated up to graduate or postgraduate level. The findings concerning the income and occupation of the respondents reveal that the majority of the respondents have engaged in service and business and earn up to ₹10,000 per month.

The findings reveal that the majority of the respondents (56.67 per cent) belong to rural areas, and 40 per cent of the respondents are living in the city for the past 10 years. The observations of social institutions and emerging attitudes manifest that the majority of the respondents belong to the nuclear family system. The findings reveal that the majority of the respondents of all age groups and education level favour the traditional pattern of marriages (58.67 per cent) and accepted that priority must be given to the opinion of parents in mate selection and favour the marriages in their own caste, in other words; the importance is given to endogamy. Besides all the changes in structure, the traditional values are still prevailing in the society. While analysing the dominant factors in marriages, the majority of the respondents favour that the importance must be given to ability of bride and groom, and a negligible percentage of the respondents favour wealth or dowry. It can be concluded that exposure to mass media, modern education and rational attitude regarding life has changed the attitude of people in this regard. The caste system has been neglected by most of the respondents; they are in favour of its elimination. The respondents from all age groups and depth of urban residence have accepted that the urban life style is full of humanitarian and equalitarian values and rationality. These are the indicators of modernization.

The findings authenticate our first hypothesis that the more the involvement and active orientation of the people in the urban community in regard to modernized means and mode, the greater the communitarian discriminations to erosion.

The observations in regard to the indicators of modernization unveil that Tables 4.2, 4.3 and 4.10–4.12 expressed the interest articulation; and as far as the assimilative tendencies in urban set-up are concerned, Tables 4.13 and 4.14 reveal empathy as propounded by D. Learner and in Indian context, associative individualism, religious tolerance and intercultural contacts have been found as the indicators of modernization. The analysis of the facts reveals that these psychological indicators are correlated with psyche of the people of both the communities, and the younger generation is flexible with regard to traditional values and religious beliefs; whereas, the older generation is the nourisher of the traditional values and ideas.

The respondents from both the communities have observed associative and cooperative relations with their neighbours. The respondents from both the communities have accepted that the mutual interactions and inter-relations between both the communities have changed and now adopt a humanitarian approach, and there is an occurrence of friendly behaviour among the people of both the communities. Modern education has changed the narrow ideology regarding the religious beliefs and has developed a reciprocal and tolerant behaviour. The majority of the respondents engaged in occupations have accepted that the attitude concerning religiosity has been changed. The majority of the respondents from all the educational levels have accepted that the appearance of modern education, recreational centres, new occupational setup, industries, hotels, restaurants, multiplexes, cineplexes, plaza markets and clubs have accelerated and enhanced the interrelations and interactions between the communities. With regard to the erosion of communitarian discriminations, the majority of the respondents from both the communities have accepted that this can be diminished only by providing specific reservations to the Muslims and abolishing the untouchability, and they conceived that the communal riots are politically motivated and nurtured by unwanted people in society. The majority of the respondents like to go to temples for prayer and worships for the well-being of their family. *The findings validate our second hypothesis that the greater the social, cultural, religious heterogeneity in the urban setup, the more multidimensional and interactional reciprocity accelerates in an urban social milieu, leading to the growth of urbanized lifestyle.*

The highly educated respondents have observed that the discriminations based on religion are the outcome of society itself, whereas the people are equal and must be seen with regard to humanitarian approach. The majority of the respondents from both the communities have accepted that they perceive that there is no hindrance in the visit of Muslim or Hindu religious places and perceived the religion as an object of respect and honour. Tables 5.1–5.9 and Tables 5.17–5.22 express associative individualism, religious tolerance and intercultural contexts as the indicators of modernization. Tables 5.14–5.16 summarize the psychological indicators such as interest articulation (the concept of Almond and Coleman), interest aggregation and achievement orientation (the concept of McClelland).

The observations of the facts concerning the inter-religious reciprocity and social adjustment reveal that the majority of the respondent from both the communities has reported that the communitarian relations cannot be ignored. The urban lifestyle is based on rational calculations. The educated respondents from young generation have a greater assimilative tendency in this regard. The respondents from both the communities have accepted that the reciprocal relations and tolerance in behaviour have been changed. The majority of the respondents have expressed that instead of all the disparities and discriminations, both the communities have the same feelings with regard to communitarian relations. They conceived that modernization, in Indian society, has changed the mutual co-relations and cooperations. Due to modernization, the religious superstitious beliefs in society have been narrowed down and the specific character of religion with a rational outlook has been developed. *The findings authenticate our third hypothesis that the more the increase of modern social values in terms of rational outlook and objective mindset, the greater the boundaries of religious separation, and the loyalties of narrow communalism are contested.*

The respondents from both the communities, in majority, are in favour of the changes in narrow religious practices and mores. The humanitarian approach and equality to all the people have been accepted by the respondents in the wave of modernization and development of science and technology. Urban development and modern occupations have contested the communitarian discriminations. The respondents in majority from both the communities have accepted that the criterion concerning religion and morality has been changed due to science and technology, whereas all the respondents from all age groups have realized an enhancement in intercultural and inter-religious contacts due to modern education, industrialization and urban development. *The findings validate our fourth hypothesis that urbanism as a way of life proceeds with diminution of superstitions and irrational social sanctions. While the rationally organized systems of faith increased with the much celebrity in both the communities. The perspectives of modernity include the accessibility to material well-being, social privileges and social security. Therefore, the religion and the tradition are also subjected to sophistication.*

A huge number of the respondents from both the communities have accepted that modernization and urban values are the catalyst for the communitarian relations. The majority of the respondents from both the communities consider an urban centre as having heterogeneity, and they consider the urban values as the responsible factor for the cooperation and accommodation among the people of the different castes and religions. The respondents in majority have considered that there is no place for separation and discriminations in urban set-up because it has its own style, personality pattern and culture. The respondents from both the communities are in favour of the eradication of superstitious and religious beliefs, and all of them have observed faith and respect for all the religions. The highly educated and younger respondents have much faith in religion of others also. It can be concluded that the appearance of modern education has modified the structure of religion, and the affinity towards religions has strengthened. *The facts authenticate our fifth hypothesis that the greater the involvement of social heterogeneity in occupational sector, the more the people of different communities and subcultures come to interact and socially exchange with one another.*

The indicators of modernization such as religious tolerance, associative individualism and active participation have been observed. Apart from these indicators, the rational end means calculations have been also perceived. The findings from Tables 6.6, 6.10, 6.15 and 6.16 indicate that there exist rational and humanist attitude between both the communities as the indicator of modernization. The intercultural contacts (Tables 6.4–6.6, 6.17, 6.18, 6.25 and 6.26) have also been validated. Demographic heterogeneity and religious pluralism as the indicators have been perceived between both the communities in Varanasi city.

In this study, interactional exchange approach has been adopted as a prime method. Then, both the communities have developed associative individualism and religious tolerant behaviour in urban set-up due to intercultural contacts. The facts reveal that the people ofboth the communities have adopted values, traditions, norms of each other by the participation in religious activities, rituals, festivals and festivities and have accepted the appropriate changes in the parameters of religion and morality in contemporary society, which is predominantly governed by modern science and technology. Thus, the people from both the communities exchange the values, behavioural patterns and norms concerning marriage, family, lifestyle, religiosity and mode of worshiping. The fact concerning attitude regarding religious beliefs reveals that the young and highly educated respondents of both the communities have observed a greater reciprocity than others.

Besides the traditional family, the respondents in majority are in favour of the friendly behaviour in urban social set-up. Education has a positive effect with regard to maintaining and strengthening cooperation and associative character with different religions, and they all believe that all the religions are only the different ways of reaching the Almighty. *The findings validate our sixth hypotheses that modernity, urbanity and industrial development have not crossed the boundaries of religious traditions, but they have emerged as behaviour friendly in heterogeneous situations.*

The respondents believe that the younger generation is the nourisher of modernity, whereas the older generation is tied with superstitions and traditional values, which creates a difference and gap between both the generations concerning values. *This authenticate our seventh hypothetical postulate that the greater and urban community involves multiple occupational specialization and dependence on scientific, technological and mechanical equipments such as systems of cybernetics and informatics, the more the changes in the traditional, communal and religious practices, the more the regulative forces of tradition that get attenuated, leading at length to differences with regard to values, ideas and behaviour patterns between the older and younger generations.*

The younger respondents from both the communities have observed a high degree of participation in the festivals, festivities and rituals of their counterparts. Education is a prime and major driving force in eradicating the differences, and all the respondents invite their friends from other communities also in their ceremonials and celebrations. The businessmen and traders have higher attitude in this regard. They believe that the mutual cooperation and participation are necessary for the economic betterment. *The findings validate our eighth hypothesis that the more the population of younger generation as against the older generation of both the communities comes into active urban social life, the greater the social arena of reciprocation, accommodation and participation.*

The majority of the respondents from both the communities have expressed a high degree of faith and honour for all the religions. The highly educated young respondents have better attitude in this regard. The critics of different religions have no sense regarding the existence of supernatural power of almighty. All of the respondents from all the age groups have expressed that the Gita and Quran must be given faith and due respect.

The indicators of modernity as empathy, religious tolerance, rational and humanist attitude are being proved and validated.

The political inclinations of the respondents reveal that the majority of the respondents from both the communities expressed their attachment with the Congress Party. The respondents from all age groups are highly active in political activities. The respondents residing in the city for a long period are participating actively in religious activities. All the respondents from both the communities have given the priority of the person who is a trustworthy, honest and devoted candidate in elections.

The attitude testing of the respondents reveals that the younger and educated respondents have the modernizing indicators given by Learner (high participation), Almond & Coleman (institutionalized political competition) and religious tolerance, rational humanist attitude as the indicators of modernization are being found in this empirical study.

SALIENT FEATURES OF THE STUDY

Present empirical study is an attempt to find out the attitude of the respondents regarding Hindu–Muslim traditions and inter-religious relations. The majority of the respondents are eager to go to school or college. The major findings of this empirical study can be summarized as follows:

1. Varanasi appeared as a confluence of tradition and modernity, par excellence, in the world.
2. The study depicts that the majority of the younger generation from both the communities have favoured the modern system of living, whereas the older generation are the proponents and nourishers of traditional and old values.
3. The study reveals that the traditional social structures are still prevailing in the communities. This means that identity specifics continue as parallel to modern changes.
4. The study highlights that caste and religion are social constructs and must be modified according to social milieu.

5. The study denotes that the people belonging to both the communities developed forbearance character, adaptability and associative individualism.
6. The study reveals that the communitarian discriminations have come to erosion due to the participation in various types of techno-economic activities. Due to application of technology in occupation and other socioeconomic activities, the knowhow technologies have brought closer the two communities on the basis of skill and efficiency and have provided scope for social reciprocation above the frontiers of caste and religion. This shows that the traditional boundaries of separation have shifted and the religious loyalties are being contested by techno-electronic efficiency between the communities.
7. Modernity, urban and industrial development have not created any hindrance for religiosity, but these have promoted and accelerated this character.
8. Religious distinctiveness and identity specifics of both the communities are confirmed in their homes and places of worship; whereas outside the family, the urban social structure is being viewed by them as a market-place, where both of them interact and reciprocate in terms of their endeavour in the area of business, trade, economic transitions and occupations.
9. The study highlights that what cannot be cured by laws and rules or even by court's provisions are being successfully overtaken by the urban agencies such as hotels, restaurants, clubs, public amenities, market and business complexes where individual's skill and efficiency of work happens to be more important than the identity of religious distinctiveness.
10. The study validates that despite the heterogeneity in urban set-up, the values prevailing in this social structure are responsible for accommodation and reciprocation. These values are basically egalitarianism, humanism and cooperation.
11. The study connotes that modernization proceeding with modern education and urban social living has rationalized

the people to interact with one another in the course of their day-to-day activities.

12. The study denotes that communal harmony can be enhanced by eradicating untouchability and religious discrimination by attenuation of fanaticism and narrowness prevailing in religions.
13. The study highlights that the education and depth of urban residence have worked as a reinforcer for the interpersonal relations and community sentiments as well as for better adjustment, cooperation and association.
14. The study connotes that most of the disturbances and communal conflicts are generated by chance monger politicians of the communities.

BIBLIOGRAPHY

Ackoff, R.L., 1957–1958, 'Towards a Behavioral Theory of Communication', *Management Science*, 4, also see, Donald M. Mackay, 1955, 'Operational Aspects of Some Fundamental Concepts of Human Communication', *Syntheses*, 9 and 1956, 'Towards an Information: Flow Model of Human Behaviour', *British Journal of Psychology*, 47.

Agrawal, C.P., 1971, *Caste, Religion and Power: An Indian Case Study*. New Delhi: Sri Ram Centre for Industrial Relations.

Ahmad, Aziz, 1964, *Studies in Islamic Culture in the Indian Environment*. London: Clarendon Press.

———, 1967, *Islamic Modernism in India and Pakistan*. London: Oxford University Press.

Ahmad, Imtiaz, 1973, *Caste and Social Stratification among Muslims*. New Delhi: Manohar Book Service.

———, 1975, *Family, Kinship and Marriage among Muslims in India*. New Delhi: Manohar Book Service.

———, 1983, *Modernization and Social Change among Muslims in India*. New Delhi: Manohar Publications.

Aktar, J., 1992, 'Muslims in Varanasi City: A Study in Cultural Geography', Ph.D. Thesis, Banaras Hindu University (unpublished manuscript).

Almond, G.A. and J.S. Coleman, 1960, *The Politics of Developing Areas*. Princeton, NJ: Princeton University Press.

Altekar, A.S., 1943, *Banaras: Past and Present*. Banaras: Nawal Kishore & Bros.

Ansari, G., 1960, *Muslim Caste in Uttar Pradesh: A Study in Culture Contact*. Lucknow: Ethnographic and Folk Culture Society.

Ashraf, K.M., 1959, *Life and Condition of the People of Hindustan*. New Delhi.

Baig, M.R.A., 1974, *The Muslim Dilemma in India*. New Delhi: Vikas Publishing House.

Bayas, K.C., 1979, 'Social Renaissance in India'. In *Indian Social Thought*, edited by G.S. Bhatt, Lucknow: Ethnographic and Folk Culture Society.

Becker, Howard and Alvin Boskoff, 1957, *Modern Sociological Theories in Continuity and Change*. London: Holt Reinehart and Winston.

Bellah, Robert (Ed.), 1965, 'Epilogue'. In *Religion and Progress in Modern Aisa*, Glencoe, IL: Free Press of Glencoe.

Besent, A., 1976, 'How India Wrought for Freedom'. In *Bhartiya Rashtrawad Ki Samajik Pristhabhumi*, edited by A.R. Desai, New Delhi: MacMillan India Ltd.

Bier, A.G., 1967, 'Migration Trends and Migrant's Characteristics', *The Cornell Journal of Social Relations*, Spain.

Blank, J., 2003, 'Ethnic Conflict and Civic Life: A Review Essay', *India Derived*, 2(2): 97–112.

Blau, P.M., 1964, *Exchange and Power in Social Life*. New York: John Wiley & Sons, Inc.

Blumer, H., 1962, 'Society as Symbolic Interaction'. In *Human Behaviour and Social Process*, ed. Arnold Rose. Boston: Houghton Mifflin.

Bogardus, E.S., 1950, *Sociology*. New York: The MacMillan Co.

Bopegamage, A., 1957, *Debhi: A Study in Urban Sociology*. Social Series No. 7. Bombay: University of Bombay Publication.

Bose, N.K., 1964, *Calcutta: A Social Survey*. Bombay: Lalwani.

Brass, P., 2003, *Production of Hindu-Muslim Violence in Contemporary India*. New Delhi: Oxford University Press.

Bryant, Clinton D. and Denis L. Peck, 2008, *21st Century Society: A Reference Book*. Vol. 1. New Delhi: Sage Publication.

Burgess, E.W., 1925, 'The Growth of the City: An Introduction to a Research Project'. In *The City*, edited by Robert E. Park, E.W. Burgers and R.D. Mekenzie, Chicago, IL: University of Chicago Press.

Burgess, E.W. and H.S. Locke, 1945, *The Family, From Institution to Companionship*. New York: American Book Company.

Chanana, D.R., 1961, 'Sanskritization and Westernization and India's North West', *Economic Weekly*, 8(9).

Chand, Tara, 1954, *Influence of Islam in Indian Culture*. Allahabad: The India Press.

Clifford, Geertz, 1965, 'Modernization in a Muslim Society'. In *Religion and Progress in Modern Asia*, edited by R.N. Bellah, New York: The Free Press.

Contu, Welter, 1949, *Emergent Human Nature*. New York: Alfred A. Knoff Inc.

Cooley, C.H., 1962, *Social Organization*. New York: Schocken Press.

Cottrell, Leonard S., 1942, 'The Analysis of Situational Fields in Social Psychology', *American Sociological Review*, 7.

Crome, James A., 2007, *How Can We Solve Our Social Problems?* New Delhi: Sage Publication.

Dahl, Robert A., 1961, *Who Governs*. New Haven, CT: Yale University Press.

Dalmia, V., 1997, *The Nationalism of Hindu Traditions: Bhartendu Harishchandra and 19th Century Banaras*. New Delhi: Oxford University Press.

Damle, Y.B., 1976, 'Educated Youth as Promoters of Modernization'. In *Tradition and Modernization*, edited by S.K. Srivastava, Allahabad: Indian International Publications.

Davis, K., 1981, *Human Society*. New Delhi: Surjeet Publications.

Desai, A.R., 1976, *Bhartiya Rashtravad Ki Samajik Pristhabhumi*. New Delhi: MacMillan India Ltd.

———, 1984, *India's Path of Development*. Bombay: Popular Prakashan.

Desai, I.P. (Ed.), 1964, *Some Aspects of Family in Mahuva: A Sociological Study of Jointness in a Small Town*. Bombay: Asia Publishing House.

Dube, S.C., 1958, *India's Changing Villages: Human Factors in Community Development*. Ithaca, NY: Cornell University Press.

———, 1965a, 'Cultural Problems in the Economic Development of India'. In *Religion and Progress in Modern Asia*, edited by R.N. Bellah, Glencoe, IL: Free Press of Glencoe.

———, 1965b, 'Study of Complex Culture'. In *Towards a Sociology of Culture in India*, edited by T.K.N. Unnithan, Indra Deva and Y. Singh, New Delhi: Prentice Hall of India.

———, 1967, 'Modernization and Its Adaptive Demands on Indian Society'. In *Papers in the Sociology of Education in India*, edited by M.S. Gore, I.P. Desai and S. Chitnis, New Delhi: NCERT.

Dumont, Louis, 1964, 'Change, Interaction and Comparison', *Contribution to Indian Sociology*, No. VII, March.

———, 1965, 'The Modern Conception of the Individual', *Contribution to Indian Sociology*, No. VIII.

———, 1970, *Homohierarchicus*. New Delhi: Vikas Publications House.

Durkheim, E., 1947, *Elementary Forms of Religious Life*, translated by J.W. Sain, Glencoe, IL: Free Press of Glencoe.

Eade, John, 1983, 'Modernization and Islamization among Members of Calcutta's Educated Bengal Muslim Middle Class'. In *Modernization and Social Change among Muslims in India*, edited by I. Ahmad, New Delhi: Manohar Publications.

Eck, D., 1983, *Banaras: A City of Light*. New Delhi: Penguin Books.

Eichler, Mike, 2007, *Consensus Organizing: Building Committees of Mutual Self Interior*. New Delhi: Sage Publication.

Eisenstadt, S.N., 1969, *Modernization Protest and Change*. New Delhi: Prentice Hall of India.

Engineer, Asgar Ali, 1995, *Lifting the Veil: Communal Violence and Communal Harmony in Contemporary India*. Hyderabad: Sangam Books.

Form and Antonie, 1951, 'Their Study of Mexico's Cities, Pub.', *American Sociological Review*, December.

Friedl, E., 1964, 'Lagging Emolution in Post Peasant Society', *American Anthropologist*, 66(3) (Part I).

Froystad, K., 2005, *Blended Boundaries: Caste, Class and Shifting Faces of "Hinduness" in North India City*. New Delhi: Oxford University Press.

Fruzetti, L.M., 1981, 'Muslim Ritual'. In *Ritual and Religion among Muslim in India*, edited by I. Ahmad, New Delhi: Monohar Publications.

Fuller, Steve, 2006, *The New Sociological Imagination*. New Delhi: Sage Publication.

Gandhi, Rajmohan, 1986, *Eight Lines: A Study of Hindu-Muslim Encounter*. Albany, NY: State University of New York Press, Chapter 1, p. 1.

Garden, Milton M., 1964, *Protestent–Catholic View*. New York: Double Day and Co., also see, Oscar C. Hadlin, 1954, *The American People in 20th Century*, Cambridge, MA: Harvard University Pressand1964, *Assimilation in American People Life*. New York: Oxford University Press.

George, Kuriyan, 1974, 'Modern Trends in Mate Selection and Marriage in Kerla'. In *The Family in India*, edited by George Kuriyan, The Hague: Mounten.

Ghurye, G.S., 1961, *Caste Class and Occupation*. Bombay: Popular Prakashan.

Giddens, Anthony, 1984, *The Constitution and Society: Outline of the Theory of Structuration*. Cambridge: Polity Press.

Goodfriend, D.E., 1983, 'Changing Concepts of Caste and Status among Old Delhi Muslims'. In *Modernization and Social Change among Muslims in India*, edited by I. Ahmad, New Delhi: Manohar Book Publication.

Gootschalk, P., 2000, *Beyond Hindu-Muslim: Multiple Identity in Narratives from Village India*. New Delhi: Oxford University Press.

Gore, M.S., 1968, *Urbanization and Family Change*. Bombay: Popular Prakashan.

Greaves, E., 1909, *Kashi*. Allahabad.

Gustchow, N., 2006, *Benares: The Sacred Landscape of Varanasi*. Germany: Buch.

Haniff, Z.N., 1983, 'Muslim Women and the Minority Mentality'. In *Modernization and Social Change among Muslims in India*, edited by I. Ahmad, New Delhi: Manohar Publications.

Harold, A.G., 1961, 'Sanskritization and Urbanization', *Economic Weekly*, 13(25).

———, 1963, 'The Adaptive-Functions of Caste in Contemporary India', *Asian Survey*, 3(9).

Harper, E.B., 1959, 'A Hindu Village Pantheon', *Southwestern Journal of Anthropology*, XV.

Havell, E.B., 1933, *Benaras: The Sacred City*. Calcutta.

Helingshed, A., 1950, 'Cultural Factor in the Selection of Marriage Mates', *American Sociological Review*, October 15.

Homans, George, 1961, *Social Behaviour: Its Elementary Forms*. New York: Harcourt Brace and World Inc.

———, 1964, 'Bringing Men Back In', *American Sociological Review*, 29(5).

Hoselitz, B.F., 1960, *Sociological Aspects of Economic Growth*. Glencoe, IL: The Free Press of Glencoe.

Houser, Philip M., 1957, *Urbanization in Asia and Far East*. Calcutta: UNESCO, Research Centre, On Social Implications of Industrialization in Southern Asia.

Hunter, F., 1953, *Community Power Structure*. Coapel Hill: University of North Carolina Press.

Hutton, J.H., 1959, *Caste in India*. London: Oxford University Press.

Ishwaran, K., 1970, *Change and Continuity in India's Village*. New York: Columbia University Press.

Jan dt, Fred E., 2006, *An Introduction to Intercultural Communication*. New Delhi: Sage Publication.

Johnson, J.H., 1972, *Urban Geography*. Oxford: Pregaman Press.

Kapadia, K.M., 1966, *Marriage and Family in India*. London: Oxford University Press.

Khan, M.E., 1983, 'Knowledge, Attitudes and Practice of Family Planning among Muslims in an Urban Setting'. In *Modernization and Social Change Among Muslims in India*, edited by I. Ahmad, New Delhi: Manohar Publications.

Krug, Gary J., 2005, *Communication Technology and Cultural Change*. New Delhi: Sage Publication.

Lateef, Shahida, 1983, 'Modernization in India and the Status of Muslim Women'. In *Modernization and Social Change among Muslims in India*, edited by I. Ahmad, New Delhi: Manohar Publications.

Lenski, Grenhard, 1962, *The Sociology of Religion in United States: A Review of Theoretically Oriented Research*. Glencoe, IL: The Free Press.

Lerner, Daniel, 1962, *The Passing of Traditional Society*. Glencoe, IL: The Free Press of Glencoe.

Lewin, Kurt, 1951, *Field Theory in Social Science*. New York: Harper and Row Publications.

Lynd, R. and Helen Lynd, 1937, *Middle Town in Transition*. New York: Harcourt Brace.

MacIver, R.M. and C.H. Page, 1981, *Society: An Introductory Analysis*. New Delhi: MacMillan India Limited.

Madan, T.N. (Ed.), 1976, *Muslim Communities of South Asia*, New Delhi: Vikas Publishing House.

———, 1981, 'Religious Ideology and Social Structure: The Muslim and Hindus of Kashmir'. In *Ritual and Religion among Muslims in India*, edited by I. Ahmad, New Delhi: Manohar Publications.

Majumdar, D.N., 1967, *raty India, Sangam Books*.

Majumdar, R.C., 1967, *The Delhi Sultanate: The History and Culture of Indian People*. Bombay.

Marriott, M. (Ed.), 1955a, 'Little Communities in an Indigenous Civilization'. In *Village India*, Chicago, IL: Chicago University Press.

———, 1955b, *Village India*. Chicago, IL: University of Chicago Press.

———, 1961, 'Changing Channels of Cultural Transmission in India'. In *Aspects of Religion in India*, edited by L.P. Vidyarthi, Meerut: Kedar Nath Ram Nath.

Masselos, J.C., 1973, 'The Khojas of Bombay: The Defining of Formal Membership Criteria during the 19th Century'. In *Caste and Social Stratification among Muslims in India*, edited by I. Ahmad, New Delhi: Manohar Book Service.

McClelland, D.C., 1961, *The Achieving Society*. Princeton, NJ: Van Nostrand Co.

Mead, G.H., 1934, *Mind Self and Society*. Chicago, IL: University of Chicago Press.

Menon, Indu, 1981, *Status of Muslim Women in India*. New Delhi: Uppal Publication.

Millar, Delvert, 1969, *International Community Power Structure*. Bloomington, IN: Indiana University Press.

Mines, Mattison, 1981, 'Islamization and Muslim Ethnicity in South India'. In *Ritual and Religion among Muslims in India*, edited by I. Ahmad, New Delhi: Manohar Publications.

———, 1983, 'Kin Centres and Ethnicity among Muslim Tamilians'. In *Modernization and Social Change among Muslims in India*, edited by I. Ahmad, New Delhi: Manohar Publications.

Moazzam, Anwar, 1967, 'Islamic Tradition and Modernity', *Quest*, 53, June.

Moore, Wilhert, 1963, *Social Change*. Princeton, NJ: Princeton University Press.

Mukherji, D.P., 1942, *Modern Indian Culture*. New Delhi: People's Publishing House.

Mukherji, D.P., 1958, *Diversities*. New Delhi: People's Publishing House.

Murdoch, J., 1894, *Kashi or Benares*. London: Muthaik

Nehru, Jawaharlal, 1951, *Discovery of India*. London: Meridian Books Ltd.

Newcomb, T.M., 1953, 'An Approach to the Study of Communicative Acts', *Psychological Review*, 60.

Oommen, T.K., 2005, *Nation Civil Society and Social Movement*. New Delhi: Sage Publication.

Pandey, A.B., 1972, *Purva Madhyakalin Bharat*. Allahabad: Central Book Depot.

Pandey, P.N., 1982, 'Approaches to the Study of Indian Society', Lecture delivered in the 'Summer Institute on Indian Society' held in Department of Sociology, B.H.U. (21 December–4 January).

———, 1987, 'Approaches to Social Change in India: A Critical Reexamination', *Journal of Social and Economic Studies*, 4(1), January–March.

———, 1988, *Education and Social Mobility*. New Delhi: Daya Publishing House.

Panikkar, K.M., 1955, *Hindu Society at Crossroads*. Bombay: Asia Publishing House.

Parsons, T., 1951, *The Social System*. Glencoe, IL: The Free Press of Glencoe.

Pocock, D., 1957, 'Inclusion and Exclusion: A Process in the Caste System in Gujarat', *South Western Journal of Anthropology*, 13.

Pool, Ethiel, 1963, 'The Role of Communication in the Process of Modernization and Technological Change'. In *Industrialization and Society*, edited by B.F. Hoselitz and WilhertMoore, UNESCO.

Puniyani, Ram, 2003, *Communal Politics*. New Delhi: Sage Publication.

———, 2005, *Religion Power and Violence*. New Delhi: Sage Publication.

Radhakrishnan, S., 1947, *Religion and Society*. London: George Allien and Unwin Ltd.

Redfield, R., 1955, 'Social Organization of Traditions', *For Eastern Quarterly*, 15(1): 13–22.

Robinson, M., 1974, *Islam and Capitalism*. London: Allen Lane.

Ross, A.D., 1967, *The Hindu Family in its Urban Setting*. Toronto: University of Toronto Press.

Rostov, W.W., 1960, *The Stage of Economic Growth: A Non-Communist Manifests*. Cambridge: Cambridge University Press.

Roy, M.S., 1970, *Urbanization and Social Change*. New Delhi: Orient Longmans Limited.

Rumi's, 1981, 'Jalal-ud-din Poems'. In *Survey of Islamic Culture and Institutions*, editedby K.D. Bhargava, Kitab Mahal, 15, Thornhill Road, Allahabad, India.

Saiyid, A.R., 1981, 'Ideal and Reality in the Observance of Moharram: A Behavioural Interpretation'. In *Ritual Religion among Muslims India*, edited by I. Ahmad, New Delhi: Manohar Publications.

Sarkar, V.K., 1979, 'The Positive Background of Hindu Sociology'. In *Indian Social Thought*, editedby G.S. Bhatt, Lucknow: Ethnographic and Folk Culture Society.

Sarvacs, Jan (Ed.), 2008, *Communication for Development and Social Change*. New Delhi: Sage Publication.

Schramm, W., 1964, *Mass Media and National Development*. Stanford, CA: Stanford University Press.

Scohle, Harry, 1961, *Leadership Heirarchies and Political Issue in New England Town*. New York.

Sellin, Thorsteen, 1938, *Cultural Conflict and Crime*. New York: Social Science Research Council.

Shah, A.M., 1964, 'Basic Terms of Concepts in the Study of Family in India', *Indian Economic and Social History Review*, 1(3).

Sherring, A.M., 1869, *The Sacred Cities of the Hindus*. London.

Shils, E., 1961, *The Intellectual Between Tradition and Modernity*. The Hague: Mouton & Co.

Showeb, M., 1994, *Silk Handloom Industry of Varanasi: A Study in Socio-economic Problems of Weaves*. Varanasi: Ganga Kaveri Publishing House.

Siddiqui, M.K.A., 1973, 'Caste among the Muslims of Calcutta'. In *Caste and Social Stratification among Muslims in India*, edited by I. Ahmad, New Delhi: Manohar Book Service.

———, 1974, *Muslims of Calcutta: A Study in Aspects of their Social Organization*. Calcutta: Anthropological Survey of India.

Singer, Milton (Ed.), 1950, *Traditional India: Structure and Change*. Philadelphia, PA: American Folklore Society.

———, 1956, 'The Great Tradition in Metropolitan Centre Madras'. In *'Traditional India' Structure and Change*, Glencoe, IL: The Free Press of Glencoe.

———, 1957, *Traditional India: Structure and Change Folk Society*. Philadelphia, PA: American Folklore Society.

———, 1961, 'Changing Level of Cultural Transmission in India'. In *Aspects of Religion in Indian Society*, edited by L.P. Vidyarthi, Meerut: Kedarnath Ramnath.

———, 1964, 'Social Organization of Indian Traditions', *Diogenes*, Spring.

Singer, M. and B.S. Cohan, 1968, *Structure and Change in Indian Society*. Chicago, IL: Aldine Publication Co.

Singh, Harbansh, 1980, *Approach to the Study of Religion*. Patiala: Punjab University.

Singh, Y., 1977, *Modernization of Indian Tradition*. Faridabad, Haryana: Thomson Press (India) Ltd.

Smith, W.C., 1946, *Modern Islam in India: A Social Analysis*. London: Victor Gollanez Ltd.

———, 1957, *Islam in Modern History*. New York: Mentor Books.

Smith, W.R., 1976, 'Nationalism and Reform India'. In *Bhartiya Rashtrawad Ki Samajik Pristhabhuim*, edited by A.R. Desai, New Delhi: MacMillan India Ltd.

Sovani, N.V., 1955, *Poona: A Resurvey*. Poona: Gokhale Institute of Politics and Economics.

Srinivas, M.N. (Ed.), 1942, *Marriage and Family in Maussor*. Bombay: Book Company.

———, 1952, 'Religion and Society among Coorgs of South India'. Further 'A Note on Sanskritization and Westernization'. In *Caste in Modern India and Other Essays*, London: Asia Publishing House.

———, 1959, *Caste in Modern India and Other Essays*. Bombay: Asia Publishing House, also see, the dominant caste in Rampurva, *American Anthropologist*, 61(1).

———, 1962, 'A Note on Sanskritization and Westernization'. In *Caste in Modern India and Other Essays*, London: Asia Publishing House.

———, 1966, *Social Change in Modern India*. California: University of California Press.

Syed, A.R., 1981, 'Ideal and Reality in the Observations of Moharram'. In *Ritual and Religion among Muslim in India*, edited by I. Ahmad, New Delhi: Manohar Publications.

Tennyson's Poem, 1981, 'Akbar's Dream'. In *A Survey of Islamic Culture and Institutions*, edited by K.D. Bhargava, Allahabad: Kitab Mahal.

Twain, Mark 1897; *Following the Equator: A Journey Around the World*, Hartford CT. American Publishing Co.

Varshney, A., 2002, *Ethnic Conflict and Civic Life: Hindus and Muslims in India*. New Delhi: Oxford University Press.

Venkatarayappa, N.N., 1957, *Bangalore: A Sociological Study*. Social Series, No. 6. Bombay: University of Bombay.

Vreede-de-Steurs, Cora, 1969, *Parda: A Study of North Indian Muslim Women*. New York: Humanities Press.

Weber, Max, 1962, *The City*, translated by Martindale and New Wirth, Collier Book Edition. Glencoe, IL: The Free Press of Glencoe.

———, 1963, *The Sociology of Religion*. Boston, MA: Beacon.

Wilicus, Philippa, 2007, *Hindu-Muslim Brotherhood: Exploring the Dynamics of Communal Relations in Varanasi*. North India.

Wilkinson, S., 2004, *Vote and Violence Electoral Competition and Communal Riots in India*. Cambridge: Cambridge University Press.

Wirth, Louis, 1938, 'Urbanization as a Way of Life', *American Journal of Sociology*.

Wright, T.P., 1983, 'Inadvertent Modernization of Indian Muslims by Revivalists'. In *Modernization and Social Change among Muslims in India*, edited by I. Ahmad, New Delhi: Manohar Publications.

Young, Jock, 2007, *The Vertigo of Late Modernity*. New Delhi: Sage Publication.

Yusuf Ali, A., 1941, 'Muslim Culture and Religious Thought'. In *Modern India and the West*, edited by L.S.S. O' Malley, London: Oxford University Press.

Zachariah, K.C., 1962, *Migrants in Greater Bombay*. Bombay: Asia Publishing House.

Zaehner, R.C., 1962, *Hinduism*. London: Oxford University Press.

Zorhaugh, 1926, 'The Natural Areas of Cities'. In *The Urban Community*, edited by E.W. Burgers, Chicago, IL: University of Chicago Press.

INDEX